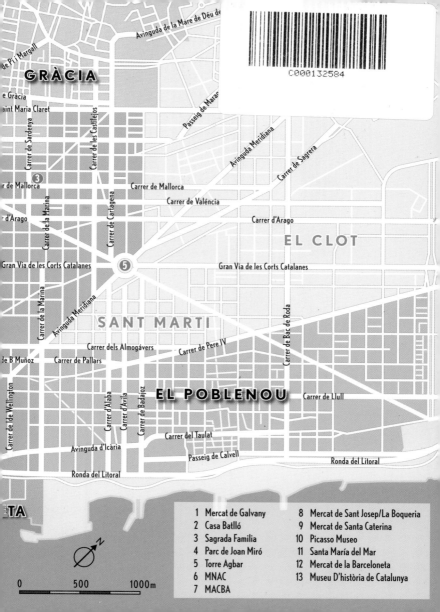

GRÀCIA

Avinguda de la Mare de Déu de
de Pi i Margall
e Gràcia
aint Maria Claret
Carrer de Sardenya
Carrer de les Castillejos
Carrer de la Marina
Carrer de Cartagena
r de Mallorca
Carrer de Mallorca
Carrer de Valéncia
d'Arago
Passeig de Maragall
Avinguda Meridiana
Carrer de Sagrera

EL CLOT

Carrer d'Arago

Gran Via de les Corts Catalanes
Gran Via de les Corts Catalanes
Carrer de la Marina
Avinguda Meridiana

SANT MARTI

Carrer de Bac de Roda

Carrer dels Almogávers
Carrer de Pere IV
de B Muñoz
Carrer de Pallars

EL POBLENOU
Carrer de Llull

Carrer d'Alaba
Carrer d'Avila
Carrer de Badajoz
Carrer de le Wellington

Carrer del Taulat
Avinguda d'Icaria
Passeig de Calvell
Ronda del Litoral
Ronda del Litoral

TA

N

0    500    1000m

| 1 | Mercat de Galvany | 8 | Mercat de Sant Josep/La Boqueria |
| 2 | Casa Batlló | 9 | Mercat de Santa Caterina |
| 3 | Sagrada Familia | 10 | Picasso Museo |
| 4 | Parc de Joan Miró | 11 | Santa María del Mar |
| 5 | Torre Agbar | 12 | Mercat de la Barceloneta |
| 6 | MNAC | 13 | Museu D'història de Catalunya |
| 7 | MACBA | | |

# MOVIDA'S
## GUIDE TO
# BARCELONA

FRANK CAMORRA
&
RICHARD CORNISH

All photography by **Richard Cornish** unless otherwise noted:
**Victoria Alexander**: pages ii, viii, x, 41, 45, 106, 113, 116, 165, 167, 177, 203, 206, 209, 213, 215, 258, 268, 269, 270-271, 275
**Casa Camper**: page 290
**Gillian Hutchison**: pages 79, 189
**Hotel Omm**: page 185 (Rafael Vargas)
**iStock**: pages 28 (Katherine Matthews), 30 (Sean Randall), 169 (fotoVoyager)
**Mandarin Hotel**: page 298
**Photolibrary**: pages 202 (Matti Hillig), 204 (Xavier Subias), 235 (Karl F Schöfmann)
**Villa Emilia**: pages 287, 292-293, 296
**W Hotel**: Pages 77, 284, 286, 289, 293

Maps by **Guy Holt**

THE MIEGUNYAH PRESS
An imprint of Melbourne University Publishing Limited
187 Grattan Street, Carlton, Victoria 3053, Australia
mup-info@unimelb.edu.au
www.mup.com.au

First published 2011
Reprinted 2011
Text © MoVida Pty Ltd, 2011
Design and typography © Melbourne University Publishing Limited, 2011

Designed by Miriam Rosenbloom
Typeset by Miriam Rosenbloom and Pauline Haas
Printed by ABC in China

National Library of Australia Cataloguing-in-Publication entry
Camorra, Frank
    Movida's guide to Barcelona / Frank Camorra, Richard Cornish.
    9780522858341 (pbk.)
    Includes index.
    Gastronomy—Spain—Barcelona—Guidebooks
    Dinners and dining—Spain—Barcelona—Guidebooks
    Barcelona (Spain)—Social life and customs.
    Other Authors/Contributors:
    Cornish, Richard, 1967–
641.013

# CONTENTS

# INTRODUCTION

**I WAS IN AN** old restaurant on the outskirts of Barcelona, the remains of my roasted pheasant sitting in front of me, when an old map of the city caught my eye. Printed in 1970, it was slightly faded and dated in style, but it included the location of the hospital where I had been born, just a year before the map was printed. There it stood, on the periphery of town, Hospital del Generalísimo Franco. Not long afterwards, Mum and Dad moved us back to their home town in Andalucía. A lot has changed in Barcelona since then. The hospital has gone and the street names have been replaced. I was born under fascist rule, when the main roads bore the names of Franco and his Spanish generals. When he died in 1975, the Catalans tore down the signs and renamed the thoroughfares after their national heroes, poets and original Catalan places. But that is the nature of Barcelona. It's a city that is constantly embracing change, with every period of invasion, conquest, revolution and evolution leaving its mark not only on the fabric of the city, but also on the way the people of Barcelona speak, think, look and, most importantly for me, eat!

I still have family in Barcelona, and I visit every few years or so. I love going back to see Dad's cousin Manola. She lives in Horta, one of the parts of town where tourists don't usually visit. I catch up with relatives and we head to the local bars, small noisy places filled with people of all ages—some places might specialise in cooking a few little pieces of fish on the hot grill, other places might be owned by Galicians, who just love their mussels and octopus. We might go to a place that serves *fuet*, cured Catalan sausage and one of the best smallgoods in the world. The family knows the lay of the land, so every eating experience tends to be a good one. I am lucky to have that connection. But they tend not to eat in the kinds of restaurant that we would hear about back in Australia, and that is one of the brilliant things I love about Barcelona—the sheer number of good-quality places to eat in such a compact city. The chefs absorb cooking influences from all around Spain and Europe and sometimes the rest of world, without heading into the domain of confusing fusion cooking. The wages for restaurant staff are low and tax on alcohol is rock bottom, which means that you can get a great dining experience at about two-thirds the price we'd pay in Australia.

It frustrates me when people come back from trips to Spain and say they didn't enjoy the food. There is so much brilliant food to be had across the nation in cafes, bars and restaurants but often the great places are hidden from the visitor. They are obscured by the glaringly obvious establishments that have obtained some great real estate by a beach or a busy tourist promenade or are simply famous for being famous and have all but forgotten how to make good food and look after people.

When I first came back to the city of my birth I was returning as an architecture student on a pilgrimage. Barcelona was gearing up for the 1992 Olympics and the change was palpable. It wasn't irrevocable destruction, but just another mantle of building and infrastructure being laid over the top of a city with millennia of history—Roman walls, gothic churches, baroque palaces, outrageous modernist façades and great expanses of apartments.

When the offer came along to create a guide to show people some of my favourite places in Barcelona, I jumped at it. With all its complexity and density, Barcelona is a city that promises so much. I wanted to help visitors go beneath the surface to explore its rich food culture and have those promises fulfilled.

This was a job far beyond one man and his liver. I teamed up again with collaborator Richard Cornish and recruited a team of friends and Barcelonese locals to work with us. It was a hand-picked team of people who share the same attitude to food and wine. This book is a collection of the places we love, from the smallest bars to award-winning restaurants, and is the culmination of months of research in the field. Some days involved researching two breakfasts, two lunches, two bars and two dinners. Luckily I am built for this type of deep investigation. Rest assured that every single place in this book has been visited by one of the team. This is a personal guide—more so than others because we have put a lot of ourselves into it.

Barcelona is not a city in which to carry a clipboard and tick off places to impress other people. It is a city that offers an intensity of experience that requires the visitor to relax into and be swept away by a myriad of different and amazing adventures. You have our permission to be swept away.

**Frank Camorra**
*March* 2011

# USING this GUIDE

**T**HE WAY WE EXPERIENCE food and wine differs from person to person. We all have different taste in décor and we all have different expectations when it comes to restaurants. Because of this, as a team we decided to do away with any façade of objectivity and simply tell it as we see it. That said, we do share a common belief that food should represent good value for money and be honest in its genre. We believe that a tiny bar that serves great tapas is just as deserving as a fine-dining restaurant to be included, as long as it delivers what it promises and is great at what it does.

There's a buzz you get when you're exposed to the dazzling display of intellect, technique and finesse of a brilliant chef in a three-Michelin-starred restaurant. There's also sheer joy in finding perfect tasty little morsels in a bar where the bar staff have well-rehearsed routines to entertain both themselves and their customers. Barcelona has these places and everything in between.

We have created a list of places we can recommend from our own experiences over the years and from the endorsements of friends and associates, people we trust. Mainly we trusted our own judgment and launched ourselves into the city with plenty of advice ringing in our ears. We came up with what we consider to be a magnificent list to present to all our friends and colleagues.

Some establishments are included because they appear in so many guidebooks; restaurants in guidebooks are a bit like splinters: easy to get in, painful to get out. We have included a few that you should be warned about just because they are recommended so often. There are some restaurants or bars we wanted to include but couldn't because they were closed for renovation or the chef/owner was away when we visited. We'll rectify that in the next edition.

What we have delivered is, as they say in Spain, from '*nuestra cabeza, nuestro corazón y nuestros cojones*'—from our heads, our hearts and our balls.

## GETTING AROUND

Barcelona is an ancient port city that has slowly grown from its seaside origins and crept up towards a low mountain range to the east. At the core of the city is a the *ciutat vella*, the old city, taking in the Gothic Quarter, or Barri Gòtic, El Raval and El Born. Almost entirely surrounding this compact core are the late 19th-century developments of Eixample to the east and Poblenou to the north.

The city is a pedestrian's dream. You can walk from one side of the old town to the base of leafy Montjuïc in half an hour, and the majority of places we've reviewed are within this area. Some of the three-Michelin-star places are a good hour from the central station Sants Estació, though, and some require a car. (If you're hiring a car, it is a legal requirement to carry an international driver's licence. However, I have only once been asked for it.) The rest of the places reviewed in this guide are generally no more than a 10€ taxi fare from the heart of town.

## BARRIS AND ZONES

Barcelona is divided into *barris*. A *barri* is a neighbourhood with its own history and sense of identity. The Spanish

Arc de Triomf, Passeig de Lluís Companys, Eixample

word is *barrio*. You can cross a street into a different *barri* and everything will change: the wealth, the architecture, the width of the streets, the people and the food. If you take time you will understand the nature of Barcelona. It's a city of many different *barris* and zones.

## CARRER OR CALLE?

*Carrer* is Catalan and *calle* is Spanish for 'street'. This is generally abbreviated to *C/–* or dropped altogether, with the name of the street followed by a comma then the street number. The abbreviation *s/n* means *sin número*, or without number.

The Catalan *passeig* is *paseo* in Spanish, meaning a passage or promenade, a slightly longer and wider street connecting two areas, and *avinguda* in Catalan or *avenida* in Spanish is an avenue, a much broader and more important roadway.

Under Franco's rule, the Catalan street names were translated into Spanish; since the the fall of fascism, the old Catalan names have been reinstated. The reality, however, is that many people still refer to the Spanish names of the streets and neighbourhoods, so in true Spanish fashion there is plenty of room for confusion.

## ESTACIÓN

Constantly rumbling underneath the city is a cheap, safe, clean and regular railway system. It costs 1.40€ per trip no matter how far you go. If you're there for a few days it's worth buying a ten-trip ticket. Buying tickets is painless, as the vending machines have multilingual functions. A few different train systems operate in Barcelona, so reaching the outer areas can require changing between systems and buying different tickets. One of the things I love about the metro is that the underground pedestrian tunnels linking the platforms are serviced by little bars selling beer and *entrepàns*. The only disappointment is that it closes at midnight.

## TAXIS

Taxis are a slightly more expensive option at around 5€ per fare in and around the old town and 15€ to the outer areas. The taxis are usually clean late-model SEATs (Spanish made cars by the VW group) and the drivers generally professional. Many don't speak great English, so having the address written down will help get you to your destination.

## SAFETY

Barcelona is a relatively safe place, even late at night. That said, petty crime such as pick-pocketing is fairly well accepted as par for the course. Stay in pairs, keep your bag in front of you and your wallet in your front pocket, don't carry too much cash and split credit cards between pockets, bags and/or purses if possible. Speaking from experience, even big blokes on their own are targets for nimble-fingered thieves.

# MAKING CONTACT

## PHONE NUMBERS

The phone numbers we have given are the local numbers. If dialing from overseas add the international dialing code plus country code (34).

## BOOK AHEAD

Good places fill fast. Some highly rated places are booked out weeks or months in advance, so avoid disappointment and make contact in advance of your visit. Many have websites where you can book online.

todo
va mejor
con
Coca-Cola

| | | PEIX | |
|---|---|---|---|
| Pan Tostado | 1'50 | CALAM. ROM. | 6'00 |
| BOMBA | 1'70 | ARENGUE | 2'50 |
| MORCILLAS | 3'30 | SARDINAS | 4'50 |
| XAMPINYONS | 3'00 | BARAT | 4'50 |
| BACON | 1'80 | CALAMAR | 6'8 |
| HABAS | 2'10 | PULPO | 3'20 |
| BUTIFARRA | 3'50 | RECORTES PULPO | 3'20 |
| CHORIZO | 3'30 | BACALAO | 5'50 |
| CAP i POTA | 3'50 | ESCABECHE | 4'50 |
| AMANIDA | 2'10 | ESQUEIXADA | 5'50 |
| JUDIAS | 2'00 | GAMBES | |
| GARBANZOS | 2'00 | ESCAMARLANS | |
| ENSALADILLA | 2'10 | BUNYOLS BAC. | 3'60 |
| CARXOFES | 3'00 | TELLERINES | 5'50 |
| ROVELLONS | 6'00 | | |

## OPENING HOURS

Many places are closed on Sundays and Mondays. Lunch is generally served between 1330 and 1500 and dinner from 2100 till 2300, but if you want to experience the buzz, book for 1400 or 2130.

Many good places in Barcelona close for the summer, and this means for most of August. Entire families pack up and head out of town, leaving many bewildered tourists behind in a city run by what seems a skeleton staff. There are also national and regional holidays, as well as religious festivals that can seem to spring out of nowhere. Check ahead.

## PLACES CHANGE

Chefs leave, businesses close, some reinvent themselves. We have chosen really solid businesses for you to explore, but as in life nothing is certain, so if things have changed dramatically since we were last at a place, please feel free to let us know.

Similarly, if you find a great place we haven't covered, we'd love to hear about it. Please email us with the name and details of your find to: **info@mup.com.au**.

# PRICES

This guide is not a list of the cheapest places in town. Unlike some travel writers, we were not forced to live on the smell of an oily backpack or told to find the places that would be the least offensive to the greatest potential market. We went out to find the places we love, and we love value for money at a range of price points. Meals that cost a few euros can sometimes be great, but sometimes not. Conversely a meal that costs 150€ could be one of the most wonderful experiences because the food, service and location are so good.

The global financial crisis has made chefs reflect on what they do, and many are now offering better value. That said, any money paid for a bad experience is too much. Hopefully we'll help you steer your way around them. The following is a rough guide as to where businesses sit in the cost hierarchy. This is not about how much you're going to pay for a main course, but how much you'll spend to get the experience that is at the heart of the operation: a little, a bit more, a fair bit or a lot.

€      This could be a pastry or a coffee, a beer and *unas bravas*, or breakfast at a bar in a market, around the 5–10€ mark, for argument's sake.

€€      A good step up from beer and tapas, but the base level for a decent meal that gets you value for money, around the 20–30€ zone.

€€€      This is going to be a good experience with a few bells and whistles, a nice fit-out, some good food and wine, and some good eye candy at around 50€.

€€€€      For most mere mortals this is going to be a bit of a splurge. Generally this is Michelin-star material and you're not going to get out for less than 100€.

## OTHER SYMBOLS

𝖸 Bars

BLUE: Cafes / bars / restaurants

RED: Shops / museums / cooking schools

# THE TEAM

### WE WERE HERE

Every restaurant, bar, museum, shop, cafe, garden, park, church, cathedral and any other establishment mentioned in this guide was visited by a member of the team and used in the appropriate manner. Some of the places are old favourites; some are new finds. Some places we love so much we keep going back year after year.

### WE PAID OUR WAY

There is no such thing in life as a free lunch. Every meal, *tapa*, beer, wine and coffee was paid for by us and no freebies were accepted. We reviewed all restaurants anonymously and only revealed that we were reviewing after paying the bill.

### WHO WE ARE

Because this is an unabashedly subjective guide, we've identified each review with the initials of the contributor. You'll notice each one of us has a different way of expressing ourselves and our own areas of expertise.

### PAUL GUINEY (PG)

Paul Guiney is a top Melbourne somme- lier, and also a good mate of ours. Among other luminaries, he has worked in London with David Thompson and with Christine Manfield in Sydney. How do I put this politely? Let's say he is a true professional and takes every op- portunity to explore all aspects of drinking culture. He's a funny bloke and has a good eye for fun places to spend a few hours. He spent time in Barcelona with us working on the book and he volunteered to write for us about bars.

### CESC CASTRO (CC)

Cesc is a local, Catalan through and through, and therefore loves food. Natu- rally. He writes about sport for Catalan TV and about food for the local food magazine *Cuina*. He's the type of bloke who starts thinking about dinner at breakfast. He's not a glutton, just loves everything about food—not just eating, but the recipes, the chefs, the traditions and the sheer fun of being in great lively places. Many of his favourite eating places have somehow escaped the Google dragnet, so you won't find them mentioned anywhere else. Local knowledge. Can't beat it.

### SUZANNE WALES (SW)

Suzanne was born in Melbourne, but was unable to contain her jealousy of the colourful backgrounds of her migrant school friends so moved to Barcelona in the early 1990s. She writes for the world's top publishers about design and architecture. We share the same belief that perfection is achieved through a marriage of beauty and practicality. She knows the hotel scene in Barcelona like the back of her hand. For me, hotels are places to crash after a day of walking and a night of eating and drinking. She is slightly more refined and likes her accommodation to provide the better things in life, like good linen, views and very comfortable beds. She has chosen some really beautiful hotels for you to stay in.

### STEPHANIE MASTERMAN (SM)
Stephanie is a Melbourne-based front-of-house superstar. She gave us a hand by writing about her time in Girona.

### SARAH STODHART (SS)
Sarah is Australian by birth, but after two decades living in Europe, she thinks like a European. She has a great restaurant called Tapioles 53 (see page 252) and travels every lane in Barcelona on her bike seeking out wonderful, honest and sometimes eclectic places where they sell food. She shares her favourites with us.

## SOME FINAL TIPS

We have found the best places not by following a guide book but by following our noses. A true foodie will always find the best places to eat. When you do find a good one, ask the waitstaff for their recommendations. Listen to their advice and to the experiences of other travellers. And when you see local people tucking into great food, you know that you're onto a good thing.

# A BRIEF HISTORY of CATALONIA through FOOD

**A**RRIVE IN BARCELONA and, while you are technically in Spain, you're also in the capital city of one of the most defiantly independent food cultures in Europe. Catalan food uses ingredients found across Spain and some other parts of Europe, but has a very distinctive style of cooking that relates to the Mediterranean Sea, the forest-cloaked mountains, the farms and the little kitchen gardens around the country. To me it is ironic that a people so connected to the land almost exclusively live in apartment buildings and that their contact with the earth comes through the food they shop for, cook and eat.

In the heart of Barcelona is El Mercat de Sant Josep, one of the most famous food markets on earth. Also known as La Boqueria, this compact undercover market—no bigger than the markets we have in Australian capital cities like Adelaide's Central Market or Melbourne's Queen Victoria Market—La Boqueria is a magnet for the best produce from Catalonia, Spain and Europe. Here you can see the raw products from which many of the best chefs of Barcelona prepare their dishes. They and many of the residents of the neighbouring *barris* shop here because of the sheer volume and quality of the produce. It's one of the best places for travellers to learn about the basics of Catalan food.

I love coming to La Boqueria in the early morning, around 8 am, before the tourists arrive, clogging the aisles while they take shaky video footage. It's enthralling to watch produce from the farms and ports around Spain being unloaded. Trucks filled with seafood from Galicia battle for spots with little vans from the Catalan countryside, like the ones carrying *ous de Calaf*, eggs from a farming area just outside the city. Catalans love their eggs, among many things, for their delicious *truites*, Catalan for *tortillas*.

Meanwhile, inside the market, Barcelona housewives are already sniffing, feeling, touching, lifting, pressing and eventually buying food for their families' meals. It is here that the food begins its transformation from raw materials to wonderfully idiosyncratic dishes.

My parents are from Andalucía in the south, so many of the dishes are a little foreign even to me. I love learning, so I really appreciate the deep knowledge that Catalan food expert Begoña Sanchis has of her native cuisine. She holds daily cooking classes (see page 102), which can start at La Boqueria. She

meets her guests at the well-known Pinotxo (see page 221) in the heart of La Boqueria, where certain local women come in and order some *tortilla* and a glass of *cava* for breakfast. Begoña points out a waiter making *pa amb tomàquet*. 'This is classic food from our region,' she explains. 'Slightly stale bread is brought back to life with the rub of garlic, a squeeze of tomato, salt and olive oil.' You can use any tomato soft enough to drag over the bread, toasted if it is too stale, but so installed is *pa amb tomàquet* in Catalan culture that they have bred a specific variety of tomato for it. The skin is so thick it can be treated roughly without breaking up. Begoña points out that the waiter doesn't peel the garlic, but uses its skin to protect his fingers from the juice. 'To stop garlic odour from permeating the food he serves?' I suggest. 'No,' said Sanchis cheekily. 'More likely to stop his cigarette from being tainted with the smell of garlic.'

Begoña takes us down to a rush of housewives descending on the mushroom stall Petràs Fruits del Bosc. A fresh delivery of *boletus* mushrooms has arrived. Mushrooms have cult status in Catalonia—the highest rating television show in the region is

Parroquia San Miguel Puerto, Barceloneta

called *The Boletus Hunters*. Hunting, fishing, gathering and making do are cornerstones of Catalan food. It's a cuisine based on frugality. Decades of poverty during the Franco era have created innovative cooks and chefs who learned to make the most of what little was available. Up until 40 years ago, most cooked on *cuines econòmiques*—charcoal-fuelled iron stoves. From these conditions comes a canon of classic dishes, almost all based on simple ingredients.

We stop at one of several stands devoted to *bacallà* (salt cod). Begoña explains that before the days of refrigeration, only people living on the coast had access to fresh fish, the food of the common people right across Spain. She listens to the conversations as the women talk among themselves and explains later that one of the women will make *samfaina*, a ratatouille-like sauce to go over a fillet of desalted and fried salt cod. Another is making *bacallà a la mel*, a dish of salt cod with honey, raisins and pine nuts. Another tosses up between buying fillets for deep-frying or buying the cheaper pieces to soak and serve raw with a hazelnut and red pepper–based *romesco* sauce in a dish called *esqueixada*.

In the fresh fish section the rapport between the shoppers and the fishmongers is playful, bordering on intimate. 'What are you making? How many people are you feeding?' goes the conversation. The fishmonger decides the best fish for the job and presents two parcels—one with the flesh of the fish and the other with the bones and offal. Nothing—repeat *nothing*—is wasted in a Catalan kitchen. But Catalans appreciate quality, and if the occasion deserves it, a home cook will fork out 75€ for a kilo of locally caught Mediterranean prawns, cooked simply, perhaps *a la plancha* or grilled on an iron hotplate.

We come to Jordi Ausiro, an immaculately dressed butcher who specialises in smallgoods and charcuterie. 'I am from a town called Vic,' he says. 'A lot of meat preserving comes from a time when Catalonia was poor. I remember my dad killing the pig. The flesh was cooked in salt and then stored under oil. It would be romantic to say it was great but it really was terrible!' He instead points us to the fermented *fuet*, a thin pork sausage stuffed into a pig's intestines and covered in a delicate white mould. It is one of Spain's best sausages. He also offers a taste of *sobrassada*, a paste of raw pig's flesh and back fat preserved with salt and smoked paprika.

'At the heart of Catalan cooking are vegetables. Anyone will grow them given enough space,' says Begoña. True, any spare patch of earth is turned into a *huerto*, or veggie patch. In Barcelona the sides of railway lines are popular with vegetable gardeners. Pulses feature heavily too in the Catalan kitchen. The traditional Sunday meal in winter is *escudella*, a hearty slow-cooked wet dish of dried beans or chickpeas, chicken, noodles or rice, with a pork sausage and black pudding floating on the top. It is the Catalan version of Spain's national dish, the *cocido*, a dish so rich and invigorating that it has no trouble crossing regional boundaries. Another pulse dish is *mongetes amb botifarra*, a white bean stew enriched with grilled sausage.

The sun comes up and La Boqueria is getting crowded. We head past the Carnicería Caballar, a butcher's shop that specialises in capon and horse, turn left at the mounds of smoky paprika sold by the kilo, past the fish stalls where a fishmonger is taking to a hake with a hatchet, and past the poulterer's large range of game birds. We pause to buy *nyores,* dried peppers, and debate if it's too early for a glass of vermouth with the market workers.

Soon the tourists amble down La Rambla, the vibrant main street on which La Boqueria has stood and fed Barcelonese for more than 170 years. With a little knowledge, La Boqueria provides a window into the soul of Catalan food, a tradition that some argue *is* the very heart of the region. FC

Alcachofa fritte (fried artichokes)

DISTRITO 1º
BARRIO 6º
CALLE
DE
LLADÓ

CARRER
DELS
LLEDÓ

# The CATALANS and
# their LANGUAGE

**O**NE OF THE FUNNIEST SHOWS on TV in Catalonia is a program called *Polònia*. It's hilarious. One comic impersonates Ferran Adrià, the man who led the molecular cuisine revolution and was chef and owner of elBulli, which was named the Best Restaurant in the World in the San Pellegrino World's 50 Best Restaurants Awards for five consecutive years from 2005 to 2009. He's parodied mercilessly and in one sketch makes a dish called Caviar of Smoke of Leek with the Texture of Plastic. The trouble is I can't understand what anyone in the cast is saying. It's in Catalan. I speak Spanish. Catalan and Spanish are two different languages. To the untrained ear they can sound similar, but I assure you they are miles apart.

I blame the Romans. Catalan comes from Latin spoken by Romans when they invaded the area two centuries before the birth of Christ, and, laced with Arabic, Visigoth and Iberic elements, has been spoken since the eighth century. It is also spoken in southeastern France, the Balearic Islands, Valencia, a small part of Sardinia and Andorra, a small country in the Pyrenees and the only state in the world where Catalan is the official language.

Barcelona is the capital of Catalonia, one of the 17 autonomous communities and two autonomous cities that make up the Kingdom of Spain. Catalan was once repressed by Spanish kings and later the fascist dictator Franco, who rejected Catalan cultural identity and its fierce assertion of independence from the rest of Spain. With Franco's death in 1975 and the arrival of democracy in the late 1970s, Catalans reasserted themselves, returning the names of towns, streets and institutions to their original Catalan. The language is taught in schools and even used for the Barcelona version of *Time Out*. Today about 80 per cent of the population of Catalonia can speak Catalan, 40 per cent as their first language. For many the language is *the* identity, a cultural unifier that represents a nation of proudly independent and resourceful people. To them they are not Spain; they are Catalonia, or *Catalunya*, as they say it.

I have seen the side of a farm building in rural Catalonia clad in old metal Spanish street signs cast off when the Catalonian order was restored. An older taxi driver from the south of Spain referred to Poblenou as Pueblo Nuevo, because that is how he remembers it. Many signs in Barcelona, such as those to the little wine-producing region of Priorat, which in Spanish is El Priorato, are written in Catalan only, as are some menus depending on the owner and just how nationalistic they are. Most places offer a Spanish version and some have menus printed in English as well. We have used a mix of Catalan and Spanish in this book, depending on the house style of the establishment we have visited. Sometimes it's confusing because the same dish will have different names depending on who wrote the menu. *Pop* is Catalan and *pulpo* is Spanish for octopus. If you know Spanish you can work it out. Sometimes an ingredient such as duck—*ànec* in Catalan and *pato* in Spanish—is harder to fathom. We have included a glossary at the end of the guide covering words from both languages. I never get caught up worrying too much about language, because all Catalans speak Spanish and many speak English.

Two points. First: if you're going to any part of Spain for some time, a short Spanish language course really helps. As food is the second language of every region, even if you only learned the words for ingredients you could still speak for hours to anyone in Spain and have a great time. Second: never call a Catalan Spanish. They are Catalan.

Miquel at La Perla

# ABOVE
## DIAGONAL

La Sagrada Família

MOST VISITORS TO Barcelona spend the bulk of their time in the old town, by the beach or in the chic shopping strips of Eixample. A little further west up towards the hills are the suburbs often referred to as Zona Alta, or the zone above Diagonal, the broad avenue that cuts through Barcelona, funnily enough, diagonally. This takes in neighbourhoods such as Gràcia, el Tibidabo and Sarrià, which are well worth exploring. A trip up to el Tibidabo offers the chance to see some of the grandest houses in Barcelona, some of them *modernista* masterpieces ... if you can manage to peer over the high fences. The view from the old fun fair on the Collserola at el Tibidabo (Parc d'Atraccions Tibidabo), however, is uninhibited, offering a panorama of the whole city. From here the story of the city unfolds. Two rivers mark the edges of Barcelona: the Besòs River to the north and the Llobregat to the south near the airport. There's the old city by the port, the business district, the ordered, bevelled squares of the Eixample, as well as the gnarled fingers of the spires of La Sagrada Família, as well as the more varied area of Horta, where one can still make out the small rural villages that have been engulfed by rows of apartments. The wealthy areas of Sarrià, Pedralbes i Sant Gervasi and el Tibidabo offer some leafy green streets, a respite from the close and compact areas in the old city below. It's worth eating in these neighbourhoods just to see the real Barcelona and, generally, the most you'll pay to get there by taxi is 15€.

Parc d'Atraccions Tibidabo

## ABAC

Avinguda del Tibidado, 1
℡ 93 319 6600
www.abacbarcelona.com
Tue–Sat 1330–1600, 2030–2400
**Modern creative**/€€€€/One
Michelin star/ Cards and euros

ABaC is surrounded by a modern timber fence dominated by security devices. It feels like ASIO HQ as renovated on a home makeover show. But don't let that put you off. On the other side of the barrier is another world again: a lush garden drops below street level, miles away from the rush of the old town. Everything about ABaC is beautiful and has been designed with a supreme understanding of the visual and tactile. The high-backed leather-upholstered chairs feel wonderful to touch, as does the linen. My God! They use Versace crockery and Spiegelau stemware. I recommend the degustation to understand what ABaC is about. This may start with a *versión de autor* Garibaldi cocktail, a lovely orange sorbet with a bitter Campari foam the head waiter sprays over the sorbet in the glass. It's refreshing fun that continues throughout the meal. A range of punchy appetizers may include little anchovy toasts—classic Catalan style with the flavour knob turned to 11—and an intense confit of baby tomatoes served in a roasted red pepper broth. Look forward to rich dishes that are intense, simple and beautiful, such as *foie gras* with variations on corn and licorice—sensational—or the surprise of a new dish the chefs are trying out. It's a big, long meal but the service is impeccable. The huge wine list has a strong Spanish leaning, but classic French and other old world bottles are exceptional value for around the 50–70€ mark. Founding chef Xavier Pellicer has moved on, but at the time of our review, ABaC was still great, although the folk at the Michelin guide thought it necessary to strip away a star to make this a one-star restaurant. Still, one of the best high-end dining experiences in town. FC

. . . . . . . . . . . . . . . . . . . . . . . . . . . .

## ⵟ BAR TOMÁS

Carrer Major de Sarrià, 49
℡ 93 203 1077
Mon–Tue, Thur–Sun 1200–1600,
1800–2200 (closed August)
**Bar**/€/Cash

When you read that a bar serves the best *patatas bravas* (basically fried potatoes and sauce) in Spain, you have to check it out—right?—even if it is a 10€ taxi ride from town. Bar Tomás is a neighbourhood bar in the wealthy middle-class area of Sarrià. Parties of young people sit outside, smoking, eating and drinking at tables and chairs under the awning. Inside the long room is a bar staffed by middle-aged waiters who bray at each other like old donkeys. 'Over there! No, the other table! More *bravas!*' Above the bar are bags of garlic, not to keep vampires away according to the barman, but for the sharp, very garlicky *allioli* they make for the *bravas*. It's good. What is better, however, are the tuna and red pepper *empanadillas*—a rich filling encased in a super-brittle olive oil shortcrust pastry. It's a fun family place and if you're in the area you should drop in. Don't be put off by the waiters: they may seem as gruff as trolls, but that's their schtick. RC

. . . . . . . . . . . . . . . . . . . . . . . . . . .

## BOTAFUMEIRO

Gran de Gràcia, 81
( 93 218 4230
www.botafumeiro.es
Daily 1300–0100
**Seafood restaurant**/€€€€/Cards and euros

Everywhere you go in Spain people tell you, 'This is where the king likes to eat.' Generally you take this with a grain of salt. However, this Barcelona institution is fit for the king. Waiters in white coats open your car door, then valet park it. This place was recommended to me by the very unregal Paco Guzmán from restaurant Santa (see page 154), which suggests to me the high esteem in which this restaurant is held by a broad cross-section of locals. This is a Galician restaurant (it's named after the great swinging incense burner in the cathedral at Santiago de Compostela), and the menu here is all about seafood, much of it, such as *percebes* (goose barnacles), spider crabs, velvet crabs and sea cucumbers. They also serve excellent versions of Galician staples such as *empanada* filled with pork, raisins and sultanas, and *pulpo a la galega*, discs of octopus leg on potato sprinkled with Spanish paprika. What I love about Botafumeiro is that it runs a full menu from 1 pm to 1 am without missing a beat. The bar is where the action is and the most sought-after place to eat. The open kitchen, where you can see chefs putting up great plates of seafood and paellas, is constantly on the move. The place gets so busy that a guy uses a microphone to call the kitchen pass, a big ledger in front of him like a race caller. Only in Spain! Owner chef Moncho Neira wanders around the packed dining rooms in full kitchen uniform, a massive head of hair, almost a caricature of himself as he oversees boisterous local families and work groups making their way through piles of seafood. It's expensive, but it's great to see how everyday people splurge on special occasions and how Barcelona Old Money spends its inheritance. FC

. . . . . . . . . . . . . . . . . . . . . . . . . .

## CATALINA

Anglí, 4

☏ 93 206 1791

www.catalina.es

Mon–Sun 1300–1500;

Tue–Sat 2030–2300

**Modern Catalan**/ €€/Cards and euros

You'd be very happy if you had this restaurant in your middle-class neighbourhood: bare brick walls, attractive casual wait staff and linen on tables set with good stemware. Chef Josep Lacambra worked under legendary chef Mey Hofmann (see Hofmann, page 42) and plays the same modern Catalan tunes but to a much more rustic beat, as seen in a simple plate of chargrilled asparagus, eggplant and zucchini with a small *quenelle* of rich *romesco*. Josep's rice dishes, however, are his tour de force. He makes his *arroz* like an Italian risotto, stirring as it cooks to release the starch. '*Bomba* rice is a friend of mine,' he told us after our meal. He cooks it for just 15 minutes (18 is the norm for paella) in a *sofrito*, then in a hot stock with perhaps wild mushrooms and a little cod. It is rich, soupy, starchy and sticky, and absolutely delicious with an aged white wine. One of the best restaurants for *arroz* in Barcelona. RC

## COURE

Passatge de Marimon, 20

☏ 93 200 7532

Tue–Sat 1330–1530, 2130–2330

**Inventive tapas**/€€/Cards and euros

This is one of my favourite places in town, just off Avinguda Diagonal in a narrow street known for its modern tapas. Coure offers great food, great value, a good fit-out and great service. It reminds me of my own place MoVida in the centre of Melbourne. I love the magnificent small bar at the entry, where they serve superb tapas and little plates to share. It's an intimate affair, low lit with dark tones. The bar menu is separate from the compact restaurant menu, which is printed daily on a single sheet with about 25 food items on one side, from small tapas to big-ticket steaks. What you notice is the quality of the ingredients—it feels as though the chef has access to the best food in Spain. Start with perhaps the finest Cantabrian anchovies available to man and move up to a piece of *ventresca*, or tuna belly, fresh and fatty and layered with thin slices of sweet figs. Move on to a soft and delicious beef cheek cooked in a deep red-wine sauce, served with a potato puree and grilled chunky *cep* mushrooms. A list of wines includes *cava* and champagne by the glass, and about six reds and whites by the glass or

# — THINGS I LOVE —

# CAVA

*Cava* is a Spanish sparkling wine that comes with permission to drink at any time of the day. The Spanish are clever. Instead of following the French and making their sparkling wine exclusive and expensive like Champagne, they made a drink that was for everyone for every day—so many more potential clients and so many more potential occasions! While you may drink Champagne at the opening of a new play, in Spain you drink *cava* at the opening of the menu. This is the perfect time to drink *cava*—while you're working out what to drink.

Most of Spain's *cava* comes from the Penedès region. It is made in the same manner as Champagne, but instead of using pinot noir, pinot meuniere and chardonnay grapes, *cava* makers use a blend of the more neutral Macabeu grapes, the slightly more flavoursome *xarel·lo* and a little crisp *parellada*, although sometimes they do use chardonnay and/or pinot noir. While the good *cava* makers create a drink that has spent time on lees, giving it a lovely brioche aroma, a good number don't, and this gives a slightly sharper tang in the mouth.

It is a different product because its grape varieties grow on a different soil type from that in Champagne, but what I really love about *cava* is that it doesn't have the snob value of Champagne. It is a drink to have in a bar while waiting for a train, at lunch with a meal or to enjoy on a terrace while reading a book. It is a drink that working men can enjoying without snide remarks being made about them enjoying musical theatre or gladiator films. It is simple, a great fizzy drink made with good tasting grape juice that makes you feel happy. It's *cava*!

bottle. Service is professional and fun at the same time. Your order is taken by either the bar staff or the owner chef, who mans the stoves and greets the clientele, mainly locals he seems to know by name. It's a busy business—even places at the bar are reserved—so make sure you book ahead. FC

. . . . . . . . . . . . . . . . . . . . . . . .

## EL ASADOR DE ARANDA

Avinguda Tibidabo, 31
( 93 417 0115
www.asadordearanda.com
Mon–Sun 1300–1530, 2100–2400
**Aragonese roast house**/€€€/
Cards and euros

Just up the hill from ABaC in this very wealthy hillside neighbourhood stands an outrageously lit ornate building owned by a national chain that specialises in the Aragonese art of roasting baby lambs over oak. This former home is a pastiche of styles—Moorish, traditional Catalan, modernista, with a few baroque touches —making it a slightly overwhelming experience. But the ostentation is part of the deal. Wealthy businessmen, local families and rich Russians all congregate in this terracotta and brick temple. At the heart of the operation is an oak-burning clay oven in which whole or parts of lambs no more than 25 days old are cooked in oval terracotta trays. Nothing apart from salt is added, and the crisp-skinned sweet flesh sits over a bath of smoky cooking juices, perfect to be soaked up with bread or, even better, a salad of plain cos lettuce. It's delicious. Typically one would start with morcilla and chorizo, but if there are *riñones*, or kidneys, on the menu the night you are there, give them a burl—they are tiny tender mouthfuls brought to the table on a steel stand over a bed of glowing charcoal; the fat encasing the kidneys drips onto the coals, which then release a delicious hiss of aromatic smoke. Finish the meal with rosquillas—aniseed flavoured short doughnuts—and some very strong orujo—grappa made from albariño marc. It's a big operation and lacks the touch of a small owner, but it is still a fun night out. RC

. . . . . . . . . . . . . . . . . . . . . . . .

## FLASH FLASH

Granada del Penedès, 25
( 93 237 0990
www.flashflashtortilleria.com
Daily 1300–0130
**Tortelleria**/€/Cards and euros

At first sight you might think this is a recent kitsch tribute to 1970s Spain, with its stark white space adorned with black female silhouettes. The silhouettes are all of model Karin Leiz, wife of one of the first owners, a photographer, who opened this fantastically chaotic place in 1970. The restaurant has been painstakingly cared for ever since and has retained its original early 70s fit-out, demonstrating the love and nostalgia the city has for Flash Flash. Beautiful and comfortable white banquettes wrap around booths that embrace the entire restaurant. The floor is covered with light-green hospital-grade linoleum, and the wait staff are dressed in stark white jackets, shirts and black ties. Some have been here since Flash Flash opened! It is popular with the locals and it can get jam packed. The menu is simple—bunless hamburgers (the norm in Spain), some fish specials and 70 different tortillas, from the classic potato tortilla to chorizo, green pepper or salt cod, all costing around the 7€ mark. FC

. . . . . . . . . . . . . . . . . . . . . . . . . . .

## FREIXA TRADICIÓ

Sant Elies, 22
( 93 209 7559
www.freixatradicio.com
Tue–Sat 1300–1600, 2100–2330
**Traditional Catalan**/€€/Cards and euros

This place is fantastically great value for what is the most delicious traditional Catalan food you will find in Barcelona. A small but luxurious room decked out in subtle white and grey tones resonates with the personal touches and the pride taken in every detail, from the fine table- and stemware to the Freixa family brand stamped on everything from the plates to the pewter table centre-pieces. The waiters reinforce the classic atmo-sphere of the restaurant with their cool, attentive air and considered silver service. For kitchenware tragics like myself, there is a large feature wall with a fantastic range of beautiful copper pots. If you can get a group together, then you'll be able to sample more of the shared dishes. The meal begins with thin-60 centimetre-long *fuet* sausages, to be eaten with the hands. Continue with salt cod or roast meat *croquetas*, both nearing perfection, then move on to the signature entrees … perhaps *macarrones a la barcelonesa*—think the best macaroni cheese in the world and triple it. There are eight classic Catalan fish and meat dishes, my personal favourite being tripe and veal *morro*, or head, with *botifarra negra* in light, super-sticky, gelatinous tomato sauce. I also love the tiny legs of slow-roasted baby goat, and the rabbit loins stuffed with eggplant. Freixa's *crema catalana* is the best I have ever tasted—a silky aromatic citrus and cinnamon–infused custard with a bitter hit from the crisp caramel top. As with most good restaurants, you get a range of *petits fours*, including chocolate pots with olive oil and salt (classic), a small tea cake and nougat. The wine list is fairly short and succinct, with mostly well-known brands from across Spain, with a bias towards Penedès. If you want a cheaper option, there is a set menu for 35€. Look out for some really interesting seasonal specials. FC

. . . . . . . . . . . . . . . . . . . . . . . . . . .

## — TOP FIVE —
# ARCHITECTURAL EXPERIENCES

### 1 BARCELONA CATHEDRAL CLOISTERS
Pla de la Seu, 3 (Barri Gòtic)
This gothic masterpiece encloses a lush green fountain and towering palms and perhaps the world's most photographed gaggle of geese.

### 2 LA SAGRADA FAMÍLIA
Mallorca, 401 (Eixample)
After a breathtaking climb up inside the spire, the beauty of Gaudí has always been in the detail. Here you get a close up and what amazing views of the city.

### 3 BARCELONA PAVILION
Avinguda Francesc Ferrier i Guàrdia, 7
Sheer poetry, a masterpiece of modernism by Mies van der Rohe, some of my architecture mates rate this as the greatest building ever.

### 4 MAGIC FOUNTAIN OF MONJUÏC
Avenida Maria Cristina (Montjuïc)
Built for the world expo of 1929, there are nightly light and water shows, cheesy but spectacular. Also great fun dodging the pick-pockets behind you while you're dazzled by the show.

### 5 PASSEIG DE GRÀCIA
This strip of Passeig de Gràcia near the metro station of the same name has an intense concentration of modernisme buildings. Coming out of the metro one is confronted with the Casa Batlló, for example, its façade a mosaic of thousands of tiles that glitter in the Mediterranean light. It's one of the most dramatic reveals in the world.

Interior of Casa Batlló

# HISOP

Passatge de Marimon, 9
( 93 241 3233
www.hisop.com
Mon–Fri 1330–1530;
Mon–Sat 2030–2400
**Contemporary Catalan**/€€€/One
Michelin star/Cards and euros
Make your way here for modern yet understated Catalan cuisine that is both restrained and delicious. Like many Spanish contemporary restaurants, the space is minimalist—the room is stark, with no decorations except for a red rose on each white linen–covered table. A red feature wall, broken into rectangles, looks like a giant monochromatic Mondrian painting. It's quite astonishing to see a waiter approach the wall, push gently on a panel, and have it open smoothly to reveal itself as a drawer. Every part of this wall is a giant waiters' station, filled with ice buckets, cutlery, Riedel stemware and so on. Later in the meal one whole portion of the wall is wheeled out as a bright-red mobile cheese table. There are two set menus, derived from the à la carte menu; both are tremendous value for money. The small two-course menu for lunch and weeknights is a 25€ steal considering the number of appetizers and *petits fours* bookending the deal. The five-course degustation costs just 50€, including all the before and after dishes. The meal may start with a sardine and tomato tartare topped with a curry sorbet. It may seem odd that Spanish and other high-end European chefs love cooking with Keen's Curry Powder until you taste it and understand that it works. The food is subdued with just a little molecular nonsense—perhaps excellent plump seared Galician scallops with zucchini flower, *cep* cream and goat's milk soup lifted by a frothy sage-spiked foam. There are nice little touches, such as a lime/mint sorbet course before dessert, served in a martini glass. Coffee comes with all sorts of wonderful little dishes—perhaps a weirdly delicious caramelised black olive, crunchy on the outside yet licorice-like inside with its pip still intact. This is a beautiful space for beautiful people. FC

. . . . . . . . . . . . . . . . . . . . . . . . .

# HOFMANN

La Granada del Penedès, 14–16
( 93 218 7165
www.hofmann-bcn.com
Mon–Fri 1330–1545, 2100–2315
**Contemporary Catalan**/€€€/One
Michelin star/Cards and euros
Legendary chef Mey Hofmann is a striking woman. With a proud mane of dark chestnut hair, neat-as-a-pin chef's jacket and dark trousers, she walks the floor and plays mine host, chatting to guests, moving easily between European languages. The dining room is off one of the area's quieter streets and is a collection of bare but warm dark wood-

panelled rooms. Hofmann, like many Barcelonese chefs, takes commonplace Catalan food, cooks it in a modern style, plates it up beautifully and then places it on a pedestal. To start, there could be a little serving of *garapinyades*, sugared macadamias (instead of almonds), a bacon-flecked madeleine or Viennese bread wrapped around *sobrassada*, sort of like a doughy *bomba*. The set menu ranges from around 55€ to 75€, depending on the time of the week and the economy in general. There may be silverbeet-lined domes filled with pine nut foam and raisins eaten with a sliver of crisp bacon, perhaps a little fillet of salt cod with cooked-down garlic and peppers, *pil-pil* and parsley sauce. This could be followed by two points of perfectly cooked lamb with an eggplant puree. My bugbear with Mey's place is that many sauces are made in Thermomixes, and all have a uniform baby-food texture. I get over it when the waiter brings a small coin-sized golden pastry and what appears to be a shot glass filled with forest fruit. With a gentle blow he knocks the glass onto the plate and smashes it. It's made of sugar! I am not a sweet tooth, but here there is mastery of skill, imagination and presentation. He swirls the mixture around on the plate and instructs you to eat the pastry whole—*crema catalana–*

flavoured cream bursts in your mouth. It is stunning. I would gladly come here for the dessert only and order three. (See also Hofmann Patisserie, page 144.) RC

. . . . . . . . . . . . . . . . . . . . . . . . . .

## VIA VÉNETO

Ganduxer, 10
( 93 200 7244
www.viavenetorestaurant.com
Mon–Fri 1300–1600; Mon–Sat 2000–2400; Closed 1–20 August
**French and Catalan**/€€€€/One Michelin star/Cards and euros

Via Véneto has been the economical and political power restaurant of the city elite for the past four decades. The Belle Époque period décor of the dining room surrounds the clients in anachronistic elegance. The carpet is kitsch and the chairs are wonderfully upholstered for all the big names that sit on them, all attended by bow-tied waiters. The formal traditionalism of this restaurant is strongly influenced by French cuisine. The chef, Carles Tejedor, arrived here from another great restaurant in 2006 and brought to the table exquisite dishes such as the soft scampi tartare with salmon caviar. There could be a superb dish of eggs from Calaf with potato and truffle, each ingredient contributing its own distinct texture. The signature dishes are the *hare à la royale*, a drum of soft and tender hare meat enveloped in a rich sauce, and the classic *duck à la presse*, a sanguine dish in which a whole rare-roasted duck is pressed for its juice and a sauce made at the table. Many dishes, including flambéed crêpes suzette, are finalised in front of the diners. Josep Monje and his son Pere manage the restaurant with unsurpassed deference and discretion. This unfortunately not-so-common style has become the emblem of a restaurant that can, deservedly, claim to have the best service in town. CC

. . . . . . . . . . . . . . . . . . . . . . . . . .

# The ESSENTIAL DISHES
## of BARCELONA

**I LOVE THE DESCENT** into Barcelona airport. If I'm coming in from London, often I look down on the snow-capped peaks of the Pyrenees and the oak-covered high country, home to game birds and wild mushrooms. The plane swings around over the Mediterranean and I can make out little fishing boats floating on the glittering water, bringing in prawns. Then, as we're coming in to land, I look out over the market gardens on the Llobregat River floodplain, and great masses of artichokes being harvested by hand. I go through customs hungry. I love the food of Catalonia, and Barcelona offers some of the best. Here are some classic dishes you should order while you are here. We give the names in Catalan, Spanish and English, which is the language order often used on Barcelonese menus. Sometimes the dish has the same name in Spanish. FC

## ARRÒS – ARROZ – RICE

There is more to life than paella, and the variety of rice dishes in Catalonia might surprise anyone not familiar with the region. They can be rich soupy affairs, loaded with mushrooms or fine mixes of crustaceans, peppers and fish stock. Served in a bowl or the pan in which they were cooked, they have one thing in common of course: the rice. It is cooked to the point the Italians would describe as *al dente* and has a lovely earthy, starchy background note. Rice is grown in Catalonia in two main regions: one is the Ebre River Delta and the other is Pals near Girona. Both have DOP or a protected designation of origin status. Some chefs, like Josep Lacambra at Catalina (see page 34), use the local *bomba* rice, stirring it as one would do a risotto, which creates a much creamier dish.

## BACALLÀ – BACALAO – SALT COD

Salt cod is the national fish of Spain, a Catholic country where the meat-free fast days were so numerous that fish became the default protein. Fish doesn't travel well, so salted fish found its way from the Atlantic to coastal ports right around the Iberian Peninsula. In the hands of a good chef, perfectly desalinated salt cod has a balance between the sweetness of the fish and the residual salt, leaving a sublime, silky series of layered flakes of white flesh such as they serve at Els Pescadors in Poblenou (see page 227). Its mild fishy taste makes it a perfect flavouring for béchamel-based *croquetas*. The Catalans will sometimes serve salt cod with a little floral honey, the trinity of sweet, salt and savoury coming together as one.

## BOLETS – SETAS – MUSHROOMS

The Catalans are mushroom crazy. In spring and autumn, when the earth is warm and the rains come in and drench the hills, the forests erupt with all manner of fungi. If you see *rovelló* on the menu, you might know these as pine mushrooms. In Catalonia they harvest their *rovellons* quite small, when they are sweet and firm, and cook them with garlic and parsley on a flat iron griddle. This is one of the dishes worth trying at tourist traps like Pitarra in Barri Gòtic (see page 115).

## BOMBES – BOMBAS – FRIED POTATO BALLS

This is a home-grown Barcelona bar snack made of mashed potato wrapped around a meaty filling, often chorizo, then deep-fried. A good *bomba* is light and crunchy and is just as much about the red pepper sauce and sharp garlicky *allioli* with which it is served. Sometimes hot, sometimes warm, *bomba* should be consumed with an ice-cold beer, or with a fat glass of vermouth, as they are at the birthplace of the *bomba* at La Cova Fumada in Barceloneta (see page 81).

Bombas at La Cova Fumada

ORIGEN Kenya  LA SEVA QUALITAT **RDURES**
VARIETAT  Gates
CALIBRE  Enfeta
CLASSE  finer
_50 _

# 7'90

P.V.P.
MERCAT
QUILO

VENDE AL EXTERIOR

## BOTIFARRA – BUTIFARRA – PORK SAUSAGE

*Botifarra*, a fresh sausage seasoned with plenty of garlic and freshly ground black pepper and served grilled, is the ubiquitous pork sausage of Catalonia. They come in a variety of flavours, and some specialty butchers make spinach or *cep* versions; there is even a super-sweet dessert *botifarra*.

## BOTIFARRA NEGRA – MORCILLA – BLACK PUDDING

This is the Catalan's answer to the Spaniard's *morcilla*, or black pudding. It's not spiced with cinnamon as its southern counterpart is, and it's far more porky than its English cousin, and there could be some onion or pine nuts or rice in the mix. In the south of Catalonia is a famous version called *baldana*. *Botifarra negra* makes appearances in a number of other dishes as a flavouring agent. It is also lovely when grilled.

## BUNYOLS – BUÑUELOS – FRITTERS

These are like *croquetas*, but are smaller and round. *Bunyols de bacallà* are delicious mouthfuls of salt cod and potato cooked together to form a light dough that is gently shaped into a ball and dropped into hot oil. Sometimes they are coated in egg wash first, and this puffs up as it fries, giving the *bunyol* a light crunchy coating—great with beer. Another version, *bunyols de vent*, is sweet, flavoured with anise liqueur and cinnamon and is a typical Easter dish.

## CALÇOTS – CHARCOAL-GRILLED LONG ONION

In the middle of winter, after the chestnuts and wild mushrooms have come and gone, the Catalans have the *calçot* season to look forward to. A long leek-like onion, the *calçot* is cooked over the embers of a fire then wrapped in newspaper. When cool enough to handle, the charred outer leaves are removed to reveal a soft slippery centre of cooked flesh that is dipped in *romesco* sauce and dropped into the mouth from above. If you're in town when it's *calçot* season make sure you order them, perhaps with a glass of young red from Gandesa or a *cava brut nature*.

## CANELONS – CANELONES – CANNELLONI

On the day after Christmas Day, the festival of Sant Esteve, housewives across the region take the leftover flesh from the *carn d'olla*, the Christmas chicken, pork or veal, mince it finely and fold it through a sweet *sofregit* of leeks and onions. This is spread out onto sheets of handmade pasta, which are rolled into *canelons*. These are covered in a light béchamel, sprinkled with a little cheese and baked. You'll find *canelons* in Barcelona throughout the year, including an exceptionally rich version at Can Vallès in the Eixample (see page 172), which has the added benefit of a little liver and cooked-down pork.

## CAP I POTA – VEAL HOTPOT

This is a slow-cooked veal dish that is just as much about its sticky texture as its rich taste. It's famous for being *esmorzar de forquilla,* the workman's breakfast. Packed with the bits of animals that one wouldn't normally talk about in polite company (*cap* means head and *pota* means foot), with the added bonus of *botifarra negra* or Catalan black pudding, this is an offal-lover's dream and the perfect foil for a glass of aged Rioja as they do at La Perla in Poble-sec (see page 244).

## CARGOLS – CARACOLES – SNAILS

The French do not have a monopoly on snails; they just made them seem appealing. I love the way snails are cooked across Spain, from the thin mint and cumin broth they serve down south to the rich pork-flecked sauces in which the

*cargols* are cooked in Catalonia. I love the snails at La Tomaquera in Poble-Sec (see page 250), cooked in a light but flavoursome tomato-based sauce.

## COCA – FLATBREAD

*Coca* is the national flatbread of Catalonia. It's as rustic as it is filling. You'll often find the savoury version *coca de recapte* covered in cooked red pepper and tiny salted herrings, a theme you'll see reprised in modern Catalan restaurants such as Alkimia in the Eixample (see page 161), where they serve it as a delicious little appetiser. A common sweet version is punctuated with pine nuts and sprinkled with sugar, the base rolled thin so the dough cooks quickly and the pine nuts don't burn. Sometimes plain coca can be used as the base for *pa amb tomàquet*.

## CREMA CATALANA – CRÈME BRÛLÉE

Think crème brûlée or Trinity cream. *Crema catalana* is an egg custard flavoured with lemon rind and cinnamon, topped with sugar that has been caramelised with a blow torch, although I have also seen the sugar burned using a branding iron heated in a fire as they do at at El Racó del Priorat (see page 277). The custard in a good *crema catalana* should have a velvety consistency and a cool base under the hot toffee.

## ENTREPÀ – BOCADILLO – BREAD ROLL

This Catalan version of a crusty bread roll filled with cheese or *jamón* tends to be more petite than others. If you don't want a whole one, order a *medio*, or half. You may also come across a finer version called *flauta*, or flute.

CABRIT
19'90

CABRIT
CUIXA 12 €/Q
ESPATLLA 30

Espardeñas with beef

## ESCALIVADA – ROASTED EGGPLANT AND CAPSICUM SALAD

There's a lot of symbolism in this dish. Red peppers, eggplant and onion roasted or grilled with garlic and drizzled with cooking juices are often served in alternating red and yellow stripes to represent the Catalan flag. According to legend, it originated when the great Catalan hero Wilfred the Hairy, Duke of Barcelona, lay mortally wounded after battle. As a mark of respect, the French emperor dipped his fingers in Wilfred's blood and ran it over his gold shield, creating the striated emblem. This is good with beer or barrel-aged Macabeu, a white wine from Penedès.

## ESPARDENYES – ESPARDEÑAS – SEA CUCUMBERS

Imagine if there were a sea creature that tasted of scallops and had the texture of squid, but looked as though it had been piped out of the star-shaped nozzle of a piping bag. This is *espardenyes*, or sea cucumber, often called *espardenyes de Roses*, after the little town on Catalonia's north coast off which they are fished. So delicious when just given a nice little browning on *la plancha*, they were once thrown away by fishermen because no one would eat them—now they are very expensive. They are often seen as a textural accompaniment in dishes such as the pressed beef and sea cucumber at Dos Cielos in Poblenou (see page 227).

## ESTOFAT – ESTOFADO – BEEF STEW

This is a beef stew that cooks down chunky pieces of beef with wine or *vi ranci*, the Catalan's answer to sherry. It could be enriched with a *botifarra*, perhaps some of the powerful herbs that grow wild in the hills and some orange peel. Sometimes this dish seems French, but then again the border with France is only just over an hour away.

## FIDEUÀ – FIDEUÁ – PASTA PAELLA

Often called Valencian pasta paella, this is a dish made in the same way as a paella, starting with a *sofregit* in which fine, short vermicelli-like pasta is cooked with shellfish and prawns in a metal pan as it is at Can Solé in Barceloneta (see page 78). There they remove the shellfish, grill the *fideus* until crisp on the top, cook them in fish broth and then return the shellfish for serving; in this case it is called *rossejat*. It tastes deliciously of the sea and is stunning with a crisp *verdejo* white wine.

## FUET – CURED PORK SAUSAGE

This is perhaps the best sausage in the world. Made with a penicillium mould, the result is a long thin sausage with an attractive white bloom, like a camembert. In fact the penicillium mould creates a rich mushroomy flavour that is reminiscent of white mould cheeses. Delicious.

## MAR I MUNTANYA – MAR Y MONTAÑA – SURF 'N' TURF

*Mar i muntanya* translates as 'sea and mountain', or in our language, surf 'n' turf. Generally it means chicken and prawns brought together in a sauce, but *mar i muntanya* could just as easily be rabbit with cuttlefish, or pork meatballs with squid. Unlike the steak and prawn offerings in Australian RSL clubs (which are just steak and prawns) this dish is about creating a sauce that is greater than the sum of its parts.

## MÚSIC – MÚSICO – FRUIT AND NUTS

Musicians (apart, perhaps, from Prince, Ronan Keating and Mick Jagger) are poor, so this is a dessert for all the rest—a mix of dried fruit and nuts splashed with *vi dolç*, a sweet fortified wine like *moscatell*. It is a simple dish, but due to the quality of local nuts and fruit, is quite beautiful and a dessert that even a musician can afford. If you see it on the menu, please consider.

Pa amb tomàquet

## PA AMB TOMÀQUET – PAN CON TOMATE – BREAD WITH TOMATO

*Pa amb tomàquet* is the benchmark dish of all restaurants in Barcelona. It simply means bread with tomato. You just cut some bread and perhaps toast it. You cut some garlic. You rub it onto the bread. You cut a tomato. You rub the tomato onto the bread. You season the tomato with a little salt, finish it with a drizzle of fresh olive oil and serve. I have shared this with vineyard workers during harvest among the old bush vines of Priorat, where it was their mid-morning snack, along with a few slurps of red wine and a few cigarettes. It is a great little dish and so easy to do, yet so many places stuff it up. If you're served *pa amb tomàquet* that was made at the beginning of service and has been sitting around getting soggy and tired, you know that will pretty much reflect the attitude of the chef or manager—soggy and tired. The food to follow generally follows form. If, however, you are served a freshly cut, perhaps toasted, piece of fresh bread, perhaps house-made, that has been freshly rubbed, seasoned and drizzled with extra virgin olive oil, you have found an establishment that cares.

## PAELLA – RICE DISH

Paella is a Valencian rice dish named after the flat pan in which it is cooked—*la paella*. In Barcelona, if you see photos of lots of different paellas on a board outside a restaurant, make like Dion Warwick and walk on by. These are generally microwaved, frozen, factory-made jobs. Paella may contain any combination of fish, poultry, beans, seafood, snails or game birds. Paella is popular in the beachside restaurants and *chiringuitos*, but that experience is more about the view than the food. The Rich Man's Paella, invented in Set Portes between Born and Barceloneta (see page 87), is a very good version of this dish.

## PEUS DE PORC – MANITAS DE CERDO – PIG'S FEET

Pig's feet are often on menus in traditional Catalan restaurants. They are split lengthways and slowly braised in a rich sauce of wine, tomato and aromatic vegetables. The sauce is so sticky with rich gelatinous texture that it almost glues your lips together. The tiny amount of flesh on the trotters is supersoft porky goodness. The bones remain, so it's the kind of dish where you're excused to use your hands as you suck away at the knuckles and bones. Sometimes cooked with other ingredients, such as snails, this is not a dish for the squeamish, but only for true lovers of pig's trotters and trust me, there are many.

## RECUIT – REQUESON – SOFT CHEESE

*Recuit* is a cheese similar to ricotta, and is often served as a delicious but simple dessert. A good example is found in the *modernista* restaurant Els Quatre Gats in Barri Gòtic (see page 103).

Arroz con necoras

## ROMESCO – RED PEPPER AND HAZELNUT SAUCE

Pounded roasted almonds and hazelnuts, rehydrated dried *nyora* peppers, olive oil and red wine vinegar are the main components of this classic sauce originally from Tarragona. There is a good modern version served at Bravo 24 on the beach (see page 72), but I prefer the rustic version Victoria makes at El Racó del Priorat in Vilella Baixa (see page 277), where it is served on top of *esqueixada*, a salad of rehydrated salt cod with onion and tomato.

## SARSUELA – ZARZUELA – FISH STEW

In Spanish, *zarzuela* means operetta or musical comedy, which reflects the collection of disparate ingredients in this rich seafood stew. It is brought together with a sauce made from cooked-down onions and tomatoes, thickened with flour dusted on the fish as it is initially fried, or sometimes with a *picada* of ground nuts.

## SOBRASSADA – SOBRASADA – RAW PORK SAUSAGE

One of the most decadent hangover breakfasts in the world is a piece of toast spread with *sobrassada*, a kind of pâté made by stuffing a piece of pig's gut with pig back fat, minced pork, salt, smoky Spanish paprika, garlic and herbs and leaving it to ferment for a few months. The result is a deep red spicy pâté that is as silky smooth as it is rich.

## SUQUET – FISH STEW

This simple dish is either a thick fish soup or a thin stew thickened with a *picada* of almonds and the starch of potatoes that have been added to a *sofregit* of garlic, onions, tomato and brandy. A variety of local fish is used to make a traditional *suquet* such as the one served in Suquet de l'Almirall in Barceloneta (page 94).

Cheese table at Dos Cielos

BARCELONETA

JUTTING OUT INTO the Mediterranean Sea is a triangle of reclaimed land about 70 hectares in size. It is so small it feels more like a village than a *barri*. This is 'little Barcelona', built in the mid-1750s by filling in the shallow water between the shore and a little rocky island, now buried somewhere under the promenade. Its 20 or so narrow streets and five slightly broader avenues were once dominated by Barcelona's fishing community, echoed in the street names such as Carrer dels Pescadors. On one side is a marina, home to millions of dollars' worth of motorboats; on the other are artificial beaches sweeping around to the new sail-shaped W Barcelona Hotel. Both waterfronts are lined with restaurants, which with a few notable exceptions, are tourist traps. The better places to eat are generally in the centre of this little area, in the streets running around the square and the new Barceloneta Market. The original was bombed by the Italians during the early years of the Spanish Civil War, along with much of Barceloneta.

Barceloneta has a good lively feel, with a mix of younger professionals blending in with the original maritime families, giving the area a nice range of traditional bars and more upmarket eateries. The beach was once lined with family *chiringuitos*—basically beach shacks that served beer and a few seafood snacks. These were removed for the renovation of the beachfront before the 1992 Barcelona Olympics, and the modern versions that have replaced them lack their rustic simplicity, although it's still a good place to get a drink on a hot night. I love Barceloneta because of this mix of people and good eateries, but also the scale of its narrow canyon-like streets and the friendly vibe of locals rubbing shoulders, quite literally, as they walk past each other on the footpaths, no more than a metre wide.

## 1881 PER SAGARDI

Plaça de Pau Vila, 3, 4th floor
(above the Catalan History
Musuem)

( 93 221 0050

www.grupsagardi.com

Daily 1300–1600, 2030–2400

**Catalan and Basque**/€€/Cards and euros

Perched above the much underrated Catalan History Museum, this restaurant has one of the best views in Barcelona, looking out over the yachts and the city towards Montjuïc. And there's hardly anyone here. The signage is appalling, which probably explains why there are hundreds of tourists dining on the waterfront while only a few curious ones who have paid the 3€ to enter the museum have made it to the top floor. 1881 is part of a national chain of Basque restaurants. At its heart is a charcoal grill over which great 1-kilogram pieces of aged Basque ox are grilled. I recommend one of these be shared—by at least four. Also consider the Catalan *fideuà*, *sarsuela* and the *favetes i pèsols*. RC

· · · · · · · · · · · · · · · · · · · · · · · ·

## ⵢ ABSENTA

Sant Carles, 36

( 93 221 3638

Daily 1100–0300

**Bar**/€/Cash

Growing up in the inner city, I feel perfectly at home in this bar. A mixed crowd of slightly grungy locals crowd together in a dark, club-like room which has a really good soundtrack of 1970s and 80s alternative/indie music. Speak English to the bar staff and you'll get short shrift. Try your Spanish and you'll get their life story. The food here is rubbish but at 2 am you're not really that fussy: what you want is good cold beer, 20 different absinthes and table service in the truly delightful outdoor drinking area in the park across the road. RC

· · · · · · · · · · · · · · · · · · · · · · · ·

## AGUA

Passeig Marítim de la
Barceloneta, 30

( 93 225 1272

www.grupotragaluz.com

Mon–Fri 1300–1545, 2000–2330;
Sat–Sun 1300–1630, 2000–0030

**Catalan and Spanish seafood**/€€€/Cards and euros

One of the most pleasurable experiences in Barcelona is to dine beside a sweeping beach on the Mediterranean. A local friend of mine loves coming here in summer with his partner, ordering a paella then going for a swim in the sea. By the time he gets back and towels off, the paella is served. There are so many restaurants along this strip so I thought I'd try a reliable one—this one run by the reputable Tragaluz group. The rustic stone wall around the restaurant is a nice barrier to the beach,

# SEAFOOD

Cod guts and hake cheeks? Love 'em. Inside of sea urchin? Served chilled with a pinch of salt—perfect. Sea anemones? Can't get enough. If it's legal and edible and it comes from the sea I will eat it. Spaniards just love seafood and the Catalans are the same. They walk the streets talking about squid and where to get the best *calamares a la plancha*. You will come across many sea creatures on your travels, but here are a few that I really suggest you eat.

The first safe bet is salt cod, *bacalao*, (*bacallà*) which you will find often. Then there's hake, *merluza*, (*lluç*) a popular fish with soft white flesh. Favoured by many is wild sea bass, *lubina*, (*llobarro*) sometimes cooked whole in a crust of salt. One of things I crave but can't get a lot of in Australia is good fatty tuna belly, *ventresca*. Pink and interlaced with fat, it's served grilled in unpretentious bars and restaurants and has become a high-profile dish in Barcelona's many Japanese restaurants.

Spanish clams, *almejas*, (*cloïsses*) caught in the shallow waters of Galicia are brilliant cooked in a garlicky white wine sauce. Galician scallops, *vieira*, are fat and sweet, as are their mussels, *mejillones*, (*musclos*). Goose barnacles, *percebes*, are tasty but expensive—they look like something out of *Doctor Who* but have a really sweet intense flavour of the sea.

The prawns, *gambas*, (*gambes*), in Spain are great. Stunning local prawns are pulled from the Mediterranean, one of the most overfished bodies of water in the world, but low supply and high demand means high prices. I saw local prawns in the La Boqueria for 77€ per kg. You often see prawns from Palamós, big red king prawns, served on a tile of slate, still sizzling from the flat grill and sprinkled liberally with salt. I treat these like life, sucking every single drop of juice out of them.

Calamari, *calamares*, feature very heavily on restaurant menus. Don't expect it to be sliced into rings and deep fried, although the very best deep-fried calamari rings I have ever had were in Barcelona (see Montalban Casa José, page 251). Often calamari hoods are stuffed and grilled. Baby calamari may be rolled in a little seasoned semolina and baptised in a cauldron of boiling oil. I could go on.

As wild stocks are depleted, farmed fish are becoming more common, so if you're after wild-caught fish look for *extractiva salvaje* on the menu or in the market.

Seafood is king in Barcelona and every time I am in town I make myself its humble subject. FC

which is—warning!—a playground for thieves. Book ahead for a table on the *terraza*, as this place is all about the location. Start with a little *jamón*, tapas, fried calamari or *boquerones*. Locals would normally move on to the soups and vegetables such as *verduras a la brasa* or *espárragos a la brasa con romesco*. While the waves are quietly beating on the shore, try the *arroz*, perhaps with lobster, then a typical seafarer-type dish like a thick steak of sweet hake baked on a *fondo* of caramelised onions and potatoes with tomatoes and herbs, or a dish of monkfish tail finished with a *refrito* of hot garlic-infused oil. They also do a reasonable *suquet*. To concentrate on the well-prepared dishes of really top-quality fish and seafood is missing the point. Take that as a given here. This is the place to come to enjoy a good time with friends, while watching the truly eclectic parade of beachgoers, one of life's great pleasures. FC

. . . . . . . . . . . . . . . . . . . . . . . . . .

## ⟁ BAR JAI-CA
Ginebra, 13
℘ 93 319 5002
Tue–Sun 0900–2300
**Bar**/€/Cash

Owner Jaime Cabot's father opened this bar in 1955 and not much has changed since then. Housed in one of the older apartment buildings in the *barri*, banners and pictures of FC Barcelona hang from the walls and there's a constant chatter of gossip from the locals, some accompanied by their dogs. Plates of squid, cuttlefish, *croquetas* and *bombas* sit above the refrigerated glass cabinet holding fresh razor clams, small sweet prawns and mussels, all waiting to be set on the hot *plancha*. Consider ordering the deep-fried baby squid, which are dusted in well-seasoned semolina that soaks up their juices, creating a rustic batter, before being deep-fried in screaming hot oil then given a decent dousing in fresh lemon juice. The ladies in the open kitchen behind the bar punctuate the bar prattle with hearty laughs and when ready will bring some of the fattest tortilla I have ever seen to the bartender to slice and serve while they are still warm. It's rough and ready but genuine fun. If you can get a table, the bar staff prodded by the occasional wave and warm smile, will come over and look after you at the table. This is one of my favourite places for a relaxing night drinking beer with local people. RC

. . . . . . . . . . . . . . . . . . . . . . . . . .

## BRAVO 24
Floor E, W Barcelona Hotel
Plaça de la Rosa dels Vents, 01
℘ 93 295 2636
www.projectes24.com
Daily 1330–1600, 2030–2300
**Produce-driven modern Spanish**/€€€/Cards and euros

Bar Jai-Ca

# — TOP FIVE —
# SEAFOOD PLACES

**1 ELS PESCADORS**
Plaça Prim, 1 (Poblenou)
Wonderfully understated top-end fish restaurant in an old tavern by
an old square.

**2 LA PARADETA**
Comercial, 7 (Born)
A busy family fish barn where you point to the raw fish and they cook
it to order.

**3 MONTALBAN CASA JOSÉ**
Margarit, 31 (Poble-sec)
Only 24 seats, no view or décor, but great fresh seafood.

**4 CAN SOLÉ**
Sant Carles, 4 (Barceloneta)
One of the bastions of old Barceloneta fisherman-style recipes such
as *rossejat de fideus*—oven-finished noodles and seafood.

**5 PASSADÍS DEL PEP**
Pla de Palau, 2 (Born)
Tell them you want seafood and they will bring it to you until you say stop.

This is the stunning new offering from Barcelona's king of cool, Carles Abellan. It's built into the base of the sail-shaped W Barcelona Hotel on the end of an arcing sand spit. The dining room is dominated by nude timber, wool rugs and other natural furnishings and has a healthy modern vibe. On the deck outside, the designers have captured the look and feel of a *chiringuito*, with rustic wooden tables and deep white vinyl couch-like banquettes shaded from the Mediterranean sun by fine bamboo blinds. Between you and the sea is a sundeck of bronzed foreigners tanning and ordering more beer and cocktails. Here provenance and produce are king, from the fat gordal olives to the bowl of arbequina extra virgin olive oil with great bread to start. Bravo 24 polishes classic Spanish dishes and takes them to another level. The meal starts with a 'complimentary' plate of tissue paper–thin *cecina*, air-dried beef from León. It should be described as 'obligatory', as it appears later on the bill for 5€. The food is deceptively simple—the *esqueixada* is a cold salad of coarsely smoked salt cod with *pil-pil*, an emulsion sauce made with very light olive oil and the juices from the fish. This could be followed by a plate of tiny tender artichokes with fat rings of calamari and sweetbreads with a butter-mounted beef jus. At the heart of the kitchen is a Holm oak charcoal grill over which big red Mediterranean prawns and, when available, sea cucumbers harvested from the coastal town of Roses are roasted. There could be steak from Galician Limousin, Charolais from France, Angus from Nebraska or Wagyu from Downunder. Desserts are adaptations of Spanish classics, like the *torrijas*, normally made with stale bread soaked in cinnamon and citrus–infused milk and eggs; here, however, brioche has been substituted. Together with a quenelle of smoked sheep's milk ice-cream it is a very happy ending. Ignore the smugness of the staff and consider the opportunity to order half serves of the dishes, which makes it possible for a couple to cover much of this very worthwhile menu. RC

. . . . . . . . . . . . . . . . . . . . . . . . . .

## CAN MAJÓ
Almirall Aixada, 23
( 93 221 5455
www.canmajo.es
Daily 1300–1600, 2000–2300
**Seafood**/€€€/Cards and euros
This place was once a benchmark for fish restaurants in Barcelona and because of that it still features heavily in guides. It's a bit like Agatha Christie's *Mousetrap* on the West End: people go to see it not because it is great theatre, but because it has been running so long. That is why we have included it. It is right on the Sant Sebastià beach promenade, offering wonderful views across the Mediterranean. It's a great

Bravo 24, W Hotel

place to watch the human theatre playing out on the foreshore, but if you want exciting food, this is not the place. If you want to eat French Belon oysters shucked to order, accompanied by some quite inspired wine choices, then a seat on the beach here could be a highlight. Their *pa amb tomàquet* is made before service. A no no. Their *esqueixada* is slices of quite good quality salt cod in an unseasoned tomato puree covered with olive oil—it's dull. Their *sarsuela* is a mix of fried fish, mussels, clams, a few prawns and squid rings in a very heavy sauce that speaks more about outdated techniques than the subtle aroma of the sea. But if you want to experience old school Spanish cooking and service in a beautiful location, you won't be disappointed. RC

## CAN PAIXANO
Reina Cristina, 7
www.canpaixano.com
Mon–Sat 0900–1030
**Old cava bar**/€/Cash

Heaving with people in the evenings, crammed at lunchtime and busy at breakfast, this is one of the cheapest places in the nation to get a drink. It seems that the prices haven't changed since this old sailor's bar opened in 1969, with a glass of *cava* starting at 80 euro cents and bottles ranging from 3€ to 6€. Push pass the crowd near the door because there always seems to be a space at the back. The incredibly fast and efficient staff won't serve booze to you unless you eat something. They offer a huge choice of *entrepans* and sausages: *botifarra*, *chorizo* and *morcilla* all sizzling on the grill, dropped into hot buns wrapped in paper napkins and almost thrown over the counter. They also serve cheese and the delicious *fuet*—it's cheap and cheerful, as this place is all about the crowd and the buzz. With *jamones* hanging from the ceiling, old wine crates on the walls and the floor covered in napkins, this is the real deal as far as bars go. There is a shop at the back that sells the *cava* and a few edible treats. FC

. . . . . . . . . . . . . . . . . . . . .

## CAN SOLÉ

Sant Carles, 4
( 93 221 5012
www.cansole.cat
Tue–Sun 1330–1600;
Tue–Sat 2030–2300
**Traditional seafood** /€€€/Cards and euros

This well-regarded seafood restaurant is a street back from the beach, so you're not paying for views but for top-quality seafood. Owner Josep Maria García, a large gentleman who obviously enjoys his *fideuà*, of which they do an excellent job here, waits at the tables. He is a member of the local food group that aims to keep the traditional fishermen dishes of Barceloneta alive. Around since 1903, it's situated on the ground floor of one of the typical low-rise narrow flats, the exterior of which has been rendered in an attractive geometric pattern. Behind the large wooden door, covered with a dozen Routard badges—generally a good omen—is a wonderfully dated (1980s perhaps) room, painted in an aquamarine colour scheme, with maritime décor and lined with photos of all the famous Spaniards who have dined here. It fills with groups on weeknights and couples on the weekends. During the day, light streams in through the windows (sunlight is a rare commodity in this cramped city). I love watching the chef taste every dish with a teaspoon as she cooks great seafood classics in her sparkling clean stainless-steel kitchen. It is in the simple Catalan braises that García's passion for tradition and the chef's mastery of classic technique really shine. The chef makes delicious *suquets* and *calderetes* but it's her *arroz a banda con bogavante*—huge live vibrant-blue lobsters, cut into sections and served in a hot cast iron pot with potatoes in an aromatic fish broth thickened with *picada*—that really entrances me. FC

. . . . . . . . . . . . . . . . . . . . .

## CHERIFF

Ginebra, 15
( 93 319 6984
Mon–Sat 1300–1600, 2000–2300
**Rice dishes and seafood**/€€/ Cards and euros

My mate Xavi, a chef who grew up in Barceloneta, simply smiled and nodded his head when I told him I had been to Cheriff. In fact, almost every native Barcelonese to whom I mention Cheriff

has a warm affection for this slightly offbeat restaurant on the city side of Barceloneta. It has a solid heart and is dependable but just a little kooky—like a favourite old uncle. Inside it is decked out in a maritime theme, with strange combinations of wooden boats' wheels, lobster and angry crab sculptures, round windows and the effusive demeanor of the owner, who is looking as well worn as his restaurant. The lunchtime business crowds and night-time families come for the good-value rice dishes, such as *paella de marisco*, and their emphasis on excellent rice, great fish stock and golden *socarrat*. These are presented to the table in the *paellera*,

then whisked away to be beautifully plated up. They also do really good wet rice dishes such as *arroz caldoso* or *arroz de bogavante*, prepared with the live lobsters in the tanks. Seafood dishes such as *almejas a la marinera*, a great clam dish, will be more expensive, but that's the deal. It's good quality, fun and just a touch bizarre. FC

. . . . . . . . . . . . . . . . . . . . . . . .

## FORN BALUARD

Baluard, 38–40
( 93 221 1208
www.baluardbarceloneta.com
Mon–Sat 0800–2100
**Bakery**/€/Cash

Top left & right: La Cova Fumada
Bottom: Lluçanès

It was the puffs of black smoke above this bakery that made me think twice. Either they were electing a new pope or this was the real deal—a wood-fired oven. Bread is not done particularly well in Spain, except in the north. Barcelona is improving, however, with bakers like Anna Bellsolà employing natural and traditional techniques to make really good bread. She uses organic wheat, sourdough and long ferments to create really tasty bread with crunchy crusts, moist interiors and bucket loads of flavour. Buy a loaf here from someone considered by many to be the best baker in Barcelona, wander through the market for some other picnic supplies and head to the beach. RC

. . . . . . . . . . . . . . . . . . . . . . . . .

## ⌑ LA COVA FUMADA

Baluard, 56
☏ 93 221 4061
Mon–Fri 0900–1520; Sat 0900–1320; Thur–Fri 1800–2020
**Bar**/€/Cash

This is home of the classic Barcelona tapa—*la bomba*! It is really hard to find, so look for the brown doors in the square at the opposite end of the market—and for people spilling onto the footpath. It opened 75 years ago, and since they got the décor right the first time, haven't touched it since. The family gets together every morning around 10 o'clock to freshly make their rather punchy garlicky *allioli*, with old Mum peeling the garlic and sons folding in the oil with a few eggs to emulsify it. Order a beer or vermouth and a plate of *bombas* or wander over to the relic of a chalkboard menu—written in a mélange of Spanish and Catalan—where you'll find *garbanzos*, a mix of chickpeas and black pudding. They also do decent salt cod *bunyols*, *chistorra*, a pork sausage hot off the grill, baby clams and seasonal dishes such mushroom and beautiful artichokes, cooked on the grill and served with a little olive oil and paprika. It's a really busy place, with the barman shouting orders to the kitchen (the chef writes the orders in pencil on the marble bench), a pall of smoke and a great mix of old and young, locals and visitors. It doesn't look like much, but the food and atmosphere have made this a Barceloneta institution. This is my kind of bar. FC

. . . . . . . . . . . . . . . . . . . . . . . . .

## LLUÇANÈS

Plaça de la Font (above the Barceloneta Market)
☏ 93 224 2525
www.restaurantllucanes.com
Tue–Sat 1330–1500, 2030–2300; Sun 1330–1500
**Modern Catalan**/€€€/One Michelin Star/Cards and euros

To find Lluçanès, go to the square in front of the Barceloneta Market and face the market. Walk through the very

# — TOP FIVE —
# MID-PRICED MEALS

**1 QUIMET & QUIMET**
Poeta Cabanyes, 25 (Poble-sec)
Wine, tapas, fifth-generation family business, beautiful old room.

**2 GRANJA ELENA**
Passeig Zona Franca, 228
Michelin-quality food in an old taverna style setting. Hidden gem.

**3 GRESCA, EMBAT**
Experience bistronomia and hook into high-end quality food at bistro
prices with the set-lunch menus at many of the hot new restaurants in
Barcelona. These are just two examples.

**4 COURE (the Bar)**
Passatge de Marimon, 20 (Above Diagonal)
Modern, fun, great value tapas at the bar.

**5 FREIXA TRADICIÓ**
Sant Elies, 22 (Above Diagonal)
The best value traditional Catalan food in Barcelona.

Quimet & Quimet

casual bistro Els Fogons on the right and head up the stairs. Here you'll find a space that feels like a tasteful airport lounge, with lots of steel, modern exposed pipes and diffused natural light. This one-star Michelin restaurant feels like a hi-tech set from the British spy drama *Spooks*—but with an open kitchen. This is where chef Àngel Pascual works his blend of modern techniques over Catalan classics. He has strong roots in the Catalan heartland of Osona, where lies the town after which his restaurant is named. A starter of a crouton smeared with squab liver pâté is a wonderfully intense way to begin a meal, along with a little bowl of pickled wild mushrooms and little tuna tartare. He plays with *canelones*, exchanging pasta tubes for rolled sheets of reduced and jellified chicken stock, the normal béchamel replaced with a brie cream. His passion for produce is not only remarkable but infectious. After we admired the baby squid he was frying for an *arroz*, he invited us to go fishing with him the next day. For the record he buys his fish daily from a fisherman mate. Àngel attracts a fairly young crowd and a good number of food tourists. Although this restaurant seems a little out of place in the very down-to-earth *barri*, it is casual enough to get away with it. We do like the good collection of lesser-known Catalan wines on the list, and the good tableware and stemware. Plus, it is just above the small but quite excellent Barceloneta Market. RC

## MUSEU D'HISTÒRIA DE CATALUNYA

Plaça de Pau Vila, 3 (Palau de Mar)

☎ 93 225 4244
www.en.mhcat.net
Tues–Sat 1000–1900; Wed 1000–2000; Sun and public holidays 1000–1430
**History museum**/Entry 3€/Cards and euros

I have never seen so much food in a national museum. Over three levels of this large brick warehouse on the shores of Port Vell tell the story of the Catalans from the Bronze Age to the present. The Catalans' self-identity is founded just as much on what they eat as the wars they fought and art they have created, proving that food is history. At the heart of a re-creation of a Bronze Age mudbrick dwelling is a grill, the forerunner of the *la parrilla* found in many restaurants. Terracotta pots are filled with snails and chestnuts and bunches of wild thyme decorate the walls, something you see in Barcelona restaurants to this day. Amphorae brimming with wine, anchovies in salt and olive oil are stacked in a mock Roman barque from the first century AD, the brittle clay bottles protected with the bough

Beach sculpture, Barceloneta.

of pine trees. A working waterwheel feeding a small vegetable garden shows the impact Moorish inventions had on the Iberian Peninsula. A man and a mule could pump enough water from underground springs to irrigate 2 hectares. This led to greater population densities. The native foods, such as carrots and artichokes, were supplemented with new foods such as oranges, dates and pomegranates from Africa and the East. With the Moors came sugar, nutmeg, cinnamon, pepper and cloves. Maps of the globe highlight the Spanish expansion into South America, which brought the staples of potato, tomato, eggplant and peppers. There is a very cute reconstruction of a little kitchen from the 1930s, with a *cuina econòmica*, a tiny charcoal-burning stove with a hotplate the size of one pot. This explains so much of the Catalan cooking that is still being eaten today—the great one-pot dishes such as *escudella* or *sarsuela*. If, like me, you are a tragic for food history, block out half a day. (See also 1881 Per Sagardi, page 69.) RC

· · · · · · · · · · · · · · · · · · · ·

## PÒSIT

Reial Club Marítim de Barcelona
Moll d'Espanya s/n
( 93 221 6256
www.posit.es
Daily 1300–1400, 2000—2300
**Seafood/€€/Cards and euros**

The Royal Maritime Club of Barcelona sounds quite posh, but it actually looks like one of those concrete buildings erected by the Tasmanian Hydroelectric Commission in the 1950s. This one, however, is on the Barcelona waterfront across the road from the IMAX and aquarium complex. Look for the flapping navy blue awning and go up the rusty iron stairs to the right of the building and into a simple square and slightly worn room overlooking a million euros' worth of yachts and the palaces on the Passeig de Colom across the water. For me this is the place to take your family on a Sunday with all the other Barcelonese families. Here you'll find the *abuelos*, *padres* and all the little *chicos* dressed in their Sunday best from El Corte Inglés. It's very middle class, with beautiful mums keeping slim with the mixed salad entree or asparagus and ignoring the *allioli* and *romesco*. The kids meanwhile are wolfing down plates of fried squid and white bait until the waiter comes around and shows off the huge *arroz negro* before going to his station to plate it up. The families continue their rabble over the shared meal—the heart of Catalan culture. The food here is better than many other seafood establishments, and this is one of three Pòsit's restaurants, the original in Arenys de Mar and the other down the coast at Sitges. The *mejillones al vapor* with super-sweet Galician mussels served with their own garlic-infused juice are good. As are the paellas; consider the *arroz con calamares en su tinta*, rice with squid ink, or even the *cazuela de rape*, monkfish fillets cooked in a scorching-hot steel pan with a tomato-based sauce and a few clams. What you pay for the crap bread roll you'll make up for in the generous servings of wine by the glass. RC

. . . . . . . . . . . . . . . . . . . . . . . . . . .

## ROSA CANINA
Baluard, 52
( 63 602 9129
www.rosacanina.eu
Open April to the end of October
Mon–Fri 1400–2000; Sat 1100–2000;
Sun 1400–2000
**Ice-cream shop**/€/Cash

This little ice-cream parlour is close and handy to La Cova Fumada. Finish up there and grab a cone with flavours including cinnamon, hazelnut, chocolate and cardamom. FC

. . . . . . . . . . . . . . . . . . . . . . . . . . .

## SET PORTES (also called 7 PORTES)
Passeig d'Isabel II, 14
( 93 319 3033
www.7portes.com
Daily 1300–0100
**Old school Catalan**/€€€/Cards and euros

You know you're in an establishment with a long history when you feel the chequered marble tile floor dip under your feet from more than 170 years of wear and tear. You'll find the Seven Doors under a portico where a line of tourists waits by the door for a table. Yes, it's famous for being famous—and maybe justifiably so when you realise that the likes of Che Guevara and Errol Flynn have come here before you. It is a beautiful room that has been lovingly maintained, and the place has soul. Above the dark wood-panelled walls is a frieze of ceramic tiles detailed in aquamarine. Black iron columns support the room, and the octagonal waiters' table in the centre is the heart of the service. With a backdrop like that this place would be busy even if they served microwaved paella. But the food is good—not great but good. *Pa amb tomàquet* is made with rustic bread and first-rate olive oil—but prepped before service so the bread is a little soggy. In season order the *rovellons*—tiny pine mushrooms just warmed through in olive oil and laced with slivered garlic and hit with salt. The house dish is *Paella Parellada*, a rice dish 'invented for the wealthy but lazy gourmet' Juli Parellada, who wanted all the meat and seafood shelled and boned. This is still a place for locals, however, and many are older diners who like the slightly starched service and the simple and quite decent classic Catalan restaurant fare. RC

## SOMORROSTRO

Sant Carles, 11
( 93 225 0010
www.restaurantesomorrostro.com
Mon, Wed–Sat 2000–2300;
Sun 1400–1600, 2000–2300
**Bistronomical/Catalan/€€/**
Cards and euros

Jordi Limon may only be 25 but he is packing out his little Barceloneta restaurant every night with locals and Barcelonese from other *barris* who come for food from his small but punchy produce-based menu. The burgundy walls of the dining rooms make the restaurant feel smaller than it is, but it is a very comfortable place, with decent bistro chairs and a soundtrack of alternative 1980s and 90s music. There are a few too many clichéd modernist foams and lots of smearing and blobs of sauce and 'soil' on the plates, but Jordi says, 'This is not molecular. We are beyond this. We are working Catalan classics into a more artful presentation.' The best bet here would be the produce-driven specials, handwritten on a chalkboard that the beautiful waitresses walk to the tables. There could be a confit of suckling piglet, slow cooked in fat for 12 hours, then cooked *a la plancha* to crisp the skin.

# BARCELONA FOOD EXPERIENCES

I met Sarah's parents by chance several years ago while researching my cookbook *MoVida Rustica*. I was out in the country for a photo shoot, making paella with a Catalan chef, when I heard people speaking with Australian accents—a middle-aged couple sitting outside the restaurant was enjoying a post-prandial glass of wine. We got talking and they suggested I meet their daughter Sarah Stodhart, a chef who had a restaurant in Barcelona.

Sarah was born in Australia but spent years criss-crossing the Mediterranean with her artist parents before settling down in Barcelona, and her Mediterranean travels show in her food (see Tapioles 53, page 252). She has strong opinions about produce and backs these up with facts and examples. So when she gave us her top five food experiences in Barcelona, we knew they would be good. And they are. FC

## THE 1.5€ EGG

Huevería Gómez-Maldonado
Mercat Santa Caterina, No 191
Francesc Cambó, 16
Mon–Sat 0800–2000
93 319 80 41

At the front of the Santa Caterina market there is a stall run by a truly wonderful woman called Encarna Maldonado García, who is incredibly passionate about her job. She sells all sorts of eggs, from chook to ostrich eggs, all of which are for eating. But her best are truffled eggs that have been stored with truffles to take on a rich heady aroma, a small slice of heaven that warms the heart after a long day.

## LUCKY DIP

Jaime J Renobell Soler
Passeig Picasso, 34
93 319 7636
Mon–Sat 0915–1330; Mon–Fri 1615–1930

Under the arches on Passeig Picasso you will see pigeons fluttering around sacks trying to steel a tasty snack of dried beans or almonds. Jaime J Renobell is a shop that opened in 1945 and sells bulk dried products, from 15 types of flour to deep brown sticky organic sugar and four different types of pine nuts. All the products are in their original 25-kilo sacks, with big metal scoops poking out the top. There is nothing more delicious than delving my hand deep into a sack of golden pine nuts when no one is looking—the sensation is unique and the smell of warm summer lingers on my hand for a few short minutes later.

## CUTTING-EDGE JEWELS

Ganiveteria Roca
Plaça del Pi, 3 (Barri Gòtic)
93 302 1241
www.ganiveteriaroca.cat

It is always great to be classed as a local but at Ganiveteria Roca it gives me great delight. I have been going there since I was just a student, about 20 years ago. This beautiful modernist shop has changed very little since it opened in 1911, and is very much like a jewellery store, with beautiful glass cases and cabinets all the way around. Instead of jewels, however, they sell knives—an amazing selection of around 9000 of them—plus scissors and other blade-related wares. They present them as if they were forged in precious metal (some are in fact worth their weight in gold, so there is little difference). Once you ask to look at a knife it will be brought out with much care and laid upon a thick green velvet display mat … very much like jewellery. They sell every kind of knife you could imagine, from cheap '3 claveles' to custom hand-made knives from Japan that can cost over 2000€ and carry the forger's signature.

. . . . . . . . . . . . . . . . . . . . . . . . . . . . . .

## THE BEST TOMATOES IN TOWN

La Cuina d'en Garriga
Consell de Cent, 308 (Eixample)
93 215 7215
www.lacuinadengarriga.com

Some women love fashion, but for me it's food and food-related things, from fresh raw ingredients to Aga stoves. La Cuina d'en Garriga is one of the gems of Barcelona. The first day I discovered this wonderful haven I was lured by the smell of fresh ripe ox heart tomatoes … it stopped me in my tracks! Walking into the shop things only got better: crusty bread, handmade cheeses and wonderful fresh milk from a small farm with just a dozen cows. At the back there is a big beautiful old wooden table where you can sit and have a coffee or sip some bubbly.

. . . . . . . . . . . . . . . . . . . . . . . . . . . . . .

## LOCAL KNOWLEDGE
Ustrell
Parellada, 51 (Vilafranca del Penedès)
93 892 0109

Most chefs have little interest in hardware stores but I find they are an amazing source of local information. Just by browsing the shelves you can quickly figure out what grows well in the area. Ustrell in Vilafranca del Penedès is nothing short of amazing. The shop opened in 1940 and slowly grew. Today it is huge: three storeys of wonders. On the ground floor the walls have huge roman stone arches, and there is an old converted well, with a spiral staircase down the centre housing their mind-blowing selection of screws, nails, nuts and bolts. But what I find most fascinating is all the grape and wine related things: wine presses, from the ultra-modern to the old-fashioned hand-turned style; wooden barrels in different sizes and qualities; and cookware, cast-iron *marmita* and *paella* pans in dozens of different sizes, the smallest to feed a small child and the largest to feed around 700 hungry Catalans.

He does a terrine of *botifarra negra* with mushroom and potato or beach fish with rissoni and mussels. He loves game, and his wild-shot pigeon is served *al punto*—dark flavours of pan-seared deep red sanguine flesh with small pockets of sweet rich fat—truly a stunning dish. RC

. . . . . . . . . . . . . . . . . . . . . . .

## SUQUET DE L'ALMIRALL
Passeig Joan de Borbó, 65
( 93 221 6233
www.suquetdealmirall.com
Tue–Sun 1300–1600;
Tue–Sat 2100–2400
**Traditional Catalan seafood/**
€€/Cards and euros
This is a real gem among a row of tourist traps on the road by the waterfront. Chef Quim Marqués is a fourth-generation cook who has worked in the top Michelin-starred restaurants in Spain, is frequently on radio and television and has penned books. He is respected for the way he prepares traditional fishermen's dishes and buys his seafood daily from the fish market just a hundred metres away. The interior has a nautical theme, tame compared with others in the area. Being a chef I poked my head inside the kitchen and was really impressed by the sparkling clean kitchen and well-organised operation. Although it's fun being out on the terrace with the fantastic parade of people, it gets bloody hot out there. The locals eat inside, most of them well-dressed middle-aged men whom Quim knows by name. There is a menu of things to share, then a long list of *arroces, fideuás*, rice and pasta, many fish dishes—mostly braises—and a blackboard of changing specials. I love Quim's 12-hour-cooked calamari, which is then

given a little *el scorchio* on *la plancha,* sliced and served with lashings of onions cooked down to total sweetness. His red mullet, fresh from the deep fryer is ultra fresh and served with strips of green peppers. If you're going to call your restaurant after a dish you better get it right. Here the *suquet* is sublime—an intense sauce of fish broth, tomato and potatoes thickened with *picada* surrounding plump clams, baby calamari and morsels of meaty monkfish. His *sarsuela* is good too. Quim lifts traditional cooking to a really good dining experience without the high prices usually associated with seafood—the *suquet* is a very affordable 20€. FC

. . . . . . . . . . . . . . . . . . . . . . .

## VINOTECA VORAMAR

La Maquinista, 14
( 93 221 1937
www.vinoteca-voramar.com
Sat 1000–1400, 1700–2130;
Sun 1100–1500
**Wine shop**/Cards

This compact but beautifully fitted out little wine shop also serves whisky and water. The wines are basically Spanish, with sections dedicated to the Catalan DOs such as Priorat, Penedès, Costers del Segre and a good range of old Rioja. It's reassuring to know that here you can get an 18-year-old single malt from Skye at a moment's notice. It's also good to know that the owners

of Voramar love their spring water so much that they have of a wall of running water in the back room as a display feature. RC

. . . . . . . . . . . . . . . . . . . . . . .

## VIOKO GELAT XOCOLATA EXPERIÈNCIA

Passeig de Joan de Borbó, 55
( 93 221 0652
www.vioko.es
Mon–Thur 1200–2300;
Fri–Sat 1200–2400
**Chocolate, ice-cream and gelato**/€/Cards and euros

Amid the fish restaurants, Vioko stands alone as a temple to sweet things. Past the perspex columns at the doorway, filled with macaroons, are chocolate truffles covered in gold leaf sitting grandly in glass boxes like precious jewellery—all made in the 'chocolate studio' on the third floor above the store. The semicircular showroom does a good trade in house-made ice-creams on hot days. There are 35 flavours—for around 2.5€ a small cup. We found their *crema catalana* flavoured ice-cream to be an amazing achievement of food science, with the flavours of lemon, cinnamon and vanilla sitting pretty well with the 'toffee'—liquid raw sugar. Vioko only opened in June 2010 and if successful, the owners, originally from Argentina, plan to roll out more of these highly designed stores across the nation. RC

GÒTIC

THERE'S A MAN pushing a trolley with a box full of fish and ice. He's heading from La Boqueria Market to the Barri Gòtic, a maze of tiny pathways through canyons of medieval buildings. He needs the trolley to get to his restaurant, as there is no room for cars or delivery vehicles in much of this area, let alone people, who can clog the little laneways on busy summer days. In the heart of the quarter is Plaça de Sant Jaume, the site of the old Roman forum built two thousand years ago. Surrounding this are the old Roman walls that once protected the small administrative town, known then as Barcino.

Most of the Roman buildings have long gone, although some do remain and have been incorporated into other buildings, such as the four remaining pillars from the Temple of Augustus, now part of an 18th-century apartment block at Carrer del Paradís, 10. The old walls pop up here and there, such as in Plaça Nova, where the old towers are now part of a much later, grander building. These Roman foundations have been built over many times, each period leaving its mark with the construction of an edifice or the removal of one from previous generations.

What this quarter offers is an intense experience of discovery—around every corner is a little square, a medieval church, an ancient fountain, a raucous nightclub, some excellent graffiti, chips on a wall where a bomb exploded during the Civil War. On Saturday nights the quarter can be packed with thousands of young people making their way between bars and eventually home in the small hours. Early morning is the best time to explore this area for the architecture, and evening the best time for the food and the bars.

Many European cities have an ancient heart, but many of them have been so gentrified and polished that they have lost their original soul. Barcelona's Barri Gòtic, with its dim night-time lighting and slightly scuffed edges, always feels a little seedy, and dare I say, gothic.

## AGUT

Gignàs, 16
☎ 93 315 1709
Tue–Sun 1330–1600;
Tue–Sat 2100–2400
**Old school Catalan**/€€/Cards and euros

Down in the bowels of the gothic quarter is this rather pleasing dining room hiding behind the bevelled panes of a mullioned window. Agut is a family business founded in 1924, and Maria Agut García still runs this old school Catalan dining room. Inside it has a warm, even cosy atmosphere, with two wainscotted rooms and cream-coloured walls. These are covered in paintings from the middle of last century by some well-known and, shall we say, 'other' local artists. Your meal could start with a dish of Cantabrian anchovies crisscrossed over slightly under-ripe tomatoes and small preserved arbequina olives, the salt from the anchovies sweetening up the tomatoes—it works! Try an *esqueixada* with good salt cod, tomato and raw onion and a *romesco* sauce made with aged sherry vinegar. You can tell that this place is a favourite with the locals, because most of the people are speaking Catalan. They are here for the grilled steaks, game and rice dishes. Agut isn't setting the world on fire—more keeping the home fires burning. RC

## ☿ BAR GINGER

Plaça de Sant Just, 1
☎ 93 310 5309
www.ginger.cat
Tue–Sat 1900–0230
**Bar**/Cards and euros

This friendly little place not far from the cathedral is where the night starts, not dies. Just off a square with a fountain that has three stone faces, Ginger has two different spaces, one with a cocktail focus and the other with a very well-considered little wine list. This is a good place to sip and chat before dinner, or before launching into one of the real late-night bars. PG

## CAELUM

Palla, 8
☎ 93 302 6993
Mon–Thur 1030–2030; Fri–Sat 1030–2330; Sun 1130–2130
**Tea room**/€/Cards and euros

Here's the perfect chance to try delicacies handmade by virgins. Nuns in fact. Nunneries used to be big business, places for the younger daughters of rich families and the surplus of girls from poor families. As idle hands are the devil's playground, nuns were set to work making delicious sweet pastries as a revenue raiser. These days the sisters are less cloistered, especially in Catalonia, where they work within the community, so these classic Spanish delicacies are gradually

Els Quatre Gats

becoming rarer. Caelum is, and I rarely use this word, a 'gorgeous' little tea room, serving coffee, hot chocolate, infusions and little cakes and pastries made to the highest standards using the best ingredients. Try the *corazones de mazapán* from the Clarisas de Ávila, chocolate truffles from the Clarisas de Valladolid or *marrón glacé* from the Benedictinos de Monlera. Some of the packaged foods here would make great gifts—you will have to declare them at Customs in Australia, but they tend to let you through. This is a very old building and in the afternoon

a fascinating 14th-century bathroom is open to the public downstairs. RC

. . . . . . . . . . . . . . . . . . . . . . . . . .

## COOK AND TASTE
Paradís, 3
☏ 39 330 21320
www.cookandtaste.net
Mon–Sat 1100 and 1700 starting times
**Cooking school**

There is no better way of understanding a cuisine than by cooking and then eating it. You can consume as much *suquet* as you want, but unless you learn how each stage of the cooking process is finessed, you're not really going to get your head around it and it will remain just a Catalan fish stew. That's why I love Bego Sanchis's Cook and Taste Catalan cooking classes. A four-hour class is 60€, but I recommend the 12€ supplement, starting the class with an hour-long tour of the world's most famous food market, La Boqueria (see pages 15–20). The setting is perfect: two large rooms in the heart of Barcelona in a reconditioned building just off the Plaça Sant Jaume. The classes are held in English and with wine, so watch your knife. You'll be cooking with a maximum of eleven other complete strangers working together to prepare some basic Catalan dishes, usually two tapas, a rice dish and a dessert. Bego can also tailor the classes for groups. I found this to be really good value. FC

. . . . . . . . . . . . . . . . . . . . . . . . . . .

## ⵙ EL PIPAS

Plaça Reial, 3
☎ 93 301 1165
www.bpipaclub.com
Daily 1800–early morning
**Bar**/Cards and euros

This is where all of Barcelona seems to come at the end of the night. It was once a pipe club, hence El Pipas, and is tucked away on the second floor of what looks like an apartment building on the Plaça Reial. Push the big white buzzer then go up to the second floor. It's a low-lit, moody space spread out with old chairs and tables, a small stage and semi-central bar where night owls of all ages and backgrounds come for the tail end of a good night. There are display cases filled with old Sherlock Holmes–like tobacco pipes and smoking paraphernalia, and it's one of the few places in Barcelona with a pool table. Drink beer or wine or hook up with the locals and drink vodka and Fanta. Fantastic fun if you can remember getting there or even leaving. PG

. . . . . . . . . . . . . . . . . . . . . . . . . . .

## ELS QUATRE GATS

Montsió, 3, bis
☎ 93 302 4140
www.4gats.com
Daily 1300–0100
**Old school Catalan**/€€/Cards and euros

For six brief years this beautiful building in the centre of the gothic quarter was the heart of the Barcelona *modernisme* movement. From 1897 Casa Martí was a cafe, restaurant and cabaret, largely financed by artist Ramon Casas (replicas of his famous paintings adorn the walls of the bar). Artists such as Santiago Rusiñol and Miquel Utrillo were also involved, and the cafe was a salon of ideas and expositions. The party ended in 1903 due to mountains of debt, and after that the ground floor of Casa Martí saw more mundane uses, including a military repository during the fascist era. It was reinvigorated as a restaurant in 1989, renamed, and is now a mecca for tourists from around Spain and the globe. The owners could rest on the laurels of their magnificently restored dining room—the painted woodwork in the main dining room and the tile work on the floor and walls are attractions in themselves—but the owners put on a really good show. It's old school food, but it is good quality and reasonably priced at around 10€ for starters and 20€ for mains. The *coca* with *escalivada* is crisp, the vegetables smoky and the *allioli* light but passable. A floured and fried piece of salt cod is served in a *cazuela* with chickpeas and wilted spinach. The salt cod isn't fried to order, but it is good quality and the chickpeas, when crushed a little, make a really sweet and earthy sauce. Pig's cheek, slow cooked until it's sweet and sticky, is on the menu. Please try the *recuit*, a ricotta-like goat's or cow's milk cheese made in Fonteta near Girona, drizzled with honey—a perfectly simple dessert. Friends of mine who live here recommend you come during the day to see the place in the natural light. They laughingly say that Els Quatre Gats, with its old-fashioned menu and old-fashioned staff, is not only a museum to modernism but a museum to food and service. Thankfully it doesn't take itself too seriously. RC

## FORMATGERIA LA SEU

Dagueria, 16
( 93 412 6548
www.formatgerialaseu.com
Tue–Thur 1000–1400, 1700–2000;
Fri–Sat 1000–1530, 1700–2000
Spanish cheese shop/€/Cards and euros

Early last century this was an artisan butter factory, the workshop about the size of half a terrace house. The original wooden refrigerator and old butter conditioner are still here. Since 2000 it has been a cheese shop, selling Spanish farmhouse and artisan cheeses. Owner Katherine McLaughlin is a Scottish cheese purist who learned from London and Edinburgh's best cheese merchants. Katherine's storage space is limited, so her stock rotation is high and she relies on the cheesemakers to send cheeses when they consider them to be at their best. Buy a selection of cheese for your picnic in the park or, even better, partake in her amazingly good-value 7€ cheese plate—only available on Friday and Saturday, 12–3.30 pm or by prior arrangement for groups of two or more. We love Katherine's passion for cheese. She staunchly refuses to vacuum pack them for tourists as she, like us, believes this smothers them. You could learn a lot about cheese from Katherine and she is happy to share. RC

# — TOP FIVE —
## CHEAP EATS

**1 CAN PAIXANO**
Reina Cristina, 7 (Barceloneta)
Eighty euro cents for a glass of *cava*!

**2 PIM PAM BURGER**
Sabateret, 4 (Born)
A big fat burger made with a real beef patty for 5€.

**3 COVA FUMADA**
Baluard, 56 (Barceloneta)
A beer and a *bomba* in a beautiful old bar for a fiver.

**4 LA BOQUERIA MARKET BARS**
Rambla de Sant Josep, 89 (El Raval)
A quick dish on a stool at one of the bars at the world's most
famous market. Try Quim de la Boqueria, Kiosko Universal or
Pinotxo.

**5 XURRERIA MANUEL SAN ROMÁN**
Banys Nous, 8 (Barri Gòtic)
A couple of churros and a bag of freshly fried chips for
a few euros.

DISTRITO 1°.
BARRIO 5°.
CALLE DE LA
DAGUERIA.

Restaurant

## KOY SHUNKA

Copons, 7
( 93 412 7939
www.koyshunka.com
Tue–Sun 1300–1500, 2030–2300
**Japanese**/€€€/Cards and euros

If I was taken blindfolded into the kitchen and then shown the ingredients and cooking methods, I would swear this place was Spanish: there is tuna, mackerel, sea bass, prawns, razor clams, eggplant, olive oil, fresh mushrooms, *la plancha*, hot oil, a grill and charcoal grill. But this stunning high-end restaurant, only a chopstick's throw from the cathedral, is the domain of Hideki Matsuhisa, a Tokyo-born Japanese chef. There's à la carte in a dining room to one side and a C-shaped wooden bar that arcs around the hi-tech stainless-steel kitchen. The bar is the stage for the set menu, where you sit side by side with Spaniards and other Europeans, mostly young and very well dressed, who come not only to eat, but to *watch* their ten-course set menu being cooked. Hideki-san knows theatre and calls the pass in a mix of Japanese and the local tongue—it's like watching *Iron Chef* dubbed into Spanish. He runs a very Japanese kitchen but has created dishes that the locals will recognise. Paper-thin slices of Spanish *mojama* are served on squares of deep-fried nori. Portions of sardine pickled in rice wine are served on top of pickled rossinyol mushrooms with a judicious dressing of soy sauce. Try a plate of charcoal-grilled Iberico pork served with three different types of mushroom over which dashi stock is poured from an iron teapot. Koy Shunka's older (but smaller) brother, Shunka (see page 117), opened in 2001 and bankrolled the 2008 opening of this place, reflecting the growing passion the Barcelonese have for Japanese food. While the Michelin reviewers might not have this on their radar, I reckon it's worth booking in for a seat at the bar. RC

. . . . . . . . . . . . . . . . . . . . . . . . . . .

## LA COLMENA

Plaça de l'Àngel, 12
( 93 315 1356
Daily 0900–2100
**Pastry shop**/€/Cash

This 150-year-old pastry shop in the heart of the old town is where locals drop in and buy their morning croissants, or maybe a post-prandial cake for the family at the weekend for which you'll need a bottle of whisky. Don't worry—there's plenty of that here. With the ladies in their white coats, the marble floors and ornate work on the columns, it has a lovely retro kitsch appeal. Look out for the *carquinyolis*—crisp almond biscuits— or the pine nut–encrusted *panellets* in autumn. For me though, anyone who goes a step beyond stuffing a buttery croissant with ham and cheese and uses a hefty spread of *sobrassada*—spiced

# BARCELONA EXPERIENCES

**1** Delicious cava and tapas while standing on the street with friends in the sun at Quimet & Quimet.

**2** The friendly atmosphere Sarah provides at Tapioles 53. It's like being in someone's home, getting fed delicious food.

**3** An early morning crispy toasted ensaïmada with fresh orange juice from Pinotxo, then a stroll through one of the world's great food markets, La Boqueria.

**4** Drinking cava among the vines in Penedès, then lunch at Cal Xim.

**5** Having a bite to eat and an ice cold Moritz at Bar Velódromo at 1 am in the morning, between bars.

and fatty raw pork sausage—has never heard of cardiovascular disease. Delicious. RC

. . . . . . . . . . . . . . . . . . . . . . .

## LA GRANJA

Banys Nous, 4
( 93 302 6975
Daily 0930–1330, 1700–2100
**Cafe** /€/Cash

*Granjas* are family places where you drink cold milky *horchata*, a refreshing beverage made from tiger lily nuts (similar to sweet almond milk), tea, coffee or hot chocolate. This *granja* has history too—literally. One of the sides of the back room is an exposed Roman wall, and the walls of the front room are covered in front pages from the local newspaper *La Vanguardia* dating from the 1930s. It's now run by a young crowd quite happy to play Leonard Cohen's later albums and serve lovely cups of tea and light snacks. Check out perhaps the world's smallest spiral staircase out the back. Perfect for something light and refreshing. RC

. . . . . . . . . . . . . . . . . . . . . . .

## LES QUINZE NITS

Plaça Reial, 6
( 93 317 3075
www.lesquinzenits.com
Daily 0900–2100, 1300–1545,
2030–2330
**Catalan and International**/€€/
Cards and euros

This place was recommended b several people and appears in man guide books, so we decided to reviev it. Judging by the queue, this plac on the sunny side of the Plaça Reial i very popular, but perhaps that's jus the effect of the no-reservations polic and people's love of joining queues Wait for a seat under the colonnade facing into the *plaça* and admire th beautiful facades of this 18th-centur square, because inside there are scan reminders of the once elaboratel painted ceilings and walls, which ar now concealed by a modern lowere ceiling and other fittings. Now—th food. This place offers internationall accepted delights such as nachos an spag bol. These are safer bets than th lifeless versions of Catalan classics w sampled. It's cheap, but you get wha you pay for. RC

. . . . . . . . . . . . . . . . . . . . . . .

## LOS CARACOLES

Casa Bofarull
Escudellers, 14
( 93 301 2041
www.loscaracoles.es
Daily 1330–2400
**Spanish**/€€/Cards and euros

I don't often recommend restaurant where the food is below par, but here I' make an exception, for this restauran is a living, breathing museum an therefore is important. Opened i 1835 by the Bofarull family, it has beer

running continually since then, slowly expanding and consuming surrounding buildings. It's a deceptive space of seemingly endless rooms attached to each other by wooden staircases and stone stairs up, around and into rooms that seem like they have been dug out of the earth like some animal's burrow. Outside there is the unmistakable open charcoal rotisserie—something that would never pass our health inspectors. There's always a young chef spending more attention looking at the cute girls than attending to his chickens roasting over the coals. Evening is an incredibly busy time, with 300 diners seated at once and more waiting at the bar. During the day, take a seat at the bar, order some *jamón* and watch the circus. When you've had enough of that, explore the labyrinth. First you'll have to pass the central kitchen, and what possibly might be the closet thing to hell I have ever seen—an army of ancient chefs and young apprentices toiling over the original wood-fired ovens in unbearable heat and black smoke—then past a series of ancient dining rooms, each with countless signed photos of celebrities such as Plácido Domingo, Charlton Heston and former US presidents who dined here in their respective heydays. The rooms get quirkier and weirder as you progress: snail statues along staircases (*caracoles* is Spanish for snails),

massive murals, painted wine barrels, beautifully set private dining rooms with *jamones* hanging from the ceiling, even a well in one. The food may not be the best, but the experience of just being here is worth it. FC

. . . . . . . . . . . . . . . . . . . . . . . . .

## NEYRAS RESTAURANT

Via Laietana, 41
( 93 302 4647
www.neyras.com
Daily 1100–0100
**Old school Catalan**/€€€€/Cards and euros

This is a three-for-one deal: wine shop, tapas bar and restaurant. The baby grand as you walk in is a giveaway as to the type of place it is. It cranks up Thursday to Sunday. This cavernous ground floor room inside a 19th-century apartment building is luxury for the hard-working middle class. We like this place because the wine focus goes beyond the usual suspects. The staff have good English and wine knowledge and can find wines to go with dishes such as a whole sea bass, cooked skin on in a crust of salt. This is served silver service as fillets with potatoes and a thin tartare sauce. There could be a veal sirloin topped with pan-fried *foie gras* or a nice little duck leg. It's a conservative choice of a decent standard. RC

. . . . . . . . . . . . . . . . . . . . . . . .

## PITARRA

Avinyó, 56

☏ 93 301 1647

www.restaurantpitarra.cat

Mon–Sat 1300–1600, 2000–2300;
Closed 16–30 August inc.

**Old school Catalan**/€€€/Cards
and euros

This place was great once and has made it into every guidebook. It has been a restaurant since 1890 and was once home to Frederic Soler, better known as Pitarra, a performer who laid the foundations of Catalan theatre. There are posters of him on the walls upstairs, dressed up as his 'characters'— drunks and criminals and pompous buffoons. The building also used to be a watchmaker's, hence the vast number of clocks on the wall quietly marking the passing of the day. It's owned by Marc and Jaume Roig, with Jaume looking after front of house. Ask Jaume to show you where the king dined and he'll take you upstairs to one of the small private chambers—so filled with manuscripts that it is more like a library than a dining room. Jaume doesn't speak English, but his determination to communicate somehow overcomes this small fact—especially after you've had a few drinks. And the wine list contains some really great Catalan wines. Allow Jaume to lead the way on this as his judgment is good. The food, however, lets the team down. Stick to the game and mushrooms here, as it seems the passion for the other dishes was lost years ago. But the whole setting, Jaume and the artwork all make up for the food. RC

. . . . . . . . . . . . . . . . . . . . . . . . . . .

Neyras Restaurant

## PLAÇA DEL PI FARMERS' MARKET

Plaça del Pi
1st and 3rd Fri, Sat, Sun of the month 1100–1430, 1700–2130
Artisinal products and farmers' market/Cash

The *Col·lectiu d'Artesans de l'Alimentació* —the Collective of Artisan Food-makers—meets every two weeks to sell their wares in this stunning square out the front of the church of Santa Maria del Pi. It's called del Pi after a pine tree that grew in front of the steps of the 14th-century church. This market has been operating since 1985 and supports people who want to make a living from the Catalonian country. Farmers, cheesemakers, fungus hunters, small goods makers and apiarists sell their products direct to the public. If you want an idea of the native flora growing around Catalonia, then see Joaquim Refa. His stunning range of wild honeys is collected in the heath country, from wild flowers and more exotic eucalyptus. The boys from Monbolet harvest and dry *ceps*, black trumpets and *boletus*, blend them with herbs and bottle them with rice or *fideus* as pre-made artisan meals—just add stock and *sofrito*. The cheeses from Formatge del Montsec Cendrat in the Pyrenees near Andorra are made from raw goat's milk and aged in caves; they are really funky tasting cheeses with a very strong acidity and may be a bit too feral-tasting for some. RC

## SAÜC

Via Laietana, 49
( 93 321 0189
www.saucrestaurant.com
Tue–Sat 1330–1530, 2030–2230
**Modern Catalan bistronomic/** One Michelin star/€€/Cards and euros

A shining light in the world of bistronomy, Saüc recently moved from its home in Eixample to the swish Hotel Ohla. Chef Xavier Franco Viles serves outstandingly high-quality à la carte food at very reasonable prices. Only 40, he has worked in the best kitchens in town including ABaC, (see page 31) Racó de Can Fabes (see page 280) and Tragaluz. There are two tasting menus, but personally I think the 27€ lunch menu is outstanding value. In this Xavier punches out amazingly tasty dishes while keeping food costs in check. The meal may start with a handful of *marcona* almonds roasted with egg white, salt and cinnamon, and a jube of tomato, garlic and thyme rolled in sugar. You might be served a plate of grilled cauliflower, leek, carrot, radish and death trumpets with a frothed saffron *velouté*. There could be a plate of shredded *jamón* and shelled prawns over which a smooth puree of green peas is poured. Xavier knows his Catalan classics and presents a great version of *cim i tomba*, in this case three pieces of gelatinous ray with a few potatoes sitting in a *suquet*.

Stunning. French skills are well honed, with a confit maryland of duck, crisp-skinned and well seasoned but not too salty. Xavier also has a great sense of humour, expressed in a dessert called *llet amb galetes*—foamed UHT milk over butter biscuits dusted with *Colacao,* the Spanish equivalent of Milo. He's serving up a version of an after-school snack in a one-Michelin-star restaurant. Brilliant! Also consider the Xavier Franco's little gastro bar in the bottom floor of the Ohla Hotel. Serving uber-cool tapas in a big windowed room on the corner of Via Laietana and Carrer Central. RC

## SHUNKA

Sagristans, 5
( 93 412 4991
Tue–Sun 1330–1515, 2030–2315
**Japanese**/€€/Cards and euros

There has been an explosion in Japanese restaurants in Barcelona, but many are ho-hum. Shunka, however, is good and an affordable alternative to its younger and flashier brother Koy Shunka. After eating so much heavy Spanish food I crave Asian cuisine, and Shunka offers the antidote. This is a no-frills restaurant down a nondescript alleyway—bamboo and Japanese fabric mark the door. Down a long corridor there's a busy army of Japanese chefs working in an open kitchen, with a bar and stools surrounding the kitchen. There's a

dining room that is barely decorated but always busy, so if you want a seat then make a booking. There is also a takeaway option. The food is generally good, with some great fatty tuna belly sashimi. It's all quite Japanese 101, but it is just what you need to kill the cravings. (See also Koy Shunka, page 109.) FC

## VILA VINITECA

Agullers, 9 and 7
( 90 232 7777
www.vilaviniteca.es
Mon–Sat 0830–2030; Saturdays
July & August 0830–1430
**Wine shop and deli**/€€/Cards and euros

Before you're overwhelmed by this fantastic wine store and delicatessen, have a look at the ironmonger across the road still belting out steel rods to make balconies. A few doors up is a cobbler who makes beautiful shoes by hand. I lifted up my foot and showed him my right RM Williams boot and he said, 'Beautiful. Hand made.' We became familiar with this area when the Vila Viniteca manager showed us around the neighbourhood. He's proud that his establishment sits in a street that has maintained its traditional artisans. It has been owned by the same family since 1932 but was given a modern facelift in 2005. Nestled in two small beautiful stone buildings either side of an alleyway, the owners have

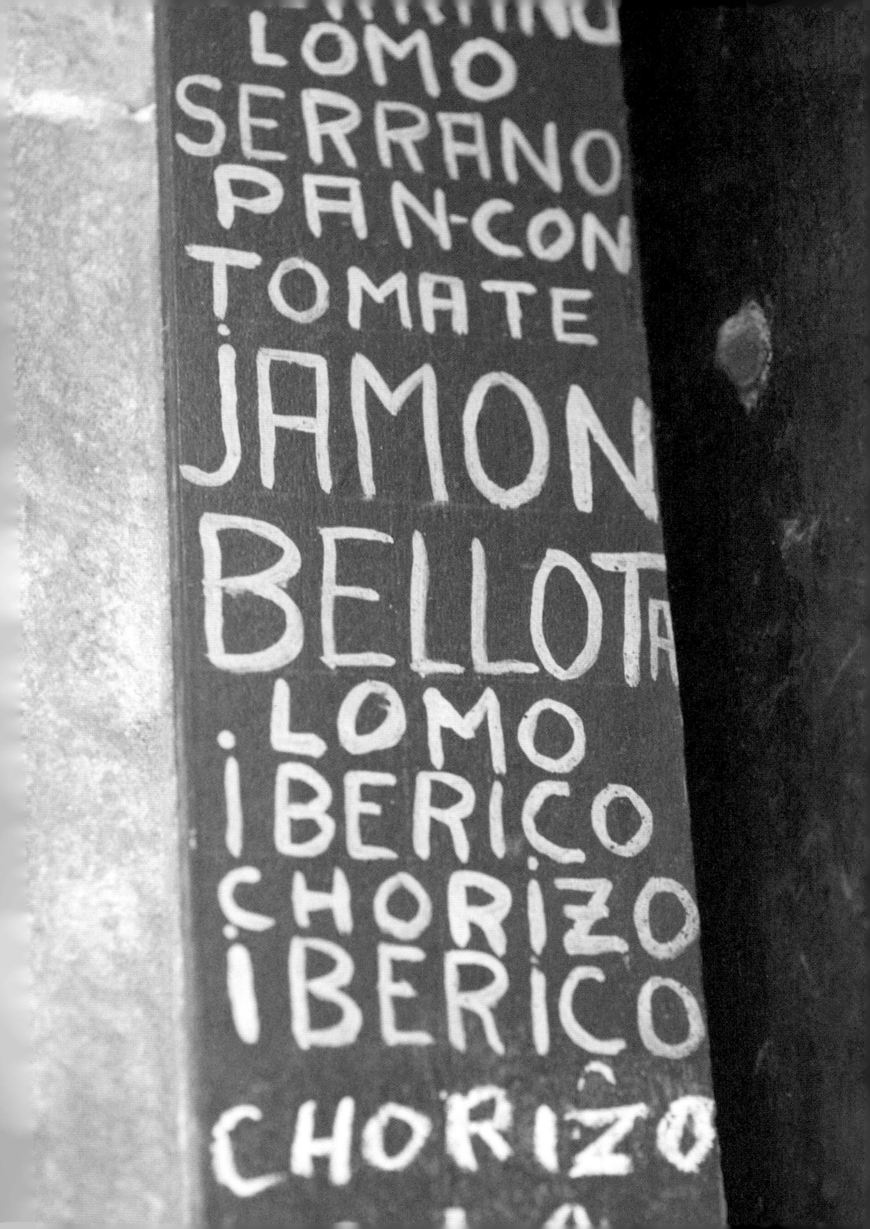

LOMO
SERRANO
PAN-CON
TOMATE
JAMON
BELLOTA
LOMO
iBERICO
CHORIZO
iBERICO

CHORIZO

put together a huge selection of wines, mostly from Spain, but also from around the world—we spied a bottle of Penfolds Grange in there. Vila Viniteca is the main wholesaler of quality Spanish wines in Catalonia, distributing an amazing catalogue of national and international brands to the best restaurants in Barcelona. This huge selection is also on offer to the retail customer. It is exciting to see so many of the brands that are too small or too idiosyncratic to make it to Australia. We are lovers of wines that come from old vines made using the natural method by lunatics—there are shelves of these wines. This is eno-heaven. Across the lane the same commitment to quality extends to an amazing deli that is a testament to the best hams, small goods, cheeses and *conservas*, mostly from around Spain. An entire wall is covered with a massive selection of tinned fish, cock's crests, molluscs and vegetables, some of these selling for scores of euros, because in Spain they only put something in a tin if it is the very, very best. This deli is a great pleasure for any food lover—the staff are incredibly knowledgeable about the products they are selling and very open to questions. There is a real pride in the way things are displayed, looked after and sold. What excites us most is that all the products they sell are available to eat on the premises at a few small tables in the deli or downstairs

in the cellar for larger groups. Try a few different types of smallgoods or *jamón*, or a few Spanish cheeses that are only found here. Choose a bottle from the bottle shop and they will pour it for you for just 6€. Very, very civilised. FC & RC

. . . . . . . . . . . . . . . . . . . . . . . . . .

## XURRERIA MANUEL SAN ROMÁN

Banys Nous, 8
( 93 318 7691
Daily 0800–1330, 1600–2000
Churros and fried food/€/Cash

Manuel San Román has been frying food in this narrow lane that leads to the Plaça del Pi for 42 years. His *churros* fit the scale of the *barri*. They are small and hooped into a teardrop shape—elegant enough to dip into hot chocolate. (Some places will let you take *churros* bought from somewhere else and enjoy them at their tables as long as you buy something else like hot chocolate or coffee.) Manuel also does a fine range of *patatas fritas* and little deep-fried potato straws that are weighed out in 100-gram lots and sold in bags. Manuel also offers a range of deep-fried pork rinds that are beautifully light, crisp and crunchy. His food tastes very rich but is fresh. When asked his secret, he says, 'I only use peanut oil. Yes, it may be expensive, but it is the best for frying.' Fry on, Manuel. RC

. . . . . . . . . . . . . . . . . . . . . . . . .

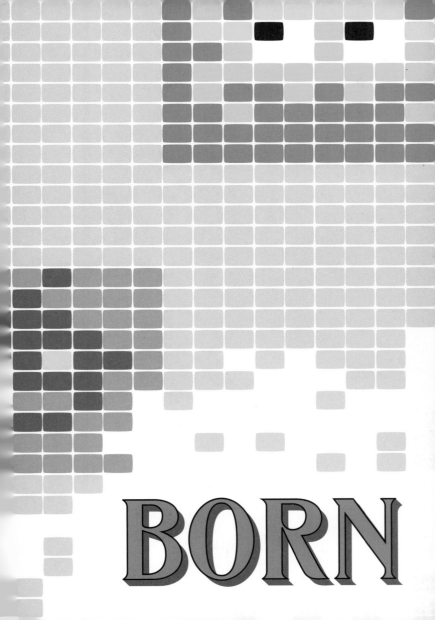

BORN

WHEN I FIRST CAME back to Barcelona in the early 1990s and headed down to Born, my family asked me, 'What on earth are you going down there for? It's so dodgy and dangerous!' So much has changed in two decades. This is now the heartland of the young, affluent, cool and hip in Barcelona, with apartments turned into modern hotels and shops filled with local designer clothes. Sitting between Barri Gòtic and Poblenou, some parts can be as labyrinthine as the Gothic Quarter, while other parts feel comparatively open and modern. It is home to the Picasso Museum, the Chocolate Museum and the city's museum for costumes worn during the fiestas. With its proximity to the water and scores upon scores of small bars and restaurants, it stacks up as a good place to stay and hang around.

The area is anchored by the landmarks of the old market and the church of Santa Maria del Mar. The old market is being transformed into a cultural centre, and once complete, this part of Barcelona will be one of the most exciting in Spain, with new galleries, restaurants, design studios and designers blending in with the generations-old businesses that already exist here. Probably the most popular area is the streets and squares around Santa Maria del Mar, a 14th-century church built at the height of the Catalonian Mediterranean empire, when the Catalan kings reigned over Sardinia and parts of Italy. It has an imposing gothic façade and an impressive yet intimate interior with quite a beautiful stone rose at one end.

One of the most exciting areas is around carrers Comerç and Portal Nou. Away from the cafes and bars that cater to the tourists are some of the younger, more fun places, just far enough off the beaten track to attract their own critical mass of locals. Since I first visited in the 1990s, Born has been born again and continues to grow as a vibrant part of Barcelona. FC

## ⍓ BAR DEL PLA

Montcada, 2
☏ 93 268 3003
www.elpla.cat
Tue–Thur, Sat–Sun 1200–2300;
Fri 1200–2400
**Catalan tapas and shared dishes**/€€/Cards and euros

Two young blokes called Jordi run this fun bar. One out the front pours some seriously good wine by the glass and one out the back cooks pan-Spanish dishes. Pan-Spanish? Yes, chef Jordi has worked in restaurants around Spain, learning how to cook regional specialities. He brings these together in a compact menu that is not a pastiche of dishes but rather his own modern style. There's a great tuna tartare, a crisp oxtail dish with *foie gras* and a dish of eggs with a big fat *botifarra*. It's a cavern-like room, reminding me of pictures of the Cavern Club in which the Beatles used to play in the early days. The crowd is young and young at heart. Here they serve one of my favourite little dishes in Barcelona—the black squid ink *croqueta*, a deep-fried dark ball of rich béchamel with loads of cooked onion, chunks of squid, squid ink and the rich aroma of the sea. Their calamari stuffed with eggplant and capsicum, dressed with almond vinaigrette and bonito flakes, is almost as good. RC

## BIG FISH

Comercial, 9
☏ 93 268 1728
www.bigfish.cat
Mon–Sun 1330–1545, 2030–2345
**Japanese**/€€€/Cards and euros

When a local fishmonger opens a sushi restaurant in the gastronomic heart of Spain there must be something going on, particularly when they have spent so much on the fit-out in this high-ceilinged room under one of the grand apartments opposite the old Born Market. Antique fittings have been beautifully applied to this large dining room—old mirrors, carved wooden statues, pillars masked by old shutters, the kitchen framed in a *modernisme* carved proscenium arch. Frank describes it as 'retro Baroque' and it's as beautiful as the crowd. Young and healthy, they're here not just to be seen, but for the quality local fish. The flavour of the raw fish used in the sashimi is stunning; the fat-enlaced raw tuna belly alone is worth the visit. The dish of the moment is tuna tartare, hand-chopped raw tuna enriched with avocado and mayonnaise, something I remember from Australia a few years ago but now gaining popularity in Barcelona—as is the whole Japanese phenomenon. The chef in charge of Japanese cooking is local Luisa Jaramillo, who trained under Japanese chefs and made the crossover, taking

Bar del Pla

beautiful fat raw scallops marinated in mirin and adding a blow-torched layer of sugar to give a crisp crust. 'In the last half-decade there has been a growing acceptance for Japanese food,' she says. 'Now it is only growing stronger.' RC

. . . . . . . . . . . . . . . . . . . . . . . . . . .

## CAFÉS EL MAGNÍFICO
Argenteria, 64
( 93 310 3361
www.cafeselmagnifico.com
Mon–Sat 1000–1400, 1600–2000
**Coffee roaster**/€€/Cards and euros

'Barcelona is the best place in Spain to get good coffee,' explains the passionate Salvador Sans Velasco of Cafés El Magnífico. He is quite right. Despite producing great wines, oils, small goods, beers and hundreds of other food products, Spaniards by and large drink bad coffee. During the Franco years, he explains, the less costly but also less flavoursome robusta variety of coffee became very popular. To extract the maximum flavour, the beans were roasted very dark, and some roasters even sprayed the beans with water and sugar to get a darker, deeper colour and flavour. These beans make dreadful coffees. Salvador's family, however, have been importing and roasting quality green arabica coffee beans since 1919. Today Salvador specialises in single-estate coffees but also produces blends. He is no coffee snob and believes there is a place for all types of coffee making. 'If coffee was alcohol then espresso would be *aguardiente* (*grappa*) and filtered coffee wine,' he says. 'On a Sunday morning before the children are awake I put the filter coffee machine on and walk down to Hofmann Patisseria (see page 144) and buy some passionfruit croissants filled with mango. You see, coffee is also about the context and the conviviality. It is something to be enjoyed with others.' If you're staying in an apartment, they generally come furnished with a stovetop coffee maker and it's worth buying some coffee from Salvador. You'll find a large selection of beautiful coffee cups here. Also, tea lovers go across Carrer Argenteria to Salvador's other shop, Sans & Sans Fine Tea Merchants. RC

. . . . . . . . . . . . . . . . . . . . . . . . . . .

## CAL PEP
Plaça de les Olles, 8
( 93 310 7961
www.calpep.com
Tue–Sat 1300–1545; Mon–Fri 1930–2330; closed August
**Catalan**/€€/Cards and euros

Cal Pep is an institution and has spawned many imitators across the globe in places like London and Hong Kong. You can wait for up to an hour for a spot at the bar—I have. In fact I have waited more than this and had to ask myself, 'Is it worth it?' Maybe. While you're pressed against the wall, standing behind and breathing down the necks of the seated customers, a glass of cava in your hand keeps you from shouting, 'Hurry up!' to the tourists squabbling over who directed *Vicky Cristina Barcelona*. It was Woody Allen already! The food is OK, but unreliable. The menu is seafood based, but there are some offerings from the garden and the paddock. It is very seasonal and they purchase whatever is good from the market, then cook it in true down-to-earth Catalan style. Doing food simply is actually not that easy to do well. It relies not only on the quality of the ingredients but also on the skill and sometimes mood of the cook. Dishes like *chanquetes con huevo*, baby white bait rolled in flour, flash fried and topped with a fried egg chopped up by the waiter, can be pure magic, but can sometimes be disappointing. The same goes for a simple dish of monkfish tail roasted with a *refrito* of garlic and chilli. Can be great; can be average. FC

. . . . . . . . . . . . . . . . . . . . . . .

## CASA DELFÍN

Passeig del Born, 36
☏ 93 319 5088
Mon–Fri 0730–0100;
Sat & Sun 0800–0100
**Seafood and Catalan**/€€/
Cards and euros

At the end of Passeig del Born is the old Born Market. Built from steel, glass and terracotta in the 1870s, it was the wholesale fruit and vegetable market until it closed in the 1970s. Renovation work started on the magnificent structure in 2002, but the discovery of important archaeological ruins of the 17th-century Ribera neighbourhood have pushed the completion of what is to be a new cultural centre out to at least 2012. So when you're sitting outside on the terrace at Casa Delfín, you'll understand why this impressive edifice is surrounded by hoardings. This is a 50-year-old restaurant that has been given a new lease of life by the owners of the group of tapas bars called Taller de Tapas. They have cleaned the place up and given it a few new fittings and a kind of French-bistro feel. The prices are really reasonable for the quality on offer. At heart, it's all about seafood. Sure there are steaks from Girona that are given a bit of el scorchio on the grill then set in the oven, and there is a breakfast menu offering great little tortillas. But it's the seafood that reigns supreme: the prawns, mussels or *peix fresc de barca*— fish fresh from the boat, perhaps sea bass or sardines—are truly stunning. Cooked in a heavy iron pan with a few sprigs of rosemary on a bed of sea salt the sardines are sweet, succulent and so fresh. One of the owners is English, so every now and then desserts like peach cobbler pop up on the menu because God bless them, there are only so many *cremas catalanas* one can eat. RC

. . . . . . . . . . . . . . . . . . . . . . .

# JAMÓN

*Jamón* is the cured meat of a pig's leg, salted and let to set and mature in the dry cold air of the mountains. *Jamón* is not a native food of the Catalans; traditionally they cured their pork in sausages such as *fuet*, *botifarra* and *llonganissa*. In the more humid climate dominated by the weather of the Mediterranean, Catalans would cure great hunks of pork under olive oil and by all accounts it wasn't something to celebrate, more something to endure during the lean cold months.

Even the most die-hard Catalan cannot turn away from *jamón*. A young Catalan chef who worked for me had to admit that *jamón* was his favourite food, even if he didn't consider himself Spanish. For visitors to Spain who are largely only spending their time in Barcelona, as many do, this is a perfect opportunity to sample one of the best food products in the world.

Ninety per cent of Spanish *jamón* is *serrano*. This is a commercial product often made in factories from factory-farmed pigs. *Jamón serrano* should have an attractive nose, deep pink-red flesh, firm texture and taste both salty and sweet. *Serrano* ham can be of exceptional quality.

The remaining 10 per cent of *jamón* is *jamón ibérico*, made from the peninsula's indigenous Iberian pigs.

The hallmark produce is *jamón ibérico de bellota*. *Bellota* (pronounced *be-y-ota*) is Spanish for acorn. Hams sold with this label must meet strict criteria. Iberian pigs about 12 months old are moved onto the *dehesa*, the holm oak

forests that cover 2.5 million hectares of south-west Spain. For a four-month period, called *montanera*, the pigs lead a supervised free-range existence consuming up to 10 kilograms of grass, acorns, insects and other small wildlife and wandering up to 8 kilometres each day. This combination of an oil-rich acorn diet and exercise helps the fat interlace the flesh, giving a distinctive nutty-flavoured fat and a texture that can range from overtly rich and luscious to lean, minerally and silky. Some of the best *jamones* can reaches 700€ per kilogram. Even though *jamón ibérico de bellota* is imported into Australia, by law it has to have the bone removed. There is a big difference in taste between the *jamón* cut off the bone by hand and imported deboned *jamones*.

Breed and feed are essential to create *jamón's* unique flavour; the third element is the curing process. The legs are salted for about 10 days then washed off and hung in *secadores*, or drying rooms, open to the outside air in the south and south-west regions just below the *sierras* or mountain ranges. There they have winters that are cool and wet and summers that are hot and dry. These climatic variations allow the salt to migrate towards the centre of the *jamón* and then migrate outwards again. The air of the *jamón*-producing towns is said to be rich with microflora—funguses that work on the meat like moulds do on a great French cheese. Enzymes already within the meat also change the flesh.

*Jamón serrano* is aged for 12 months or more and *jamón Ibérico* is aged for 36–48 months, during which time the flavour concentrates and the flesh darkens and hardens. The process is part mummification, part transubstantiation. The end product is a deep ruby red and slightly stiff delicacy that offers flavours from forest floor to cigar box to mushroom.

The best way to carve a *jamón* is in *lonchas.* These are 3–4 cm wide titbits carved by a professional *cortador* or 'cutter'. *Lonchas* fit perfectly on the tongue and are pressed onto the roof of the mouth to feel the texture and experience the aroma before the teeth get involved. Good Barcelonese restaurants serve their *jamón* this way, as they do everywhere in Spain.

*Jamón* is offered in bars and restaurants across Barcelona. The price point will differ markedly depending on what sort of *jamón* it is, but if you're in a bar and want a salty snack and *jamón* is on offer, it is most likely *serrano* unless otherwise stated.

The best drink to have with *jamón* is sherry, which is not so easy to find in Barcelona. If it's a casual bite, have it with beer, or if the *jamón* deserves a bit more body for company, a tempranillo. If you're going into serious *ibérico de bellota* territory, then there's nothing better to accompany it than a really good oak-aged Rioja. FC

Celler de la Ribera

Sardines at Delfin

## CELLER DE LA RIBERA

Plaça de les Olles, 6

☏ 93 310 7845

www.cellerdelaribera.com

Also Lonja de Tapas, Plaça del Palau, 7, El Born;

Lonja de Tapas, Plaçeta Montcada, 5 El Born;

Celler de Tapas, Plaça Universitat, 5, L'Eixample

All restaurants: Sun–Thurs 1200–2400; Fri & Sat 1200–0100

**Fast tapas**/€€/Cards and euros

You'll see this tapas joint and its doppelgangers all around the tourist areas of Barcelona. These restaurants are sit-down places offering fast and reasonably priced little dishes and wine, proving the point that not every tourist trap offers bad food. It's fast and efficient, but dull. What is more entertaining in this location are the 100 or so balconies overlooking the square and the residents who wander out onto them to watch over you. Vegetarians rejoice as there are six vegan and ten seafood dishes on the menu. There are fat *bombas* with super-crisp shells and a nicely sharp *allioli* and *mojo rojo*. The *mojama* with almonds may be swimming in olive oil, but the almonds are good and the *mojama* passable. If you need to eat, the food here won't be great but it will restore you. RC

● ● ● ● ● ● ● ● ● ● ● ● ● ● ● ● ● ● ● ● ● ● ●

## COMERÇ 24

Comerç, 24

☏ 93 319 2102

www.comerc24.com

Tue–Sat 1330–1530, 2030–2300

**Modern Spanish**/€–€€€€/Cards and euros

This was one of the places that inspired me when I was developing ideas for MoVida. Chef Carles Abellan worked under Ferran Adrià for many years before opening Comerç 24 and has lifted tapas to a new level. He serves food that stirs opinions and debate. It has all the molecular bells, whistles and pyrotechnics: foams, thickeners, gels, spherification. I wonder if this will remain in vogue now that elBulli has closed? The restaurant has a great informal feel compared with most Michelin restaurants, with bright primary reds and yellows. The kitchen is open, and as a chef I love hearing all the action—it's loud and fun. If you want an intimate dinner, however, ask for a table in the back dining room. The service is extremely well drilled but does feel a bit like airline stewards going through the safety instructions prior to take-off. Even if the service is a little lacking in heart, it is very attentive to detail. The wine list fills two large books, one for whites, one for reds. You have the choice of two menus: six courses for 72€ or nine for 98€. A great succession of appetisers begins

the meal, my favourite being a fantastic cold white asparagus soup with what looked like a bocconcini but is in fact a spherified coconut ball. It's not the only time you see spherification—there's a delicious *consomé* with sphere of egg yolk, truffle and parmesan—a play of texture and umami. I do love the delicious duck rice mixed with a *foie gras* mousse. Compared with most Michelin restaurants, desserts are a little different here as they are designed to share and pass around. There could be a little sheep's milk yoghurt mousse with mint granita or a berry sorbet. Carles's signature dish combines the classic Spanish flavours of chocolate, salt, olive oil and bread. Although Carles is still opening new places in Barcelona, you can just feel that this place's glory days are past. FC

. . . . . . . . . . . . . . . . . . . . . . .

## CUINES SANTA CATERINA

Santa Caterina Market
Avinguda Francesc Cambó
( 93 268 9918
www.cuinessantacaterina.com
Bar open daily 0900–2400
Restaurant open Sun–Wed
1300–1600, 2030–2300;
Thur–Sat 1300–1600, 2030–0030
No reservations
**Tapas and Sushi**/€€/Cards and euros

This huge space inside the Sant Caterina Market was designed by top architects Enric Miralles and Benedett Tagliabue and is part of the successfu Tragaluz group. Three kitchen dominate the space and Wall Street style digital graphics scroll through th dishes of the day. As you enter ther is a tapas bar, open from breakfast

The classic tapas are simple but well executed, with great-quality produce like fried artichokes, anchovies and grilled baby calamari, plus some more interesting dishes like a carpaccio of beef with *foie gras*. There is a section of tall tables and stools serviced by the sushi bar and finally a huge open dining space filled with large olive-wood tables separated by hibiscus trees. This is a great place, especially on Sundays, when all else seems to be closed. It's busy then, so service can be patchy, but the atmosphere is vibrant. Don't be afraid to sit at the main bar; a service person is always stationed there, and as a chef I love watching the staff cope with such a behemoth of an operation. I had a few dishes from the bar here and enjoyed them all, a favourite being the Iberico pork ribs, slow roasted in the wood oven until they where coming off the bone. It was enough to feed two people and only cost 24€. Bargain. FC

. . . . . . . . . . . . . . . . . . . . . . . . . . .

### ⍟ EL BITXO

Verdaguer i Callís, 9
📞 93 268 1708
Mon–Thurs 1300–0100;
Fri–Sat 1300–0200
**Bar**/€/Cards and euros

Small, smart and cute, this is a bar run by women, which is unusual as most are run by men. That would explain the vases of fresh flowers and neatly handwritten specials signs. It serves plates of cheese and smallgoods and good wine by the glass. Simple and elegant, it's always busy before the opera at the nearby Palau de la Música. RC

. . . . . . . . . . . . . . . . . . . . . . . . . . .

## ⛾ EL BORN BAR

Passeig del Born, 26

☎ 93 319 5333

Daily 1730–0200

**Bar**/Cards and euros

You can't pass up drinking in an old codfish shop, especially when it's right on the main drag and so close to the Picasso Museum and all the other bars in Born. The awesome shuttered windows, the cool old coot behind the bar, the rattan furniture and modern art make it a great place to sit down for a few drinks. There's an interesting collection of people, from laid-back locals to those a bit more dialled in to the Barcelona cool. They have a good selection of spirits and bottled beers, and serve *conservas*—quality tinned seafood—until closing. And if you haven't finished your drink by then, they'll pour it into a plastic cup so you can be on your way! PG

. . . . . . . . . . . . . . . . . . . . . . . . . .

## ⛾ EL XAMPANYET

Montcada, 22

☎ 93 319 7003

Mon–Sat 1200–1600, 1830–2330

**Cava bar**/€€/Cards and euros

The family who owns this popular little bar has perfected keeping the tourists happy while also serving locals. Being so close to the Picasso Museum, there are hordes of tourists, and the staff seems to have a sixth sense about what they want even before they sit down.

Generally it's a bottle of house cava, a selection of tapas and some of their really outstanding anchovies. The rest of the food won't set the world on fire, but the tortilla is acceptable. Don't worry that the place looks packed— you will have a glass in your hand and a place to sit within minutes. I remember coming here for the first time more than a decade ago with my partner Vanessa and two old friends from uni days. The place was bright, vibrant, noisy and looked so great with its fantastic zinc bar along one side, barrels of wine above and colourful tiles on all the walls. This place is magnetic. Who doesn't enjoy drinking a bottle or two of cava with friends in a busy, fun place? FC

. . . . . . . . . . . . . . . . . . . . . . . . . .

## ESPAI SUCRE

Princesa, 53

☎ 93 268 1630

www.espaisucre.com

Tue–Thur 2100–2330;

Fri–Sat 2030–2300 or 2400

**Dessert restaurant**/€€€/Cards and euros

This restaurant is the baby of the Espai Sucre Escuela de Postres. It's a big boxy room painted chocolate brown with touches of orange, and the door is locked so you'll have to ring the doorbell on the right. At the rather cool end of Carrer Princesa, the restaurant opened its doors in 2000 with a dessert-only

menu, reflecting the pastry school's core business. The menu has broadened somewhat since then and now includes more savoury elements, but you're never going to get a steak here. What you will get is a pretty amazing experience! Some of the offerings are variations and interpretations of classic Catalan dishes—think Miles Davis working on a theme—so you might not get just how out-there an olive oil gallette with pear gel and sobrassada and honey is. It's iconoclastic! But it works. It's sweet and sour and a mix of textures. And that's what they do here. They play with primary flavours and textures and the way we taste things with such a high level of skill that the experience can be rapturous. The set menu is probably mandatory,

as is the matching wine. They have picked a textural white from Rioja to go with a bowl of rice that has been cooked in milk flavoured with gelatinous cod tripe and dressed with tomato ice-cream and pieces of crisp cod skin. To me it is a fishy *arroz con leche*. There could also be rolls of cucumber gel with pineapple cubes and tarragon ice-cream with a little glass of Moscato d'Asti. It's the baby of masters Jordi Butrón and Xano Saguer, but cooking the food day to day is Ricardo Martínez, a former student of the school. It is still possible to have a dessert-only menu for around 30€, but for 45€ plus 16€ for the matching wines, I really recommend the tasting menu. RC

Gispert

## ⅋ GIMLET

Rec, 24

☎ 93 310 1027

Mon & Sun 2200–0300;
Tues–Sat 1900–0300

**Bar**/€/Cards and euros

When it's busy this place is packed, but it's worth it to rub shoulders with the hipsters who hang out in the Born. Not to be confused with the famous cocktail bar of the same name, the only give-away that this is a bar is the sign outside featuring the drink after which the bar is named. Gimlet, that glorious blend of gin and lime juice, is a great starting point for those who want to drink martinis but can't (or won't). The long narrow room is dominated by a full-length bar where they prepare some really great low-key cocktails, which are more about flavour and mood than colour and movement. When it's not busy, Gimlet has a really chilled small-gin-joint vibe reminiscent of old Hollywood movies, but it's a great spot at any time of the night. PG

• • • • • • • • • • • • • • • • • • • • • • • •

## GISPERT

Sombrerers, 23

☎ 93 319 7535

www.casagispert.com

Mon–Sat 0930–1400, 1600–1930
(Closed Mondays Jan–Sep)

**Nuts and dried fruit**/€€/Cards and euros

The smell of wood smoke and toasted almonds hits you long before you stumble across the carved wooden shopfront, painted black and detailed with mirrors and gold writing. This shop sells nuts and dried fruit, a few spices, a little rice and some coffee. The layout and fixtures haven't changed since it was built by Dr Josep Gispert for his two sons Enric and Alfons. There's still the long wooden counter, baskets of fresh nuts in woven baskets lined with hessian, jars of cloves, whole nutmegs and sticks of cinnamon bark individually wrapped in decorative paper. At the end of this dark alley-like shop is the original roaster. The walls and ceilings are blackened from the wisps of smoke emanating from a great brick box fuelled by Holm oak that slowly burns away, roasting the almonds inside a perforated steel cylinder. Roaster Marc Martínez i Uribe goes backwards and forwards between his customers and his almonds. 'These are *marcona* almonds. They are the best in the world. I am checking to see the colour,' he says. (He speaks several languages fluently—the Japanese love him.) 'They should go from white to this slightly darker colour. The oils should be coming out of the almonds to give them this gloss.' He reaches in and hands me a few almonds. They are scorchingly hot. The almonds are taken into a tumbler and mixed with a few handfuls of salt to make salted almonds. Fresh from being roasted over oak and still warm, they are absolutely stunning. In 1999 the French association Les Gourmands Associés awarded E & A Gispert a Coq d'Or for their nuts. RC

. . . . . . . . . . . . . . . . . . . . . . . .

## HOFMANN PASTISSERIA

Flassaders, 44
( 93 268 8221
www.hofmann-bcn.com
Mon–Thur 0900–1400, 1530–2000;
Fri–Sat 0900–1400, 1530–2000;
Sun 0900–1430
**Patisserie**/€€/Cards and euros

The smell of baking pastries fills this cute little patisserie, found down a cobbled lane off Passeig del Born. It's the bakery arm of the Mey Hofmann school and Hofmann Restaurant (see page 60) with graduates from the cooking school (just around the corner) baking throughout the day in the kitchen above the shop. A recent award for the best butter croissant in Spain is greatly deserved. 'I only use French butter,' said Hofmann when we spoke with her. 'Spanish butter has too much water and goes …' She pulls a face to indicate it's no good for fine pastry work. The sweet treats here

Hofmann Pastisseria

are costly but delicious. Consider the butter biscuits or traditional *panellets,* a frangipane filling covered in toasted pine nuts. In summer there are white and dark chocolate mousses or a small tart filled with berries ready to take home. Salvador, the coffee merchant from Cafés El Magnífico (see page 129), recommends the croissant filled with mango crème. RC

. . . . . . . . . . . . . . . . . . . . . . . . . . .

## LA PARADETA
Comercial, 7
( 93 268 1939
www.laparadeta.com
Also Riego, 27 in Sants;
Passeig Simò, 18, Sagrada Família;
Sant Pere, 24, Sitges;
Pacific, 74, Meridana
Tue–Thur 2000–2330; Fri–Sat
2000–2400; Sat–Sun 1300–1600
**Fish restaurant**/€€/Cash

There is absolutely no service at this place. That is not a criticism; it's simply the business model. It's a glorious family fish barn where you wait outside until a table is available. Then you stand at what appears to be a market stall of raw seafood. You point to what you want, and if you speak Spanish you tell the dude how much you want and how you want it cooked: *a la plancha, al vapor* or *frito.* He gives you a number and you go to the next counter, order the drinks, pay and find a table. They call out your number when the dish is

ready. If the lady on the microphone has to call your order out more than twice she gets real shirty. It is like every seaside pub or country RSL I grew up with. Even the décor is seaside cafe circa 1988, with yellow and blue walls and the odd bit of nautical flotsam. The difference is that here they serve excellent red prawns, baby squid, razor clams and other amazingly fresh seafood, including crayfish for around 35€ for two. It's stunning value for money, and that is why this great cavern of a room is always full of locals rather than tourists, as language can be a barrier. My advice is learn to count to a hundred in Spanish, come here and wait for your number to be called out, then hoe into a seafood feast. RC

. . . . . . . . . . . . . . . . . . . . . . . . . . .

## ⍟ LA VINYA DEL SENYOR
Plaça de Santa Maria, 5
93 310 3379
Mon–Thur 1200–0130; Fri–Sat
1200–0200; Sun 1200–2400
**Bar**/€/Cards and euros

This cool little—and I do mean little—wine bar on Plaça de Santa Maria is an inside/outside affair, with a tiny upstairs area that looks straight out at the beautiful Santa Maria del Mar. There are only two tables up here—so be quick, lucky or well connected to get this stunning view. Small plates of wine-friendly food, like *fuet,* freshly shucked oysters and cheese, complement a wine list that is not too long to navigate. The selection by the glass changes twice a month in the middle of the month, so if you time your holiday just right you can investigate a number of Spanish wines in just two visits. There are some really fantastic wines here that we just don't see in Australia. You can order by the half and whole glass, so it's possible to cover a lot of territory without getting too squiffy. Some classic jazz in the background makes sitting inside on a sunny day not so bad after all. PG

## MUDANZAS CAFE/BAR

Vidrieria, 15
☎ 93 319 1137
Mon–Thur, Sun 1000–0230;
Fri & Sat 1000–0300
**Bar**/€/Cards and euros

When Australia's best barman, Gerald from Gerald's Bar in North Carlton, tells you to go to a bar in a foreign city, it's a good idea to listen. To give you an idea of the sort of neighbourhood place this is, I watched a woman in her eighties wander down from her apartment in her dressing gown, sit at the bar, order a coffee, drink it with a cigarette, and then head back home. This is a little split-level place, with black-and-white tiled floors. The barman serves freezing-cold beer on tap, plus there is a back bar filled with about forty different scotches, twenty vodkas and and an eclectic mix of other spirits. Funky music and a constant flow of people of all ages, all of whom appear to live nearby, make this a cool little bar. PG

## MUNDIAL BAR

Plaça Sant Agustí Vell, 1
☎ 93 319 9056
Tue–Sun 1300–1600, 2100–2400
**Seafood**/€€/Cards

From 1936 to 1965 this was the Peña Bartos boxing club. The image on the menu of a boxer in a loincloth feeding his trophy belt to a lion is Vicenç Febrer, uncle of the present owner of this locals' bar and bistro. Pull up a seat under the mural facing the busy bar. This is where the action is. There's an à la carte menu that serves the two little dining rooms out the back, but they are literally outback. Because Mundial is all about the fun of the busy bar, a quick bite of mussels *a la plancha*—hot salty and deeply concentrating the flavour of the sea—is the go here. That said, the *cecina* here is well sourced: fine slices of deep red and rich air-dried beef that have developed the secondary characteristics of curing, those rich glutamic flavours. The bistro menu gets a little effete, with things like veal sirloin grilled and served with a truffled reduction on a plate smeared with strawberry puree and topped with *foie*. I wonder what old Vicenç would make of that? Well, he *is* nearly naked with a

Mundial Bar

lion. I am a big man and the cheap and flimsy furniture in the bistro doesn't instill in me a lot of confidence in its weight-bearing capacity! RC

. . . . . . . . . . . . . . . . . . . . . . . . . . .

## MUSEU DE LA XOCOLATA

Comerç, 36
℡ 93 268 7878
www.pastisseria.com/en/
PortadaMuseu
Mon–Sat 1000–1900; Sun 1000–1500
**Museum**/Entry 4.3€

Remember the sheer ecstatic anticipation that Charlie felt when he was about to step into Willy Wonka's chocolate factory? That's how I felt as I waited in line to get into this museum entirely dedicated to chocolate. I imagined rivers of 70 per cent grand cru, whole forests of single-estate cacao beans with cocoa butter rabbits you could catch and eat. I bought my ticket, held my breath and stepped into a large, lifeless room of cobbled-together, static displays curated with all the passion of an agnostic Sunday school teacher. For the most part this is a bland collection of artifacts—a timeline of chocolate from the pre-Columbian bitter beverage sipped between blood sacrifices to the European sweet beverage and confectionary block enjoyed between pan-continental wars. Cynical? Yes. The word Nestlé—a major sponsor—pops up often. But for true chocolate nerds there is some cool stuff among the dross. There's a *melate*—a C-curved piece of granite from Central America on which the Aztecs once crushed their cured beans to make cocoa powder. There are some ceramic serving cups from Spain's colonial period, some made from rough terracotta, others from fine china showing how cocoa was enjoyed across various classes. With so many great pastry schools in Barcelona there are some really cool chocolate sculptures on display, from a dismounted Don Quixote, who tilted too far at a windmill, to a full-colour depiction of Asterix and Obelix, characters from a French cartoon originally published in 1959. The sculptor captures the sheer energy of the cartoon so well in 3D that you can't help but smile. Further on is the Solé Graells kitchen and that's where your heart melts. It's a chocolate cooking school sectioned off by glass. Seeing 30 eight-year-old school children squeal with delight as they ogle a running vat of liquid chocolate is worth the visit. In this room the temporary displays of chocolate sculptures are open to the air so you can smell the rich, sweet dark chocolate. Chocolate nerds will also love seeing the 1940 granite conching machines, 1930s Easter-egg moulds and stamps for printing the wrappers of chocolate blocks. But in the end it's the wonderful smell that turns you into a big kid. RC

. . . . . . . . . . . . . . . . . . . . . . . . . . .

Kangaroo loin, Picnic

As the name suggests, they sell a lot of olive oil here: thirty different brands, all top shelf, some around 50€ a litre. Imagine frying your eggs in that, folks. Which is a good reason to chum up to Agnes Roukoz, the manager. She is a gentle soul who is absolutely passionate about extra virgin olive oil and will lead you through a free tasting of five different oils. These are no ordinary oils. Take Full Moon for example. It's made from arbequina olives by Pago de los Baldios de San Carlos from Cáceres in Extremadura. Pressed within hours of harvest, it has an acidity of 0.1 per cent (to be considered 'extra virgin' an oil has to have an acidity of at least 0.8 per cent or lower) and comes in a matte black square bottle designed by architect Mariano Martín. It is buttery, with the aroma of tomatoes and a very refined piquancy in the middle palate. It's 25€ for 250 millilitres. Agnes explains that the owner of Olive is French, which would explain the large number of syrups and confitures. Some would say that it is outrageous decadence to create a retail temple to household staples such as oil, jam and soap and turn them into expensive

objects of desire. However, that is wh· has happened to the handmade artis· products of Europe. RC

· · · · · · · · · · · · · · · · · · · · · · · ·

## PASSADÍS DEL PEP

Pla del Palau, 2
℡ 93 310 1021
www.passadis.com
Mon–Sat 1330–1530, 2100–2330
**Catalan and Seafood**/€€€/Card·
and euros

The entrance of this place is a bit li· platform 9¾ in Harry Potter. You kno· it should be around here somewhere b· you just can't see it. But if you find th· number 2 above a doorway to a rath· elegant apartment in the plaza, you· see beneath it a dark corridor that lea· deep into the building, and at the e·· of the corridor is a door with dappl· glass glowing with warm light. Insi· is a series of large rooms divided ·· ancient stonewalls and archways. The· is no menu. You sit down. A bottle · cava is poured and food is brought · you. It keeps coming until you say sto· This has been the way of the place sin· it opened in 1979. One of the waite· cheekily comments that as the dish· change daily according to what is in th· market, the owner saves money by n· having to print new menus every da· Another, Vicente, a classic prankste· says they don't stock water when yo· order it and pours more wine into you·

glass, only to return with a bottle of water and ice bucket. The meal starts with a plate of *jamón serrano* and a little *pa amb tomàquet*. I love the plate of little murex snails cooked on a bed of sea salt and dusted with fine breadcrumbs and garlic. The way chef Joan Manubens uses a bit of *jamón* with his clams gives the natural juices and olive oil extra body, turning the juices into a sauce. His red prawns, sacrificed for a second on the screaming hot *plancha*, are a super-sweet, crunchy eat-the-whole-lot affair. A plate of *xanguet*, tiny

deep-fried fish, follows. The extra-salt Mediterranean prawns—deep red an heads filled with mush—are truly grea There is more, so much more, includin succulent milk-fed goat, plates of hak and monkfish if you want. Here yo find old school generosity that you jus don't get in Anglo countries. Whe the meal's over, Modesto brings over bottle of whatever spirit you feel like puts glasses down on the table an leaves you to help yourself. (See als Cal Pep, page 129.) RC

## PICNIC

Comerç, 1
( 93 511 6661
www.picnic-restaurant.com
Mon–Fri 1300–1630;
Tue–Sat 2000–0100
Brunch Sat–Sun 1200–1630
**Global**/€€/Cards and euros

I always wondered why on summer weekends there were so many people holding numbered red helium balloons in Parc de la Ciutadella just off Passeig Picasso. Then I saw a girl on a bike deliver a cardboard box to a couple with a balloon tied to their picnic blanket. She rode off and the couple took out containers of what appeared to be quite delicious food. I followed the girl back to a restaurant around the corner called, yes, Picnic. It's a small place, just 40 seats and high chairs at benches. The owner is Chilean Jaime Riesco, who, with his Californian wife, has worked in food around the globe. This is his first restaurant (he has been backed by an Australian bloke called Andrew Cameron), and he has defied the odds by serving pan-American-style food, modern Californian with a strong South American twist, to an audience consisting of some of the fussiest eaters in the world—the Catalans. 'They do not like to have their foods mixed on the one plate,' he says. 'If there is a stack of kangaroo loin with green pickle stack on top, they will put each part to one corner of the plate and nibble each bit separately to taste it, then try a little bit of the falafel with the pickle, then the kangaroo with the pickle.' He has, however, won them over and needs to expand his seating. What I like about Jaime's operation is that he has understood the sensibility of the locals and modified his cooking accordingly. He'll make a chowder with smoked salmon and extra virgin olive oil—something the locals can understand. He makes fusion tapas and tasting plates so people don't have to invest in a big expensive plate. He also keeps his food costs to a minimum by value adding to cheaper cuts like hanger steak as opposed to sirloin. While it's not everyone's cup of tea, it is a good example of how new styles of cooking are being formed in this amazing gastronomic city. RC

## PIM PAM BURGER

Carrer Sabateret, 4
( 93 315 2093
www.pimpamplats.com
Daily 1300–2330
**Burgers**/€/Cash

Sometimes, after a hard night on the *pisto*, you want a burger to recover. Bad luck. Good burgers in Barcelona are thin on the ground. A *hamburguesa* in a restaurant will give you the rissole but not the bun. There are fast-food burgers from American chains, but a good burger can be found a few streets off

Carrer Princesa in Born. You can get the Aussie style with the lot (no pineapple or beetroot, I'm afraid) or some more exotic choices—one with Roquefort cheese for example. Around the corner is Pim Pam Plats, which sells ready-to-eat takeaway salads and quiches if you want to dine in your apartment. RC

• • • • • • • • • • • • • • • • • • • • • • • • •

## SANTA

Avinguda Meridiana, 2
( 93 309 7078
www.santamania.biz
Tue–Sun 1330–1600;
Thur–Sat 2030–2400
**Inventive tapas**/€€/Cards and euros

This is Paco Guzmán's second and much larger restaurant after Santa Maria a few blocks away. It's in a good location, just across the Parc de la Ciutadella, in a quiet part of town. It's like the best Spanish bar of old but with a modern polish—all dark, slick colours, wooden floors, and black glass-lined walls. Small terrariums filled with frogs add to the quirkiness. The place is filled with large groups of hip young locals sitting at the long communal wooden tables, and through the dining room you can see the partially open kitchen where more often than not Guzmán orchestrates the kitchen, floor and tunes for the dining room. Nearby one poster reads '¡Hoy vuelan los cuchillos!' or 'Today the knives are going to fly'. Weekdays

there is a fantastic value special for 16€, which includes three courses, wine and coffee. Come night-time there is a long list of small dishes served either as a *raciones* or half *raciones* and covering totally delicious versions of classic Spanish dishes such as *jamón* and chicken *croquetas*—the best I have ever eaten. Guzmán says, 'My mother, she doesn't speak to me any more because I stole her recipe!' I also love his *tigres,* gratinéed stuffed mussels. Guzmán has also embraced Asian ingredients, using Vietnamese mint and *wakame*, even making Vietnamese rice paper rolls with salmon. What I do love is an extraordinary dish of grilled artichoke heart, filled with a quail egg and topped with *arenque* or imitation caviar. This is a fun place; the waiters are cheeky, almost flirtatious. May I suggest the signature Dracula dessert. It's a surprise! FC

• • • • • • • • • • • • • • • • • • • • • • • • •

EIXAMPLE

Bar Velódromo

EIXAMPLE WAS TO BE an example of socialist utopia when it was planned in the mid–19th century, but capitalism got in the way and the result is a huge swathe of a European city that is more tightly planned than Haussman's Paris but as intensively developed as New York—without the skyscrapers. It's a huge tract of uniformly sized and shaped blocks that surround the old town of Barcelona.

When Philip V invaded Barcelona in the early 18th century, he constructed the Ciutadella, a giant fort to house the soldiers who would keep the Catalan capital under his rule. When it was pulled down in the mid–19th century, after much social upheaval, citizens took pickaxes to stone, and the great medieval walls that had stymied the city's growth were destroyed. Barcelona expanded for several generations on a plan laid out by a progressive socialist designer called Cerdà. Cerdà's vision, with its great parks and canals, was never realised because developers took over the grand design. They built out every last square metre and later filled in the courtyards that were to be private parks for every apartment. One of the few parts that reflects Cerdà's plan is the Joan Miró Park on Carrer Aragó. It was built in 1976 on the site of a former slaughterhouse, but it imparts the idea of free space that was central to his plan. There is also a unique smaller scale development on Passatge de Gaiolà just above Diagonal.

The blocks of Eixample are 113 metres square with the corners chamfered or cut off. This means getting around Eixample involves negotiating the bevelled corners of block after block. Without communal gardens in the centre of their apartments, residents spill out onto the streets, creating demand for remarkable bars, restaurants, food shops, cafes and some of the best retail shops and boutiques to be found in Europe. There's money in Eixample, but the Catalans are canny with their coins, so there is also some amazingly good-quality food to be found at prices that are above entry level but reflect the earning capacity of the residents of one of the most elegant and massive apartment developments in Europe.

## ALKIMIA

Indústria, 79
( 93 207 6115
www.alkimia.cat
Mon–Fri 1300–1530, 2100–2300;
closed Sat & Sun
**Modern Catalan**/One Michelin
star/€€€/Cards and euros

There's a foot-long onion *grissini* poking
out of a glass sitting on the table in
front of me. It's ludicrously long and in
defiance of all hospitality norms. But it
is fun. As is all the modern Catalan food
served from Jordi Vilà's kitchen in this
small, modern dining room in the leafy
residential strip of Carrer Indústria,
just four blocks from La Sagrada
Família. Dividers between tables
give the dining space a very intimate
atmosphere, and the staff move easily
between Spanish, European languages
and English. Vilà is a showman who
does the usual modern food trickery
without sacrificing the integrity of the
ingredients. He may send out a little
glass of tomato water with cubes of
bread and olive oil floating atop—a
nod to *pa amb tomàquet*. He may get
the mouth prepared with a little bowl
of fresh beans in a chive sauce served
with a single tiny seared squid hood.
The traditional *coca amb escalivada* may
be enriched with a little truffle followed
by that classic—chicken *canelones* with
scant almond béchamel and parmesan
crumbs. Then a rice dish—*bomba* rice
cooked in *sofrito*, then in stock, topped

with a single langoustine and a John
Dory fillet surrounded by the world's
tiniest vegetables sprinkled with shreds
of delicious *jamón* fat. It's a fantastic
mix of theatre—the tables are spotlit
and the light bouncing off them
illuminates the room—and it's fun. RC

. . . . . . . . . . . . . . . . . . . . . . . . . .

## BAR MUT

Pau Claris, 192
( 93 217 4338
Mon–Sat 0800–2400; Sun 0800–1700
**Cafe and tapas**/€€€/Cards and
euros

The first impression on entering Bar
Mut is that it must be some kind of
weird offspring of French and Spanish
parents. The noise and the fun crowd
are Spanish, but the elegant dark wood,
bronze fittings and etched glass give
it a distinctively French air. A waiter
greets you at the door, welcomes you,
looks around the room, points to a
small section at the corner of the bar
and nods. That's your space. There
is no written menu; it's all on three
blackboards with a broad range of
options written in Spanish. One lists
smallgoods, another lists seafood and
eggs served with different rich additions
such as *sobrassada* or *foie gras*, and a third
lists a dozen other delicious creations:
charcoal-grilled octopus, *mar y montaña*,
tuna tartare, *foie gras* with cherries. Give
the waiter an idea of how much you'd
like to spend and let him order for you,

as the food is of such high quality that some of the top-end dishes can be pricey. They serve a line of top-quality *conservas* from behind the bar, but as the Spanish only put the best in tins, a can of preserved clams could cost 36€. They have a ripping wine list, but what sets it apart is a great selection of wines by the glass. This place deservedly gets extremely busy, so reserve a table, be prepared to wait, or come during the day when the crowds of sophisticated Barcelonese and well-heeled tourists are out doing other things. FC

. . . . . . . . . . . . . . . . . . . . . . . .

## BAR VELÓDROMO
Muntaner, 213
( 93 430 6022
Daily 0600–0300
Spanish/€€/Cards and euros

Founded in 1933, this was once a 24-hour a day Barcelona institution. It's the sort of place you can mention to a cab driver without giving an address. In fact, sometimes it's more important to get them to concentrate on the road because they are enthusiastically telling you about some night they spent there in their younger days. Velódromo has had a very colourful history. At the time of the Spanish Civil War it became the unofficial headquarters of the exiled Republican government. During the 1960s and 70s it was a home for left-ing politicians, artists and bohemians, a haven from Franco's authoritarianism.

In 1977 it was the birth left-wing magazine *L'A* 1980s and 90s it was a fa venue. In 2000 it close decade it remained dorr family who owns Moritz beer poured in a small fortune to give the old girl some of her early glamour back. In 2009 it reopened. It really is a spectacular place: floor-to-ceiling windows cover the entire front façade, bathing the huge space with natural light. The ceilings soar above the diners, allowing the back area to be used as a mezzanine accessed by a grand wooden staircase. Downstairs, large, comfortable green banquettes encircle the room, the floor covered in beautiful patterned marble. Along one wall is the original zinc bar, where, naturally, they serve ice-cold Moritz, fresh from the brewery. Open at dawn, it serves coffee and breakfast until 3 am—and you might drop in two or three times a day if you're in the area—I have. The huge menu is designed by Michelin-starred chef Carles Abellan. It covers typical breakfast pastries and the usual rich braises to eat with a spoon for breakfast, like tripe or *botifarra*. Yes, for breakfast. It's delicious. For the rest of the day there is consistently good food, a long list of tapas, everything from almonds, conserved razor clams and *pulpo* to salt cod, *esqueixada*, *patatas bravas*, *ensaladilla rusa* and a list of quality smallgoods. One of my favourite things on the menu is *guiso*,

# ARCHITECTURE

**THE FIRST TIME** I travelled to Barcelona as an adult, my main reason was to marvel at the architecture. I had just finished my Bachelor of Arts in Architecture and had taken a year off to travel to Europe to be inspired. I was particularly interested in seeing the city of my birth, Barcelona, through adult eyes.

## LA SAGRADA FAMÍLIA

It was the crazy spires of Gaudí's La Sagrada Família that drew me in; those dark fingers reaching skyward seemed to border on the profane. When I first stood under them I wasn't disappointed, I was moved. Despite the brutalist additions that have been tacked on since Gaudí was knocked down by a tram, his outrageous organic shapes and contours that draw upon both the darkness of Gothic architecture and the renewal of nature left me gobsmacked. He had married the beauty of birth and the dread of death, capturing that combined power in stone, in a vision that is dreamlike but speaks with a voice that is new and different. It is distinctively Catalan and still a work in progress.

There is a saying in Spanish that goes, '*Que pide más que la Sagrada Familia!*' You ask more than the Sagrada Família!', referring to the charity that you keep on giving to, as the cathedral

is still in completion. Although it was consecrated in 2010, stonemasons are still at work in the knave, hammering away at lumps of stone, slowly completing the building one piece at a time. Anyone who can walk through this awesome (I use this word in its original sense) building and not be moved quite possibly could have coolant running through their veins.

What I hadn't realised until I had started my pilgrimage in 1990 was that while Gaudí may have been working at the peak of Barcelona modernism, a style of architecture that has a lot in common with Art Nouveau with a very Catalan twist, there were many more architects and buildings to be discovered. In fact, what really excited me was that such a specific building style had permeated so deeply into the fabric of the city. It was everywhere: in the curved, almost mouth-like, carved archways around the doors to apartment buildings, in the audacity of using mosaic to paint the skin of an entire building or fill a park with what simply is art.

## CASA BATLLÓ

The beauty of Barcelona, especially in Eixample, is popping up from the subterranean metro to be slapped in the face by an astonishingly beautiful building. That is why the hordes crane their necks at the reptile-like Casa Batlló (Passeig de Gràcia, 43). Modernism is everywhere, from lamp posts to the interiors of bars and cafes. Cadafalch's Casa Amatller next door to Casa Batlló may not be as well known, but shows the breadth of expression of form during this incredibly bright period of Catalan culture. One could also go into the foyer of Domènech's stunningly beautiful Palau de la Música Catalana, but buying a ticket and seeing a show puts you inside this beautiful jewel box of a building and makes you part of the experience itself.

## LANEWAYS

The pleasure of a European city like Barcelona is being drawn into a labyrinth of endless winding streets like Barri Gòtic, lanes and walkways that were never planned by a greater authority, just paths worn into the city by people going about their lives between markets and churches and the city gates. Streets too small for cars, just wide enough for two people to walk shoulder to shoulder, surrounded by stone buildings can be like walking along an ancient canyon.

I remember many years ago when we where looking for a site for MoVida in Melbourne's CBD, what drew me to Hosier Lane were the same basic emotions I felt when walking in the little lanes of Barcelona. A mix of slightly frayed beauty, graffiti, small discoveries along the laneways, opening up onto a lovely open space or in the case of MoVida, onto a landmark building like Federation Square.

Casa Batlló

Torre Agbar

## MACBA (The Museum of Contemporary Art)

Barcelona is not just about the past. The sheer unapologetic mass of Richard Meier's MACBA in the heart of El Raval could have ruined the fabric of this old *barri*. Instead it regenerated El Raval. The great white concrete edifice, filled with a wealth of modern art, drew a new crowd brimming with creative energy into an area that had been seedy, bordering on slothful. It also had a power of its own—so new and white and so obviously concrete the contrast between the old Raval created its own potential.

## BAC DE RODA

The list of contemporary architects who have worked in Barcelona is astonishing for almost any city in the world. I love Santiago Calatrava's bridge Bac de Roda in La Sagrera. The white steel curves of the arches holding the suspension cables cut through the air with same audacious confidence that modernists brought to the apartments of Eixample.

## TORRE AGBAR

I also love French architect Jean Nouvel's giant gherkin in Poblenou. It's real name is the Torre Agbar. At night it shimmers and glows with 4500 different coloured lights. Nouvel also designed the new Moritz Fàbrica in Eixample.

The lasting impression I get from Barcelona is the specific character of each *barri*. To me this has much to do with the architecture which, of course, is a product of the history, culture and economy of the location. Just like food. FC

a wonderful tripe, chickpea and chorizo stew. The package here is great. Good staff. Good food. Good price. While the crowd isn't as bohemian as it once was, it's the type of place where you can rub shoulders with students, workers and politicians—a true Barcelona experience. FC

. . . . . . . . . . . . . . . . . . . . . . . . . .

## BLAU

Londres, 89 and Passatge Lluís Pellicer, 16

( 93 419 3032

www.blaubcn.com

Mon–Sun 1330–1630, 2030–2330

**Modern Catalan bistronomic/** €€/Cards and euros

Any chef who has the balls to put artistic photographs of models posing with pigs on the walls of his restaurant wins my respect for sheer lunacy. But Marc Roca is not a lunatic. He's a driven young chef who has worked at Zuberoa in San Sebastián and Gaig in Barcelona. In 2007 he opened the doors to his own establishment in this long, narrow, mellow-lit restaurant (an entrance at either end) and has been just about full every service since. His young front-of-house crew stumble around a bit, and aside from the pre-cut-bread-in-the-basket deal it's a really good quality and value for money menu. He may serve up a plump piece of boned chicken seasoned with a little

rosemary and the merest of *manchego*—it is roasted with perfect brown skin and the juiciest flesh. I really like the little iron *cazuelas* in which he serves a fillet of salt cod in *pisto*. You may finish with a peach soup and yoghurt sorbet or a mango and grapefruit frozen jelly with a soft, coconut-flavoured Italian meringue. A nicely managed wine list concentrates on local wines and others from classic Spanish regions. There's a good vibe in the room, with a business crowd during the day and more mixed groups at night. RC

. . . . . . . . . . . . . . . . . . . . . . . . . .

## CAFE ZURICH

Plaça de Catalunya, 1

( 93 317 9153

Mon–Sun 0800–2300

**Cafe terraza**/€/Cash

When I was 21 I remember being asked by one of my cousins to meet at Cafe Zurich, which turned out to be a bit like what we do in Melbourne, meeting under the clocks at Flinders Street Station. This iconic meeting place is over eighty years old on the very busy Plaça de Catalunya at the head of La Rambla. Sit outside and enjoy the passing parade. The service is fast, sometimes bordering on a little rude. It's a bit more expensive than drinking off the beaten track, but the same goes anywhere you pay for position, because although the coffee is OK and the pastries good, it's all about watching the people and rubbing shoulders with real Barcelonese. FC

## CALDENI
València, 452
( 93 232 5811
www.caldeni.com
Mon–Sat 1330–1515;
Thurs–Sat 2100–2230
**Creative Catalan**/€/Cards and euros

Caldeni is roughly a block away from La Sagrada Família, making this a perfect location to have lunch before or after your visit there. This simple-looking restaurant is tiny, so plan and book ahead. They serve a very good three-course lunch here for 19€, a give-away. At night it is great value at 35–55€, with *aperitivos*, snacks, dessert, *petits fours*, bread and coffee. Dishes may include an appetiser of carpaccio of Nebraskan Angus, thinly sliced and topped with a carrot sorbet or a lovely tartar of beef with a soft chunk of real truffle butter to mix through the dish. In fact beef from Galicia, the US and Japan is king here. Their bread is wonderful and artisanal, and just reinforces the idea that the quality of the ingredients is all-important. It's minimalist without being molecular and with really large portion sizes. A great package. FC

## CAN RAVELL
Aragó, 313
( 93 457 5114
www.ravell.com
Sun 1000–1600; Tue–W(
1000–2100; Thur–Sat 100( ....00
**Traditional Catalan**/€€/Cards and euros

You could easily walk past what looks like another quality local grocery and wine store without realising what wonders await inside. Perhaps the Catalans want to keep this place for themselves. Although there's an amazing array of food packed from floor to ceiling, beautiful displays of cheeses in cabinets, and wines piled to the roof, there's no sign that some of the most deliciously prepared Catalan food is being served here. To find the beautiful dining room, you have to walk boldly through the kitchen doors, through the working kitchen and up a set of spiral stairs, not one but two levels—it's an adventure. The same menu is served all day, but there is also a specific breakfast menu offering eggs with *jamón*, or eggs with *foie gras*. Also consider tripe with spicy *chorizo*, pig's feet with snails or salt cod *tortilla*. Trust me, this is really great stuff. The main menu might have superbly tender pigeon, cooked in two ways with fresh *cep* mushrooms for just 24€. There are classics like *fideuà*—braised pasta with seafood in a garlicky fish broth and

ghtly in the oven to crisp the
mities of the pasta, served with
llioli so powerful it could put hair on
your chest. What's more, you can order
from an extensive list of wines from
the bottle shop downstairs and pay not
much more than retail. The quality
of everything here is great: Riedel
glassware, fresh silverware, mature,
well-trained waiting staff. FC

• • • • • • • • • • • • • • • • • • • • • •

## CAN VALLÉS
Carrer Aragó, 95
☏ 93 226 0667
Mon–Sat 1300–1600, 2100–2330
**Old school Catalan**/€€€/Cards
and euros

This nondescript restaurant is a few
blocks away from the Joan Miró
neighbourhood park. To say the room
is ugly would be harsh, but being
businesslike and styleless is the kind of
aesthetic that fits in with the lunchtime
suits and night-time locals. And we're
not here for looks. We're here for
really good Catalan food. You might
get some of the best scallops outside
of Galicia, seared on the grill with just
a brush of oil. Consider the *canelones*,
filled with cooked-down chopped pig's
trotter flesh, enriched with mushroom,
seasoned with a little nutmeg, and
covered with béchamel and just a little
*manchego*. There could be a plate of tiny,
tiny chickpeas with crayfish-tail pieces
in a rich lobster bisque thickened with

*roux*. Finish with a plate of *bunyols* filled
with chocolate custard. It is not the type
of place used to dealing with tourists,
but it's highly recommended by many
Barcelonese chefs and foodies. RC

• • • • • • • • • • • • • • • • • • • • • •

## CASA CALVET
Casp, 48
☏ 93 412 4012
www.casacalvet.es
Mon–Sat 1300–1530, 2030–2300
**Catalan**/€€€/Cards and euros

This restaurant is located in Casa
Calvet, which was designed by Antoni
Gaudí for local textile manufacturer
Andreu Calvet. Gaudí acknowledges
this in the bobbin-shaped columns
either side of the doorway. Completed
in 1899, it is conservative for Gaudí,
with a plain tiled interior and hints of
industrial steel girder. The accounting
offices, management and boardrooms
of the Calvet textile business were
converted into a restaurant in 1994.
Slide into a carved wooden booth
surrounded by posters and artworks
of the modernist period and immerse
yourself in a pile of cushions. There
could be an egg from Calaf on a bed
of potatoes with a subtle *jamón* sauce
or sautéed mushrooms and chestnut
on *coca*. Imagine sheets of lasagna
filled with prawns and sharp cheese.
There are many meats to choose from
lamb ribs, beef fillet, slow-cooked
pig's cheek. The food is good, as is th

service. It's a safe bet—nothing over the top—a long-lunch kind of place. RC

. . . . . . . . . . . . . . . . . . . . . . . . .

## CATA 1.81

València, 181
93 323 6818
www.cata181.com
Mon 2000–0030; Tues–Sat 1330–0030
**Modern tapas/€€/Cards and euros**

*Cata* is Spanish for *tasting* and usually refers to a wine tasting. And while that may have been the case nine years ago when Cata first opened, the food has become more elaborate and taken centre stage. The action happens in an overpowering room with bright lights, white-tiled walls and fluoro orange touches. It reminds me of being in a 7/11 late at night. However, once your eyes have adjuste___ in the hands of the fr___ educated staff, it's all good___ appear immediately, firm t___ delicious; strangely they are not that easy to find in Spain. The menu is divided into seven sections from light to heavy to dessert. Most mains sit in the 8–10€ zone, with small tapas under 3€. There could be a delicious dish of sweet fresh sardines, lightly cured in vinegar and aromatics on *coca,* or the classic Catalan bikini, a toasted ham and cheese sandwich with a shaving of truffle. For something unusual, try the *brochetas* of octopus or a roast beef sandwich with curry. There is definitely that element of fusion in the food, like the *mar y montaña*—sweet Iberico pork neck, pan fried with calamari, with a rich mushroom and miso jus and nori on top. Although some of the dishes

feel ___
d

Casa Calvet

little outdated, they are really delicious. It's just so good to be in a place where wine is so respected, with a great list by the glass, mostly from Catalonia but also from all over Spain. They willfully boast 2005 Vega Sicilia Valbuena from Ribera del Duero by the glass for 20€. FC

• • • • • • • • • • • • • • • • • • • • • • • •

## CINC SENTITS
Aribau, 58
( 93 323 9490
www.cincsentits.com
Tue–Sat 1330–1500, 2030–2300
**Progressive Catalan**/One Michelin star/€€€€/Cards and euros

Cinc Sentits, Catalan for 'five senses', is a total experience, serving some of the most exciting food in Barcelona. The room is beautiful, balancing overt style and modernity. And thankfully, it's comfortable, as meals here can take several hours. The staff are young and immaculately polished. The food is fresh and market-driven, a spirited response to the heaviness of classic cooking and the flavours and textures dictated by the dogma of the molecular school in Barcelona. There could be garlic foam over tomato sorbet with a slice of *fuet* and crunchy bread cubes—a play on the more rustic *migas*—or a funky young chef's version of *ajo blanco*, an almond granita with raw sardine pieces, peeled grapes and

beautiful almonds. They could be bold enough to do red mullet with a pesto sauce (almost no one uses basil in Spain except the migrants) or a poached egg with a sauce made from *chistorra* sausage. Yes, this place is lovely, and it is full of beautiful and lovely people from all over the world who are here to eat beautiful and lovely food. It's called Five Senses; however, it is missing the sixth, the sense of humour. It's all far too serious for me. RC

• • • • • • • • • • • • • • • • • • • • • • • •

## COLMADO QUILEZ
Rambla Catalunya, 63
( 93 215 2356
www.lafuente.es
Mon–Fri 0900–1400, 1630–2030;
Sat 0900–1400
Food shop/€€€/Cards and euros

This is high-end food shopping at its best. Colmado Quilez was founded in 1908 but was bought out by large food retailer Lafuente. They haven't changed any of the workings or signage but have kept it as it is. You could be traveling on to the UK and want to impress friends— say it with *jamón*! Buy a leg and take it to London with you. Here they have a fantastic collection of acorn-fed *jamón* from around the DOs. They also have cheese, chocolates and everyday veg and seafood. The quality is high, but then so are the prices. FC

• • • • • • • • • • • • • • • • • • • • • • • •

## ☂ DRY MARTINI

Aribau, 162–166
☎ 93 217 5072
www.drymartinibcn.com
Mon–Fri 1300–0230;
Sat–Sun 1830–0300
**Bar**/€/Cards and euros

It was late and I kept on saying to the taxi driver, 'I can't remember its name; it's just this really good bar.' He turned the corner, stopped the car and, by coincidence, said, 'This is a good bar,' and let us out. The dark timber-panelled walls have that slightly old New York feel, and the white-jacketed waiters in ties don't try to dispel that visual myth. Sit back in cyan leather chairs and couches, puff on Cuban cigars and mix it up with the hip and wealthy. For added interest, a 60-something drag-queen flowerseller comes in throughout the night. Although there are plenty of other cocktails, such as frappes and fresh fruit martinis, there is only one drink to have here, and if the digital readout is to be believed, they have sold over a million of them. Dry martini is king, and the back bar groans under the weight of the fantastic array of gin and vodka waiting to be shaken or stirred into the world's most famous cocktail. PG

• • • • • • • • • • • • • • • • • • • • •

## EMBAT

Mallorca, 304

( 93 458 0855

www.restaurantembat.es

Mon–Fri 1300–1530; Sat 1400–1530;
Thur–Sat 2100–2300

**Modern Catalan and Spanish
bistro**/€€/Cards and euros

Bistromania has hit Barcelona in a big
way and this is textbook bistronomy.
It's about simple, small restaurants
serving high-end food but with the
fit-out and price point of a bistro.
Lunchtime is very busy, with the
waiters buzzing you from the door
to your table (book ahead) or the bar,
which isn't the most comfortable in
Spain. The six starters may include
the classic *canelones* filled with a rich
mix of duck and truffle or a plate of
perfectly cooked assorted vegetables
with Gruyère cheese and roasted
hazelnuts. Second course could be a
confit salt cod fillet spotted with an
intense tomato sauce on cauliflower
puree and fresh basil—beautifully
balanced sweet/salty/creamy, an
assured dish for under 10€. Desserts are
simple but so delicious, like *borracho*,
literally 'drunk'—a cake soaked with
rum topped with chocolate foam
and tiramisu ice-cream—4€! Thank
you, good night. The downside is
that they are only open three nights a
week. FC

. . . . . . . . . . . . . . . . . . . . . . .

## FÀBRICA MORIT

39–43 Ronda de San

When we were resea
I was shown around a
what will become on
dining destinations. In the 1860s, when
Eixample was first being developed
Alsatian brewer Louis Moritz built his
first factory in the new quarter of the
Catalan capital. By the 20th century the
Moritz family had three buildings side
by side in Ronda de Sant Antoni. The
Moritz family have now redeveloped
these into their headquarters and
a multi-purpose site they describe
as a 'temple to beer'. Not a lager
swilling barn but a sophisticated place
where beer is not the objective, but
conviviality is.

I was impressed at the audacity of
the new design by one of my favourite
architects Jean Nouvel. The way he has
integrated the old reinforced concrete
fermenting tanks into the new bar, café
and restaurant areas. The industrial
rawness is offset with Nouvel's
minimalist touches balancing out the
yin and yang.

On the ground floor the cerveceria
was taking shape. This is not an intimate
tapas bar but a large and boisterous bar,
the type many Australians would be
used to. To one side is a beer museum
displaying Moritz's sense of humour
and irony—there's an old definitely
not PC poster of a lady breast-feeding

### 1 PICASSO MUSEO
Montcada, 15–23 (Born)
We sometimes forget that this great artist worked hard to become an accomplished figurative artist before anything else.

### 2 FUNDACIO JOAN MIRÓ
Parc de Montjuïc (Montjuïc)
Miró's bold colours and robust forms have been used to market the Barcelona Olympics and now Spain in general. Here in beautiful Parc Montjuïc is a great concrete temple of a building housing 14 000 works of art, including many of his sculptures.

### 3 MACBA–MUSEU D'ART CONTEMPORANI DE BARCELONA
Plaça Àngels, 1 (El Raval)
The Museum of Contemporary Art near the university zone of Barcelona is a great white concrete building filled with a great collection of modern art.

### 4 MNAC–NATIONAL D'ART DE CATALUNYA
See pages 234–35.

### 5 UNDACIO ANTONI TÀPIES
Aragó, 255 (Eixample)
Even if you're not interested in seeing a great collection of modern art, which we're sure you are, then it's worth seeing this rejuvenated modernisme building by Lluís Domènech i Montaner.

whilst drinking a caña of Moritz. The baby has an exceptionally rosy glow.

At the time of print the menu was not finalised but word was out that Moritz was hiring a Michelin starred chef. I believe there are to be two restaurants, one serving great casual food, the other a 40–50 seater high end restaurant.

Although it was yet to open when I toured I got the impression that this was a space that was going 'to go off'! FC

. . . . . . . . . . . . . . . . . . . . . .

## FONDA GAIG

Còrsega, 200
☏ 93 453 2020
www.fondagaig.com
Tue–Sun 1330–1530;
Tues–Sat 2030–2300
**Traditional Catalan**/€€€/Cards and euros

This is the new outlet for chef Carles Gaig. It's the sibling of the original Gaig restaurant which was founded in 1869, and based in Horta on the outskirts of Barcelona. Carles moved the operation to the heart of Barcelona (Carrer Aragó, 214, phone 93 429 1017) in 2004. Gaig has one Michelin star. The new Fonda Gaig, however, feels like a bistro, but you can see by the attention to detail that there is some fairly serious high-end aspiration here: large numbers of impeccably groomed staff, white linen on tables, fine cutlery, stemware and crockery. Silver trays filled with

plates of traditional Cat[...] to serve a diverse, most[...] The room feels spacious [...] of comfort, with plush ba[...] super-comfy upholstered [...] The room is mostly white with splashes of red—it feels sophisticated, yet it's great value with a three-course lunch menu for 28€. There could be salt cod *canelones* or *ceps* with *botifarra negra*—intense, woody grilled mushrooms served with fall-apart black pudding. Suckling pig, boned out flat into bricks of crispy porkiness and served with quince, could also be on offer. Desserts are classics from the Catalan and Spanish repertoire, but done extremely well. What we have here is a modern interpretation of a typical Catalan eating house, with high aspirations, good food and professionalism. FC

. . . . . . . . . . . . . . . . . . . . . .

## GRESCA

Provença, 230
☏ 93 451 6193
www.gresca.net
Mon–Fri 1300–1530, 2030–2300;
Sat 2030–2300
**Bistronomic**/€€/Cards and euros

When I asked chef Rafael Peña what the term 'bistronomic' meant, he said, 'That's what people call us. We do what we do. We serve gastronomic food at low bistro prices.' If that's the case, I'm all for it. Gresca is small, just ten tables in a long thin minimalist whi[...]

characteristic of the spaces of ...ample. Peña's wife runs the floor with some really good staff. The quality wine list suits the food and the size of the room. Most bistronomic places use cheap, everyday ingredients, but here it's not the case, with costly produce such as *foie gras*, pigeon with John Dory making appearances. In fact the *foie gras* is a wonderful chilled dish served in a delicate *escabeche*. The signature dish is an egg soufflé, a savoury meringue around a soft yolk on creamy potato—sublime. The highlight is half a pigeon, cooked to perfection, the breast slightly bloody, with a ginger sauce. All the food was simply presented but pretty, with really interesting flavours on the plate. Peña's food is very intelligently and skilfully cooked. FC

. . . . . . . . . . . . . . . . . . . . . . . . . .

## LA BODEGUETA PROVENÇA

Provença, 233
( 93 215 1725
www.labodegueta.cat
Mon–Fri 0700–0145; Sat 0800–0145; Sun 1830–0145
**Catalan**/€€/Cards and euros
This is the younger sibling of a classic called La Bodegueta (La Rambla de Catalunya, 100), and while the original might be older and more 'authentic', ...'s a lot smaller and doesn't offer ...ndard of food or wine they do ...'s the catch—some places ...d traditional serve old-

fashioned food, so the younger version in Eixample is always busy. It has a decent outside area, a gorgeous bar and a good-sized *comedor* or dining room at the back. At the bar they carry forward the tradition of the old place by serving a variety of wines from old barrels, including the interesting *vi ranci*, a dessert wine from Priorat. There is a fantastic list of classic Spanish tapas to choose from—salt cod *croquetas*, *salpicón, mojama*—and an extensive *conservas* offering. They have an ever-changing list of handwritten specials, which may include charcoal-grilled tuna belly or suckling pig with unbelievably toffee-brittle skin. The action goes on in a space that reflects the essence of an old *bodega* without succumbing to Disney-like pastiche, so it's dark colours, old wine barrels and black and white tiles on the floor. FC

. . . . . . . . . . . . . . . . . . . . . . . . . .

## LA CLARA

Gran Via de les Corts Catalanes, 442
( 93 289 3460
www.laclararestaurant.com
Mon–Sat 1300–1600, 2030–2400; Sun 1300–1600; Bar open 0800–2400
**Catalan**/€€€/Cards and euros
Don't be deceived by this fairly typical looking tapas bar on Gran Via. It ha. the usual refrigerated display of *tortilla* anchovies and seafood. It looks good but wait, there's more! Find a waite. to take you around the corner, pas

# — TOP FIVE —
# SPLURGE

**1 ABaC**
Avinguda del Tibidado, 1 (Above Diagonal)
Top-end luxury and food in a ritzy neighbourhood.

**2 RACÓ DE CAN FABES**
Sant Joan, 6 (Sant Celoni)
The fires still burn at the late Santi Santamaria's 3-star temple to Catalan and Spanish produce.

**3 SAÜC**
Via Laietana, 49, in the Ohla Hotel (Gòtic)
Nightime a la carte at this understated restaurant is sublime.

**4 BOTAFUMEIRO**
Gran de Gràcia, 81 (Above Diagonal)
This is where the king eats ... or should.

**5 MOO**
Passeig de Gràcia, 104 (Eixample)
The famous Roca brothers from Girona have a cool city operation in the heart of town.

the open kitchen and into either the downstairs room with its rustic stone walls or upstairs to a room stripped back to minimalist white, all linen-covered tables and comfortable upholstered chairs. This is a place where it is best to share, as the serves are large but oh so good. Perhaps a starter of tiny beans, onion and anchovies followed by some rich fleshy cuttlefish stuffed with wild mushrooms. Consider some meaty treats, such as grilled goat chops or super-succulent pig's trotters deep-fried and served with a rich *samfaina*. This is also the sister restaurant of L'Oliana, a classic Barcelona restaurant at Santaló, 54, phone 93 201 0647. FC

. . . . . . . . . . . . . . . . . . . . . .

## LOIDI

Hotel Condes de Barcelona
Mallorca, 248
( 93 492 9292
www.loidi.com
Mon–Sun 1300–1530;
Mon–Sat 2000–2300
**Modern Basque**/€€€/Cards
and euros

This is the Barcelona eatery of three-Michelin-star Basque chef Martín Berasategui. Although he's not behind the pans, it's his show—in fact he is referred to as 'director' (we'd use the term 'executive chef'). The restaurant is inside a rather swish hotel with a slick glass façade, the only real hint of the restaurant's existence being a small menu stand beyond which is one glass door and then another … you wait for the staff to open it, a trend in Barcelona. As you enter there is a long high table with stools—perfect for dining alone. The room is done out in monochromatic grey and pastel tones, with very vibrant and colorful works of abstract art—more interior design than a heartfelt touch. For me this is a lunchtime spot, a great opportunity to eat the man's food from a very accessible bistro-type menu. You'll be joined by a mostly Spanish business crowd, hopping into the recession-busting set-menu options of 22€ for two courses and salad, 39€ for four courses, and 47€ for six courses based on a constantly changing á la carte menu. The dishes generally pay homage to Berasategui's Basque roots, with maybe a pasta thrown in or an occasional Catalan favourite like *rossejat de fideos con almejas*, baked pasta with clams, or salt cod on *piperrada*, a classic Basque red pepper stew. Reminiscent of the cider houses near his restaurant in the hills above San Sebastián are the famous lamb *costillas*—chops served rare but made extra tender by slow cooking—served with *rossinyol* mushrooms. The efficient staff are mostly young and professional, and the food is great and superb value; just don't expect great atmosphere. FC

. . . . . . . . . . . . . . . . . . . . . . .

## MANAIRÓ

Diputació, 424
( 93 231 0057
www.manairo.com
Mon–Sat 1330–1530, 2030–2300
**Modern Catalan**/€€/Cards
and euros

This understated modern Catalan restaurant is just a block away from the bullring of Plaza de Toros Monumental. Bullfighting is banned in Catalonia, so please feel welcome to walk around this dinosaur of a monument to Spanish federalism. After that, come to Mainaró and be prepared to go with the flow. This is a restaurant that demands the complicity of the diner. Jordi Herrera is a joyous chef and his cuisine unleashes a playful spirit with a strong tendency towards fun re-creations of Catalan classics and some innovative surprises. The meal may begin with the gracious dish of *xof de pa amb tomàquet*, a revolutionary methodology of the avant-garde spherfication invented by Herrera himself, applied in this case to the Catalan classic, where a sphere of liquefied bread and tomato sauce is served in a jellied sphere on a spoon. The exciting menu also offers the spherical *gorgonzola* pizza or a chicken *croqueta* made with roast chicken and wrapped in Greek *kataifi* pastry, instead of being crumbed and fried. The pièce de résistance is a magnificent dish of egg, potato, a little onion, *botifarra* and quid, where each ingredient is cooked

to resemble another. However, the crown is, and will always be, the fakir grill—a bed of hot nails over which meat is beautifully cooked. It's a fun experience with more emphasis on the gastronomic than the molecular. CC

. . . . . . . . . . . . . . . . . . . . . . . . .

## MAURI

Rambla de Catalunya, 102
( 93 215 1020
www.pasteleriasmauri.com
Mon–Sat 0800–2100; Sun 0900–1400
**Patisserie and cafe**/€/Cash

Walking into Mauri is like going back in time. The original decorations outside have not been obliterated as many in La Rambla have. Even the window displays hark back to 1929, the year Mauri first opened its doors and set itself on the path to becoming one of the finest pastry shops in Barcelona. As you walk in you are confronted with a massive dark wooden cabinet filled with *flautas*, pastries filled with crème, all sorts of delicious croissants, *ensaimadas*, *magdalenas*, chocolate cakes. The choice is huge. You get the feeling that the owners are set not just on producing great pastries, but on preserving the style of service of a bygone era. The idea is that you order what you like at the counter, you are given a ticket and you take your pastries to a table, where a waiter comes along to take your drink order and add it to your ticket. As you leave you take the ticket to the old-fashioned cash-register station. To say this is a museum piece is wrong. Sure, the tables and chairs are old and the marbled floors are worn, the ceiling mural slightly faded and the customers wonderfully middle-class regulars who look like they have been coming here for years, but the food is great. The almond croissant has a real marzipan filling and a crisp crumbly pastry exterior that is just perfect. FC

- - - - - - - - - - - - - - - - - - - - - - - - -

## ⵢ MONVÍNIC

Diputació, 249
( 93 272 6187
www.monvinic.com
Wine bar Mon–Fri 1300–2330;
Library Mon–Fri 1100–2330;
Culinary space Mon–Fri 1330–1530, 2030–2230
**Wine bar/library/culinary space**/€/Cards and euros
Monvínic is a temple to all things vinous, with more than three thousand wines on offer between the wine bar, library and 'culinary space'. It's refined, modern, urban and urbane, fitted out with lots of stone, wood and glass. There is classy lounge seating near the entry, with a restaurant at the back. Small tasting rooms are available for the serious investigation of those inclined, or a more relaxed feel for those who want a glass of something interesting. Wines by the glass are sold in various serving sizes, so you can cover a broad range of wines in one sitting without spitting or getting too blootered. The cellar itself is the jewel in the building, and for the boffins who get a chance to take a tour, the staff are very proud to show it off; alternatively you can explore it virtually, on the house iPads. PG

- - - - - - - - - - - - - - - - - - - - - - - - -

## MOO

Hotel Omm
Passeig Gracia, 104
( 93 445 4000
www.hotelomm.es
Mon–Sat 1330–1600, 2030–2300;
Closed in August
Modern Catalan/One Michelin star/€€€€/Cards and euros
Although this restaurant has a menu created by the famous Roca brothers (see En Celler de Can Roca, page 267), its approach to fine dining is contemporary and casual. The entry is directly through the foyer of Hotel Omm, through its sister restaurant Moovida. There are no walls, just sculptures separating the restaurants. In fact, everything about Moo cries 'designer'. The tables, beautifully crafted from one thin piece of curved metal, are topped with linen and set with great tableware and cover plates handpainted by the likes of Ferran Adrià. I was blown away by a dish of *cigalas*, scampi-like creatures presented three ways: confit tails with spiced green beans, the heads and

Hotel Omm

legs served intact to crack open and pick over, followed by a small cup of warm white bean and shellfish soup. Magnificent! The degustation meals cost between 55€ and 85€ and take about three hours to get through. The wine list is encyclopaedic, arranged not by variety but by *bodega*, Catalan first, then Spanish, then the rest of the world. You could try to make sense of this or surrender yourself to the truly brilliant leather apron-clad sommeliers. Towards the end of the night the room changes as a DJ sets up in Moovida next door and the bar turns into a haven for poseurs and pretty girls. FC

. . . . . . . . . . . . . . . . . . . . . . . . . .

## MÚRRIA

Roger de Iluna, 85
℡ 93 215 5789
www.murria.cat
Tues–Thurs 0900–1400, 1700–2100;
Fri 0900–2100; Sat 0100–1400,
1700-2100
**Fine food shop** /€€€/Cards
and euros

The old woman at the cash register sits in a tiny cubicle taking cash from the customers, just as she has done for decades. The floor-to-ceiling shelves in this 100-year-old *modernisme* shop are stacked with some of the finest food in Europe. *Foie gras*, stunning acorn-fed Iberico *jamón* from the south,

caviar, outrageously good extra virgin olive oil, fine wine, *cava* and Moritz beer. This isn't a self-serve affair; it's a boutique, and as such one waits for one of the assistants to help you with your selection and only then can you visit the old lady in the cubicle and hand over your money. On the way out glance back and look at the assistants in their blue and white striped shirts, the ornate shop front, the windows framing the beautiful display. This is a way of shopping that is dying around the globe, but it's alive and well in Barcelona. FC

. . . . . . . . . . . . . . . . . . . . . . . . . . . .

## ORXATERIA VERDÚ

Bruc, 126

℡ 93 207 5630

Daily 1000–2300 (closed October and November)

**Ice-cream and *horchata*/€/Cash**

This tiny hole in the wall has been serving ice-creams and *horchata* to the neighbourhood's children and adults for 30 years. The signage proudly proclaims that the *horchatas* are made from *chufas*, or tiger nuts. Imagine very sweet almond milk with an earthy nutty flavour. It may be an acquired taste, but I love it. Verdú is like walking into a refrigerator, all shiny white surfaces and stainless steel, a cool respite after romping through the streets ogling the *modernisme* architecture. They also serve granitas, ice-cream and wonderful

semi-frozen *leche merengada*—sweetened milk infused with lemon and orange rind and cinnamon. Avoid Verdú when school ends for the day as it is packed with noisy kids. It's closed in winter but open before Christmas to sell *turrón,* nougat from the owner's home town of Jijona, a town to the south. FC

. . . . . . . . . . . . . . . . . . . . . . . . . . . .

## RACÓ D'EN CESC

Diputació, 201

℡ 93 453 2352

Mon–Saturday 1300–1530, 2030–2330

**Traditional Catalan**/€/Cards and euros

This is a classic formal Barcelona eating house with unusually young front-of-house staff. Not inexperienced in the least, they are dressed in dark uniforms and full-length grey aprons. I would say they offer exemplary service, especially the sommelier. The fresh-faced waiters and the good value of the food give this place a pleasant modern energy. Make sure you get the right door though as there are two—one to the restaurant and one to the apartments above—but with true crazy Barcelonese logic both have signs for the restaurant above them. The dining room is decorated in subtle pastel colours with expressionist paintings on the walls, frilly decorative features and large tables covered in top-end tableware. Looking around, there's not a tourist in sight—in fact the surprised waiter asked me how I found out about it. On arrival the waiter sets down a serve of homemade potato crisps and a plate of *fuet*, two of my favourite things. Ask to share some of the dishes—such as a carpaccio of octopus. In season there could be a potage of white beans with wild mushrooms and a slice of seared *foie gras*. Exceptional! Mains may include slow-roasted legs of baby goat, rich, tender, and glazed in its sauce, with tiny baby calamari and sweet baby onions, or slow-cooked pig's feet, boned then pressed, made crisp on *la plancha*, a classic so often forgotten by modern cooks. The food is renovated classic Catalan cooking, rich and filling, very well executed—it's the type of place I would come back to again and again. FC

. . . . . . . . . . . . . . . . . . . . . . . .

## RESERVA IBÉRICA

Aragó, 242
( 93 272 4974
www.reservaiberica.com
Mon–Thur 0830–1330;
Fri–Sat 0830–1400
*Jamonería* and *charcutería*/
€€€/Cards and euros

This is the place to begin your love affair with Spanish ham. As soon as you walk into this gleaming modern room you are overwhelmed by the scent of mushrooms, pine, cigar box, funky pork and forest fungus—the idiosyncratic aromas generated by the microscopic flora that inhabit and transform *jamón*, and this is the best. Ten different *jamones* sit in their *jamonería*—cradles where they are sliced into bite-sized *lonchas* by the *cortadores,* professional *jamón* slicers. Past them and the counter is a small tasting room where you can try some with a glass of wine. Civilised! There are other pork products such as top-quality *chorizo*, but it is the *jamón* made from the Ibericos, the Spanish breed of pig, some of which are fed on acorn *bellota*, that people come here for. You can buy the *jamón* in vacuum packs, but there is nothing better than hand-sliced *jamón*. Also, their original store is at the Mercat de Boqueria. FC

. . . . . . . . . . . . . . . . . . . . . . . .

## TAKTIKA BERRI

València, 169
( 93 453 4759
Mon–Sat 1300–1600;
Mon–Fri 2030–2300
**Basque**/€€/Cards and euros

Football ignites the most passionate discussions in the crowded bar of this Basque restaurant. Speak well about star footballer Lionel Messi and you will earn heaps of friends and, who knows, maybe even a free *pintxo*. If you criticise FC Barcelona and reveal yourself as a Real Madrid supporter you will understand why, as British football manager Bill Shankly said

football is not a life or death matter—it's much more serious than that. But as there are no differences that can't be resolved by sitting at a table in Barcelona, Taktika Berri offers one of the most well-arranged selections of *pintxos*, *montaditos* and *raciones*. They have achieved such success that there is a constant fight to earn a good spot in the bar. Just one piece of advice: train your bob and weave movements. You will need them if you want to avoid all the defenders, including the regular customers, to reach a bit of *morcilla*, *chistorra* or the sought-after European hake *pintxo*. If you are one of those people who is never satisfied with regular victories and who aims for the major titles, ask for the omelettes, either the Spanish one or, even better, the cod

one. Both are juicy. Then you'll witness how these delicacies are able to mute any controversy in just one bite. CC

. . . . . . . . . . . . . . . . . . . . . . . . . .

### TAPAÇ 24
Diputació, 269
( 93 488 0977
www.carlesabellan.com/tapac24
Mon–Sat 0800–2400
**Modern tapas**/€€/Cards and euros

Just a few convenient steps off the Passeig de Gràcia is Carles Abellan's informal tapas bar (see Bravo 24, page 72). It's a busy place so come early to avoid waiting on the staircase until a spot becomes available. The bar itself is brightly lit and wraps around a service area and central kitchen decorated with strings of garlic and baskets of tomatoes—all heavily stylised but still really fun, with cute printed paper napkins and tin lids used as bill folders. The menu is written on the cutlery pocket and a tiny blackboard on the table lists specials. Carles's *croquetas jamón ibérico* are perhaps the best I have eaten—and that is a lot! I love his bikini—little triangles of toasted sandwich filled with buffalo mozzarella, *jamón* and truffle—a recipe good enough to appropriate. There are also some great small portions of slow braises such as *rabo de toro*. Be adventurous when ordering and ignore the amateurish service and you'll have a ball. FC

. . . . . . . . . . . . . . . . . . . . . . . .

## TOC

Girona, 59
( 93 488 1148
www.tocbcn.com
Mon–Fri 1300–1600;
Mon–Sat 2030–2330

**Bistronomic**/€€€/Cards and euros
This restaurant was recommended to me by Sarah Stodhart, chef from Tapioles 53 (see page 252). To be honest, if it wasn't for her recommendation, I would probably have kept walking. The stark cafe feel doesn't encourage walk-in trade. But the ground-floor entrance does not do justice to what is a very nice restaurant, with some fine cooking and a lovely small dining room. The six-course 50€ degustation may start with a great little appetiser of a *foie gras* bonbon

with smooth glazed exterior served with crunchy apple. The meal then launches into uber-fresh, lightly cured sardine fillets above a tart tomato tartare, served with a raspberry vinegar sorbet. Sharp and delicious! The classic *escalivada* is served with soft gelatinous salt cod enriched with a slow-cooked egg and the skin of the fish, crisped for texture. Weirdly I felt like I'd had one of my own dishes served up to me: a plump, expertly pan-seared scallop with crisp leaves of *jamón* and a rich potato puree. It's great food, with fine use of seasonal ingredients prepared in the Catalan manner. Ignore details like loose ceramic floor tiles and enjoy. FC

• • • • • • • • • • • • • • • • • • • • • • • •

Vila Vinateca

# WINE in
# BARCELONA

**THE CATALANS HAVE** a healthy relationship with wine. They appreciate the good stuff but don't idolise it. And they have much to appreciate: Catalan wine has come a long way since the middle of last century, when much of it was pretty rough stuff made in co-operative wineries.

Widespread modernisation and an influx of some really serious and passionate individual producers have resulted in Catalonia now producing some of the best wines in Spain, particularly textural whites, fine sparkling and warm, generous reds.

What is truly outstanding is the sheer value for money of the wines served in bars and restaurants in Barcelona. The low taxes paid on wine here—and the unfortunately low wages paid to staff—means mark-ups on wine are minimal (around 25 per cent) and prices are kept low: really good wines can sell for just 4€–5€ a glass or 20–25€ a bottle.

If you're willing to spend a few more euros you can venture into serious wine territory; the top Michelin restaurants carry wine from all around the world, but the wine lists in Barcelona tend to be fiercely parochial, dominated by Spanish wines in general and Catalan wines in particular. Most of these wines are remarkably good but—apart from the few that are exported—many are unknown outside Spain, or even outside the region.

If you do find yourself in unfamiliar territory when confronted with a wine list in Barcelona and want to stray from the easy bets of Albariño from Galicia, or a red from Rioja, here's a guide to the local stuff.

*Paul Guiney*

## LOCAL WINE WORDS
. . . . . . . . . . . . . . . . . . . . . . . . . . . . . . . . . . . . . .

Some traditional Catalan wines to consider are *Vi ranci* and *Vi dolç*. *Vi ranci* translates as 'rancid wine'—like *oloroso* sherry, *Vi ranci* has a *'rancio'* character, a pleasantly oxidised, nutty, spicy flavour (the wine is intentionally oxidised by storing it in glass demijohns on rooftop terraces). *Vi dolç* means 'sweet wine'; this is a luscious version of *Vi ranci*, and tastes a bit like an old Australian muscat.

The words *crianza, reserva* or *gran reserva* on a bottle mean the wine has been aged in oak barrels. The Spanish word for oak is *roble*. Another word also used often by winemakers and restaurateurs is *autóctono*: this refers to a grape variety that is indigenous to its area.

Some older style restaurants have not moved with the times and still serve appalling house wine. In this case it is perfectly acceptable to 'shandy' the wine up with some lemonade or *gaseosa*. The locals do it all the time.

## WHITE GRAPES

**MACABEU**—A white grape used in sparkling *cava* but often also made into still table wine. Sometimes fermented like New World Chardonnay, with lees contact and a few months in oak, it can produce a lovely clean and slightly textural white wine.

**PARELLADA**—Like Macabeu, this white grape is used to make *cava* but is also made into still wine. Apple-like crispness and a clean finish make this a good wine with which to start a meal.

**XAREL.LO**—The last of the *cava* white grape trio, Xarel.lo ('char-ello') can make a pleasing white, with aromas of ripe stone fruit, and is often blended with other grape varieties.

## RED GRAPES

**CARIÑENA**—This grape (known in France as Carignan) makes deep red, acidic wines, often blended with *Garnacha Tinta* (France's red Grenache).

**MONASTRELL**—Also known as Mataró or Mourvedre. In lower altitude vineyards this produces wine with black fruit flavours, spices and leather, but from vineyards higher up, Monastrell wines can taste more herbaceous.

**TEMPRANILLO**—Spain's best-known red grape, responsible for full-bodied wines in Ribera del Duero and medium-bodied wines in Rioja and Navarra, is known here as Ull de Llebre—Catalan for 'eye of the hare'.

## REGIONS

Catalonia boasts a number of regions with a DO or *Denominació d'Origen*, a quality classification similar to the French AOC and Italian DOC system. You may come across this on wine lists in restaurants and bars in Barcelona.

**DO ALELLA**—Catalonia's smallest DO is just 15 kilometres north of Barcelona and is slowly shrinking as Barcelona swallows up its wine heritage, just as Adelaide's urban sprawl is threatening neighbouring wine regions such as McLaren Vale. Vineyards here are cooled by the mountains on one side and the Mediterranean on the other. The main grape varieties are Garnacha Blancq, Pansa Blancq and Garnacha Tintq. Look for these top producers: Alta Alella and Marqués de Alella.

**DO COSTERS DEL SEGRE**—This low-rainfall, poor-soil collection of subregions to the west of Catalonia produces an increasingly large range of wines: *cava*, crisp whites and tasty reds of the *joven* or young drinking style made from local Tempranillo, Garnacha and Monastrell) plus the French varieties Pinot Noir and Syrah. Also look out for Riesling made here from vineyards 800 metres above sea level. Good producers include: Cérvoles, Raimat and Tomàs Cusiné.

**DO EMPORDÀ**—This DO stretches from the Costa Brava right up to the French border and is more famous for elBulli and Dalí than its wine, but the region does produce some tasty ones: whites made from Macabeu and Garnacha Blanca as well as reds made from Garnacha, Carinyena and Cabernet. Look for the wines of Espelt and Perelada.

**DO MONTSANT**—The DO of Montsant, to the west of the city of Tarragona, encircles the more prestigious Priorat DO, but this elevated country boasts the same slaty *llicorella* soil for which Priorat is famous. Montsant means 'holy mountain' and the vineyards here are mostly planted with Garnacha, Carinyena and Tempranillo. You'll find juicy gluggable *rosado* (rosé) here, and while much of the red production is fairly rough, there are some quality-minded producers, including Portal del Montsant, Acústic Celler, Capçanes and—if you can find it—Espectacle.

**DO PENEDÈS**—Penedès is the *cava* region, the epicentre of Spanish fizz. *Cava* is ideally drunk young and fresh, but with some age becomes rich, full and brioche-laden. Look for *cava* from Raventós i Blanc, Gramona, Juvé y Camps and Albet i Noya. *Cava* is not the only gig in Penedès, though. There are some tasty and delicious whites and reds that should not be overlooked; these wines can be outstanding value for the money as Penedès is still not trendy. Look for the pinot noir–like *autóctono* Penedès red grape, Sumoll: the Gaintus winery produces a great version.

**DO PRIORAT**—This region, about 90 minutes south-west of Barcelona and encircled by DO Montsant, came to fame early in Catalonia's wine renaissance. The wines from here, many of them blends of old, bush-vine Garnacha, Carinyena and Cabernet, are a powerful, balanced and focused expression of the stoniness of the *llicorella* soil in which they're grown. These are perhaps the best-known Spanish reds outside Rioja, and their fame means that Priorat wines are also some of Spain's most expensive. Are they worth the high price? You be the judge. Start saving now, and then look for wines from Costers del Siurana (Clos de l'Obac), Clos Mogador, Álvaro Palacios and Mas d'en Gil. PG

# EL RAVAL

NOT FAR FROM the docks, El Raval was once the haunt of hookers, pimps, strippers, fraudsters, pickpockets and the usual grafted-on artists and bohemians. This is pretty much how the south of the *barri* remains. What a lively little area. It was once called *Barri Xino* because with all the nefarious goings-on of the inhabitants, their behaviour was so foreign to the Catalan sensibility that they may as well have been Chinese. Today the place has been gentrified, with the building of the MACBA, Barcelona's Museum of Contemporary Art, and the FAD design institute, making it a haven for artists, musicians, students and funky cool types. It's a blend of late-medieval buildings, 18th-century apartments, some beautiful *modernisme* buildings and some brand-spanking-new urban redevelopment projects. The northern part of El Raval is packed with galleries, comic shops, vintage clothing outlets and book stores.

About half of the people living in El Raval were born overseas, and in the southern part there is a large Pakistani population, so if you're hankering for a spicy korma, head down Carrer de l'Hospital and drop into one of the many local Pakistani restaurants. Then there is the Rambla del Raval (not to be confused with the other great boulevarde, La Rambla), which divides El Raval from the Barri Gòtic, the haunt of tourists and all those who prey on them. Rambla del Raval is a broad avenue lined with cafes and a centre strip on which there is often an outdoor market. There are still some seedy areas, such as Carrer Sant Ramon, the no-go area for most locals as it is just packed with street prostitutes. El Raval is a lively place, with a greater proportion of 'real' Barcelonese than other *barris.*

## ÀNIMA

Àngels, 6

☏ 93 342 4912

Mon–Sat 1300–1600;

2000–2400 à la carte menu

**Modern Catalan**/€€/Cards and euros

The set price menu, *menú del dia*, is a Spanish tradition. Most Spaniards will look for one when it comes lunchtime. It's generally two courses, bread, water and a glass of wine at a very reasonable price. There is usually a lot on offer, but unfortunately not all is good quality. This is not the case here at Ànima. This has to be one of the best value meals you would find anywhere in Barcelona— 10€ for two courses, a glass of wine and coffee. In fact, *menú del dia* is the only daytime offering, although the menu switches to à la carte at night. It's packed with locals, very hip, trendy ones, who come for the fresh, light and mostly organic fare. I was really impressed with their asparagus and salt cod soup followed by juicy fried morsels of dogfish followed by a wonderful orange cake with a coconut foam. The restaurant is minimalist but is beginning to feel well worn in with some great artwork on the walls. Service is attentive and straight to the point—perfect for a quick bite to eat before heading to the nearby MACBA. At night try one of the tables outside for a really interesting parade of cool El Raval locals. FC

## ANTIGUA HOJALATERÍA SUCESOR DE PEDRO APOLLARO

Petxina, 8

☏ 93 317 7584

Mon–Sat 0930–1430;

Mon–Fri 1700–2000

**Kitchenware shop**/Cards and euros

'*Muy pequeña pero llena*' is the best way to describe this fantastic little kitchenware shop one street to the left of the Boqueria Market. It's 'small but full', packed with every single piece of cookware a Spaniard may need, from a *jamón* knife to a chestnut roaster to a *perol* or paella pan. FC

. . . . . . . . . . . . . . . . . . . . . . . . . . .

## AVINOVA

Mercat Sant Josep/La Boqueria

Rambla Sant Josep, 89

☏ 93 301 3071

www.boqueria.com

Mon–Sat 0800–2000

**Poultry stall**/€/Cards and euros

Spanish chicken is fantastic. If you're staying in an apartment, buy yourself a big fat chicken, its skin deep yellow from the corn it has been fed, and cook it any way you like. It is fantastic. The people here at Avinova inside La Boqueria stock some of the best birds in Barcelona. They also carry some great *foie gras*—raw *foie gras* packed in atmosphere-controlled packs. They sell ducks slaughtered but not bled,

especially for restaurants serving duck *à la presse* (see Via Véneto, page 62). In season they stock a large range of game sold in fur and in feather—the sight of a wild pheasant with its iridescent plumage is quite unforgettable. FC

. . . . . . . . . . . . . . . . . . . . . .

### ⍦ BAR CAÑETE

Unió, 17
☎ 93 000 4484
Daily 1200–2400
**Bar and Catalan tapas**/€€/Cards and euros

Brand new in mid-2010, the food critics screamed praise for this long brightly lit bar that feels like an odd mix between the Love Boat and a hacienda. The waiters are dressed in white jackets with black braid epaulettes, yet the boss wears a fedora and black T-shirt, and who thought neon lighting strips would work with the agaves in the terrace? The food definitely plays to the locals. *Croquetas*, normally filled with a rich béchamel, are unbelievably light, with loads of chopped chicken. The friend who brought me here is Barcelonese, and with his eyes closed he said, 'This tastes like Christmas.' He explained, 'This is a classic filling for *canelones* served on 26 December using the leftover chicken from the Christmas feast.' Seafood on offer might be a piece of sea bass with a chive-infused *velouté*, or try something more meaty like little pieces of steak topped with a slice of *foie gras*. It's fun, slightly pretentious, self-conscious and expensive. RC

. . . . . . . . . . . . . . . . . . . . . .

## Y BAR MUY BUENAS

Carme, 63

( 93 442 5053

Mon–Fri 0900–0200; Sat 1100–0200;
Sun 1900–0200

**Bar and Cuban food/€/Cards and euros**

I would love this to be my regular bar, a place where I could sit and quietly drink beer as the untouched *modernisme* interior silently decayed around me. There's football on the TV above the cigarette machine, the fruit machines blink and beep, and between the two a cat is staring at the wall, either stark raving mad or waiting for a mouse. This is not everyone's cup of tea, but if you're an inner-city bar type, you'll love this. Out the back is a small dining room serving Cuban food for 9€ a meal. This place is about the atmosphere and the great *mojitos* served Cuban style. FC

## BARCELONA REYKJAVIK

Doctor Dou, 12

( 93 302 0921

www.barcelonareykjavik.com

Mon–Sat 1000–2100

**Bakery/€/Cash**

I have never tasted bread with the complexity of the organic sourdough breads baked by David Nelson in his white tile–lined bakery. He champions organic methods of farming, using extra virgin olive oil instead of butter, and agave instead of sugar. Try making a brioche with those sorts of handicaps. Yet he pulls it off to create a really delicious little bun-shaped, brioche-like pastry. It's no longer brioche but it is light and rich with that unmistakable tang of sourdough. David also uses biodynamic fermentation cultures in his bread-making, as well as more traditional sourdough mothers. An advocate of the Slow Food philosophy, he is working with Catalonian millers to find, preserve and bake with grains that for generations have been grown and fed to Catalonians but now are at risk of being replaced by modern hybrids. The results are in the tasting. RC

## Y BETTY FORD'S

Joaquín Costa, 56

( 93 304 1368

Mon 1800–0130; Tues–Thur 1100–0130; Fri–Sat 1100–0230

**Bar/€/Cards and euros**

An aptly named den of libations with plenty of cocktails and strong long pours of fine spirits, Betty attracts both locals and expats and is run by a bloke from Adelaide who has called Barcelona home for about nine years now. It's a mid-30s rocker tattoo set, who like comfy chairs, table service and the video screen that plays classics like *Easy Rider*. Clearly the regulars love it, and they create a warm and welcome vibe. PG

# MARKETS

Barcelona's markets are sacred sites to me, temples to food, with La Boqueria, Spain's most famous market, being the cathedral. It is not because it is the biggest, as there are others with more floor space, but because of the extreme quality of the food.

Markets are a mixture of commerce, agriculture, theatre and gastronomy. They are public spaces where people congregate and socialise, particularly in the outlying areas, and where home cooking is discussed at length between the customers and stallholders.

Most of Barcelona's markets were built in the mid 19th century, with soaring ceilings supported by cast-iron columns and light streaming in through stained-glass windows. I suppose that is why they remind me of cathedrals. Other markets, particularly in the newer *barris*, were built in the early 20th century, *modernisme* palaces of brick and concrete with strong straight vertical lines typical of many Catalan public buildings of the period.

Early morning is usually the best time to visit the markets. Arrive when the delivery vans are coming in from across the country and you'll hear the shouting and banter of the stallholders and porters as the produce is brought in and stacked. Or should I say 'artfully displayed'.

Usually there is a bar at the entrance where shoppers and workers congregate for coffee, brandy, *vermut* and meals that blur the line between lunch and breakfast—sometimes hearty fare to feed the hard-working porters, truck drivers and stall holders.

Walking through a market and not buying anything, for me, is like going to church and not taking communion—you're just a visitor and not a believer. Barcelona markets need to be shopped in to be fully appreciated—even if just for a few snacks. FC

## MERCAT DE LA BARCELONETA
Plaça de la Font, 1 (Barceloneta)
www.mercatdelabarceloneta.com
Mon–Thur, Sat 0700–1500; Tue 1700–2000; Fri 0700–2000

The Barceloneta Market was a glass-and-steel edifice similar to the market at Concepció in Eixample and would still be so if Mussolini's airforce hadn't bombed it and much of Barceloneta under General Franco's invitation during the 1930s. Many school children were killed during that bombing. Rebuilt in the last few decades, it has a sweeping awning on the façade that looks out onto the very quaint town square where there are some great shops and bars, including La Cova Fumada (see page 81). This is a nice little neighbourhood market whose diverse produce would put many Australian cities to shame.

## MERCAT DE GALVANY
Santaló, 65 (Sant Gervasi)
www.mercatgalvany.com
Mon–Sat 0700–1400

Built in 1929 this market, with its soaring concrete structure supported by brick archways, combines *modernisme* and Moorish influences and unlike other markets has not suffered a recent upgrade that obliterates all the charm of the mid-20th century. Some of the façades of the stalls date back to the 1960s. There is an old merry-go-round for the kids and some very serious seafood sold by the same family who own Big Fish in Born (see page 127). Apart from the opulence of this rich neighbourhood and its very good restaurants there is a fantastic cheese shop, Al Petit Savoya, which specialises in French, mostly raw milk cheeses. Yum.

· · · · · · · · · · · · · · · · · · · · · · · · · · · · · ·

## MERCAT DE LA CONCEPCIÓ
Aragó, 313-315 (Eixample)
www.laconcepcio.com
Mon–Sat 0800–1500

Designed by the same architects as the Sant Antoni Market, Concepció was named after the nearby church of the Conception. Built of glass and iron, its address is in Carrer Aragó but the entrance in Carrer València is rather more attractive, a tree-lined street with some rather attractive apartments and unusual castle-like follies.

· · · · · · · · · · · · · · · · · · · · · · · · · · · · · ·

## MERCAT DE SANT ANTONI
Cnr Ronda de Sant Pau and Carrer Comte Urgell, 1 (Sant Antoni)
www.mercatsbcn.com
Mon–Sat 0800–1430, 1730–2000

The beautiful old steel-and-glass building takes up a whole block and is surrounded by some really good cafes and food stores. The building is being renovated, with its reopening expected sometime in 2012–13. A temporary replacement market has been erected nearby and offers the same range of excellent produce as was (and will be) in the old building.

## MERCAT DE SANT JOSEP/LA BOQUERIA

Rambla de Sant Josep, 89 (El Raval)
www.boqueria.info
Mon–Sat 0800–2000

See pages 15–20.

. . . . . . . . . . . . . . . . . . . . . . . . . . . . . . . . . . . . . . .

## MERCAT DE SANTA CATERINA

Avinguda Francesc Cambó, 16 (La Ribera, Born)
www.mercatsantacaterina.net
Mon 0730–1400; Tue–Wed, Sat 0730–1530; Thur–Fri 0730–2030

A modern renovation has given this market one of the most interesting rooflines in Barcelona. Curved and wave-like and patterned with multiple colours, it somehow reminds me of a chameleon. One stallholder in this market sells some very delicious truffled eggs (see page 91). A great locals' market in the heart of the old town.

. . . . . . . . . . . . . . . . . . . . . . . . . . . . . . . . . . . . . . .

## OTHER FOOD MARKETS IN BARCELONA

Mercat de l'Abaceria Central (Gràcia)
Mercat del Ninot (Eixample) www.mercatdelninot.com
Mercat de Poblenou (Poblenou)
Mercat de Sants (Sants)Mercat d'Hostafrancs (Hostafrancs)
www.mercathostafrancs.com

For a comprehensive list, check out
www.barcelona.angloinfo.com.
It has great information but is hard to navigate. Click on what's on on the left then click on markets on the right.

La Boqueria

## BIBLIOTECA RESTAURANT

Junta de Comerç, 24

( 93 412 6221

www.bibliotecarestaurant.cat

Mon–Sat 2000–2330

**Catalan and Mediterranean**/€€€/
Cards and euros

This very sexy-looking space has a casual feel and a whiff of romance. It's a lovely old shop that has been stripped back to reveal its classic bones then had some subtle modern touches of softness and ambience added. You know you're in for a great meal when the waiter brings you fantastic home-baked bread and quality olive oil. The meal might begin with a wonderfully balanced chilled melon soup. The food here also shows lovely restraint, drawing on Catalan influences in a truly delicious *esqueixada* salad, moist shreds of salted cod mixed in with the sweetest tomato and ripe peppers. It's a very well-priced affair at around 40€ for the meal and wine from a lovely little wine list. FC

. . . . . . . . . . . . . . . . . . . . . . . . . . . .

## CA L'ESTEVET

Valldonzella, 46

( 93 302 4186

Mon–Sat 1300–1600;
Tue–Sat 2000–2300

**Classic Catalan and
Spanish**/€€€/Cards and euros

Ca l'Estevet has been here for over a hundred years. During the 1960s and 70s it was the mecca for intellectuals.

The photos on the walls tell the story: Orson Wells, Salvador Dalí and Joan Manuel Serrat, one of the most important figures in both Catalan and Spanish music. The place has been recently renovated without being gentrified, giving the old girl a new lease of life, and it is a lively place full of locals and business people. It's a real pleasure to hear children enjoying themselves as they eat with their parents, a contrast to the uber-cool that can permeate El Raval. The food, such as baby goat slow roasted with thyme garlic and a few potatoes, is simple and tasty. FC

. . . . . . . . . . . . . . . . . . . . . . . . . . . .

## CA L'ISIDRE

Les Flors, 12

( 93 441 1139

www.calisidre.com

Mon–Sat 1330–1600, 2030–2300

**Old school Catalan**/€€€/Cards
and euros

How do I explain my love for this place? There are restaurants that you know don't have the best food or wine or décor in town, but you still go there. Right? There's a feeling in the large room at Ca L'Isidre that everything in the world is going to be all right—and that is the theatre and magic that can happen in a great restaurant. Mine host Isidre Gironès welcomes you and explains: 'What's good at La Boqueria will be good here too. We go man

times to the market each week and that's what we cook and serve.' A platter of delicious sliced *fuet* and *bull* is placed on the table. Then you notice the raised dining area on the other side of the room, where well-turned-out couples are as much on display as they are there to dine. The waiter arrives with cloche-covered plates and whips the lids off to reveal a single fried egg, the white and yolk cooked separately, almost hidden beneath a pile of shaved Alba truffles, a nice prelude to a plate of pine mushrooms cooked with a few slices of *botifarra*. I hesitate to use the term 'museum food' for fear that it might put you off, but the foreleg of milk-fed goat is a stunning dish—silky, sweet and tender—but served with an old-fashioned brown demi-glace. There's a great selection of French cheeses, many made with raw milk. 'The Spanish prefer French cheeses when they dine out because they have Spanish cheeses at home,' explains Isidre. Opened in 1969, Ca L'Isidre is the kind of place where Spanish people from out of town come to eat when they're in Barcelona. Isidre says he loves everything on the menu, but it's the lamb's brains cooked in brown butter and served with capers that he eats when he can. RC

## CAFE DE LES DELÍCIES

🍸 Rambla del Raval, 47

☎ 93 441 5714

Mon–Sun 0900–1500; Mon–Sat
2000–0200; Sun 2000–0100

**Bar**/€/Cash

Along the Rambla del Raval is this
quirky little cafe-cum-bar. None of the
furniture matches, and it's cool antique
feel reminds me of a great Melbourne
institution, The European. The first
thing going for this cafe is that it serves
decent coffee. Inside, it has a great
local feel; outside is good for people-
watching, and as this is down near the
red-light district, there is usually some
seediness going on … in the most
colourful kind of way. FC

. . . . . . . . . . . . . . . . . . . . . . . . .

## CASA LEOPOLDO

Sant Rafael, 24

☎ 93 441 3014

www.casaleopoldo.com

Mon–Sat 1330–1600, 2100–0100

Closed Mondays in August

**Classic Catalan and
Spanis**h/€€€/Cards and euros

Open since 1929, this restaurant has
seen the changing face of El Raval.
Rosa Gil, the original owner, was both
the daughter of a bullfighter and the
wife of one, hence the conservative
Spanish décor. It's not the most
popular theme these days—Catalonia
banned bullfighting not long ago—but

it's still a great place to get a sense of
what Catalonia was like before the
death of Franco in 1975. Businessmen,
celebrities and tourists rub shoulders
here, and the service is like that of most
restaurants of this type throughout
Spain: surprisingly laid-back, friendly
and professional, without continental
pompousness. The food here isn't much
different from some of the more casual
bars in La Boqueria only a stone's throw
away. The seafood is cooked simply, as
fresh seafood should be, on the flat grill.
You'll also find some delicious braised
dishes such as super-sticky braised pig's
trotters, succulent tripe, or for the less
adventurous *mar y montaña*—braised
veal and pork meatballs with cuttlefish
and prawns. And if you want to have
a good *pan con tomate*, this is just the
place. FC

. . . . . . . . . . . . . . . . . . . . . . . . .

## DOS PALILLOS

Elisabets, 9

☎ 93 304 0513

www.dospalillos.com

Tue–Wed 1930–2330;
Thur–Sat 1330–1530, 1930–2330

Closed 7–29 August inc.

**Asian and fusion tapas**/€€€/
Cards and euros

Albert Raurich, the owner and former
chef of Dos Palillos, was head chef
at elBulli from 1999 to 2007. This is
part of the very cool Camper Hotel

a brand more often associated with footwear than accommodation and hospitality. It's a bar and a restaurant that specialise in a fusion of Spanish and Asian cuisines to create innovative *tapas*. You enter through a simple long thin Spanish bar with lots of stainless steel and what looks like beer boxes stacked against one side. These on further inspection turn out to be stools. The wait staff are dressed as chefs. Cool. You can eat food from the restaurant menu in the bar, but it can be a little cramped. Walk through a set of red chain curtains into a dark and sexy dining area, a U-shaped counter around a central kitchen where the chefs cook meals in front of you. Here you're committed to a 13- or 18-course degustation menu for 50€ or 65€ respectively. Waiters come to discuss wine choices to go with the dishes. The highlight is what translates as 'rolling your own joint', using nori as a 'cigarette paper', and marinated tuna belly, rice and wasabi as the filling. Delicious. Other standouts include a fishy *foie gras*—monkfish liver with grated daikon and seaweed salad—or the 63-degree cooked egg served in a dashi stock and soy powder. The theatre is great fun, but to be truthful, we do this food better in Australia. That said, it is a great light and fresh antidote to the sometimes rather rich offerings of Spanish and Catalan kitchens. FC

## EL QUIM DE LA BOQUE.
Mercat Sant Josep/La Boqueri.
Rambla Sant Josep, 89
( 93 301 9810
www.elquimdelaboqueria.com
Tue–Thur 0700–1600;
Fri–Sat 0700–1700
No reservations
**Traditional Catalan**/€€/Cash

One of the true pleasures in Barcelona is eating wonderfully prepared food while sitting on a stool with a placemat in front of you that reads 'the art of eating on a stool', surrounded by the heady cornucopia of La Boqueria Market—a truly beautiful place. What I love about the food in the bars like Quim in La Boqueria is the honesty. The chefs almost reach over and pick the ripe fresh ingredients from the stalls as they need them. The cafes serve up a range of dishes, with breakfast and lunch all mixed up. Nobody raises an eyelid when a market porter sits down to a plate of tripe with a beer at 9 am—he has been up for hours. I always come here and order freshly squeezed juice—the aroma from the oil in the skin cuts through the jet lag and confirms that I am back in Spain. Egg dishes are great here but I can't go past a *botifarra amb mongetes*—Catalan sausage with white beans. It's real, it's fun, it's fast and it's a great way to start the day. A good time to come here is before 10 am, when the crush of tourists starts. FC

## DE ARAGÓN

...agon.es
... ..00–1600, 2000–late
**Aragonese roast house/€€€/**
Cards and euros

I stumbled across this place a few years ago after arriving in Barcelona with my business partners when all of us decided that we wanted meat, and lots of it. We were in El Raval and I could smell the telltale signs—woodsmoke and the sweet aroma of roasting flesh. Only come here at lunchtime. With most *asadores* or roast houses you order the day before. Here, however, they have to roast enough to get them through lunch and by night service a lot of the food seems like leftovers. Part of the attraction is the tiny entry along a narrow bar, all dark and wood-panelled, then past the kitchen, with all the delicious cooked produce lined up on the bar—suckling pig, goat, cuts of beef—ready to be ordered, and then into two lovely old dining rooms with wooden floors and exposed wooden beams. It's a family-run affair, with the matriarch warmly greeting and keeping an eye on her old regulars. I usually stick to portions of lamb and goat. Start with a little *jamón* and a bottle of old Rioja and you would think you were in the high Pyrenees not five minutes' walk from the sparkling waters of the Mediterranean. FC

. . . . . . . . . . . . . . . . . . . . . . . . . .

## ♉ NEGRONI

Joaquín Costa, 46
☏ 61 549 8465
Mon–Fri 1900–0230;
Sat–Sun 1900–0300
**Bar/€/**Cards and euros

Joaquín Costa is one of El Raval's more grungy laneways and off this you'll find this tiny split-level designer bar where Campari is king second only to the house specialty Negroni. You can chill at the bar on the first level, or if you get there at the right time you might snag a small couch in the little lounge. Check out the wonderfully puerile collection of school-boy graffiti of genitalia drawn on the bar and preserved under a layer of clear lacquer. There's a good crowd here and a good vibe. As in the rest of Spain, the pours are lethal, so a few gin and tonics on a Tuesday night will see you wake up on Friday. PG

. . . . . . . . . . . . . . . . . . . . . . . . . .

## PASTISSERIA ESCRIBÀ

Rambla de les Flors, 83
☏ 93 301 6027
www.escriba.es
Mon–Sun 0900–2200
**Cake shop/€/**Cards and euros

This institution offers the opportunity to sit in a room covered in a wonderful mosaic lit by light filtered through stained-glass windows designed by a *modernista* set designer in 1902. I find it a treat to sit here and enjoy a crisp pastry cone filled with cream. It's great being tucked just away from the action of La Rambla, sipping a nice coffee next to a display of wedding cakes inside a wedding cake of a building. Escribà also has a *chiringuito* on the beach at Bogatell (see page 229). FC

. . . . . . . . . . . . . . . . . . . . . . . . . .

## GRANJA M.VIADER

Xuclà, 4–6
( 93 318 3486
www.granjaviader.cat
Tue–Sat 0900–1330;
Mon– Sat 1700–2030
**Cafe**/€/Cash

On a hot Barcelona day, when the breeze from the sea fails to penetrate the old city, the tight streets can feel mean and sweaty. Over the years the Barcelonese have created their own little urban oases—*granjas,* cool, clean cafes where iced drinks and ice-creams are served to families. Granja M. Viader is a 125-year-old institution in an interesting old building with a great tiled interior. Here they serve a host of delicious cool drinks such as *horchata* and *leche mallorquina*—sweet milk flavoured with cinnamon, lemon and orange rind. They also dish up delicious granitas, cream desserts, yoghurts and *mató*—kind of like junket. FC

. . . . . . . . . . . . . . . . . . . . . . . . . .

## KASPARO BAR AND RESTAURANT

Plaça Vicenç Martorell, 4
( 93 302 2072
Tues–Sat 0900–2400
**Cafe**/€/Cash

Under the colonnades of this apartment by the park is a little cafe. It's in a sun trap that overlooks a children's playground—perfect for families travelling with kids—and serves good coffee. It also sells good-quality BLTs by day and transforms into a bar later in the night. Simple. Good. RC

. . . . . . . . . . . . . . . . . . . . . . . . . .

## KIOSKO UNIVERSAL

Mercat Sant Josep/La Boqueria
Rambla Sant Josep, 91
( 93 317 8286
Mon–Thur 0700–1600;
Fri–Sat 0700–1700
**Seafood**/€/Cash

Once I have had time to salivate over the wonderful seafood displayed in the market, all I want to do is cook some. Unfortunately from my experience, cooking a piece of monkfish in your hotel room isn't appreciated—and there is only so much one can prepare with a kettle and the contents of a minibar. That's why I head to Kiosko Universal to get my fill of some of the best seafood fresh from the market. There's a list of seafood on the blackboard reflecting the fresh fish on ice under glass in front of you. Mussels, razor clams, prawns and a variety of fresh fish are all cooked on *la plancha* with a little olive oil, garlic and parsley. The aroma of the juices as they hit that great slab of super-hot steel is just beautiful. With a beer in hand it's the perfect way to satisfy your seafood cravings before heading off for a proper lunch. FC

• • • • • • • • • • • • • • • • • • • • • •

## MAM I TECA

Lluna, 4

( 93 441 3335

Mon–Fri 1300–1600, 2000–2400; Sun–Sat 2000–2400

**Catalan**/€€€/Cards and euros

It was the image of a Slow Food snail on the door that drew me into this relatively new little restaurant. It's very much a local's place, with just a few tables and a small bar, simply decorated and serving a range of cured meats and cheeses. The tiny kitchen still manages to produce some lovely Catalan dishes. They serve a *botifarra* and *bacallà a l'all traginer*—a good-quality cod fillet quickly cooked in olive oil with loads of garlic and chilli. There's a great terrine with wild mushrooms, and it's all complimented by a nice little wine list with some great *cavas*, whites, *rosados* and reds. Seeing as this is meant to be a Slow Food place, my only disappointment was seeing that the desserts are brought in—but then the kitchen is minuscule. FC

• • • • • • • • • • • • • • • • • • • • • •

## ☖ MENDIZABAL

Junta de Comerç, 2

Mon–Sun 0830–2300

**Cafe and Bar**/€/Cash

This is a hole-in-the-wall bar, literally, serving the tables in the small plaza. You'll recognise it from the cool graffiti on the outside. In the morning they do great juice and at night it transforms into a bar that can get a bit messy when it gets late. It's a gathering point for locals and visitors, and one of the few places to get *churros* in El Raval. You can buy pastries from shops nearby and eat them at the tables as long as you order drinks at the bar. Across the Carrer de l'Hospital is the L'Hospital de la Santa Creu, a 15th-century hospital, now a library with a very cool and quiet garden courtyard that is open to the public. Depending on the availability of heroin in Barcelona and the quality of policing, junkies sometimes frequent the area. FC

• • • • • • • • • • • • • • • • • • • • • •

## PATISSERIA LIS

Calabria, 137

( 93 425 3904

Mon–Sat 0830–1430, 1700–2030

**Pastry shop**/€/Cash

You have try to *xuixos* which are crisp cones of pastry filled with *crème pâtissière*. Perfect with coffee. Ask first There are great sweet treats to take away—sweet almond *cocas* made with flat flaky pastry sitting in big glass case

In a room lined with lacquered wood. Or try *cabello de ángel*, a pastry made with angel's hair—or sweet preserved strips of gourd encased in sweet pastry, sometimes made with lard. They are large so you'll need some chums to wolf one of these down. FC

. . . . . . . . . . . . . . . . . . . . . . . . .

## PINOTXO
Mercat Sant Josep/La Boqueria
Rambla Sant Josep, 89
Tue–Thur 0700–1600;
Fri–Sat 0700–1700
No reservations
**Traditional Catalan**/€/Cash

Every time I arrive in Barcelona I visit Pinotxo. It's like dropping in on an old friend to say hello. It's a bar that serves great food fresh from the market.

There really isn't much of a menu here, but that's what makes it fun—you have to interact and ask what's good today. I always start with a shot of *anís* (the coffee here ain't that great) and an orange juice and perhaps an *ensaïmada*. I ask for mine *tostada*, toasted. Pure heaven. After that they have a great range of *bocatas* or little rolls, their best filled with vegetable *tortilla*. There's always some seafood but you'll need to ask for this. This is the place to see the matriarchs come first thing in the morning before they go shopping, to sit down, and to order some *tortilla* and a nice icy glass of *cava*. FC

. . . . . . . . . . . . . . . . . . . . . . . . .

POBLENOU

SOMEWHERE IN THIS large, mixed *barri* of iron-balconied petit-bourgeois apartments and derelict late–industrial revolution factories is a handful of little villages. They have been swamped by a large development that extends from the Mediterranean to the new suburbs to the north, but somehow they give a certain down-to-earth soul to Poblenou that its more genteel contemporary Eixample doesn't have. Poblenou has been described as the Catalonian Manchester, and they share some similarities. They were both locations for soap operas, they were both home to bands in the early 1990s, and they are still great places to find massive nightclubs. Poblenou, however, has a beach. Although the beachfront has been well and truly developed, the renaissance of Poblenou is not yet complete, with long streets still lined with derelict warehouses and factories. Because most of this area is not a major tourist district, it is possible to walk around and still feel as though you're making discoveries.

## DOS CIELOS

Hotel ME
Pere IV, 272–286
☎ 93 367 2070
www.doscielos.com
Daily 1300–1600, 2030–2400
**One Michelin star**/€€€€/Cards
and euros

On the 24th floor of a sanitised glass-and-steel hotel tower in the 'ready for a renaissance' part of Poblenou is a temple to the Torres brothers. These disarmingly handsome young twins (I say this because chefs are normally neither twins nor handsome) were justifiably awarded their first Michelin star in 2010 and some say are headed for another. Javier and Sergio have worked for some of the best chefs in Europe and it shows in their food. They understand the canon of French cuisine and the foundations of Catalan cooking, bringing the two together in this impossibly clean stainless-steel kitchen and improbably white dining room. I love the tasting menu of around eight faultless dishes with wines for 130€. Presented by the immaculate floor crew on blown-glass bowls or hand-thrown fine crockery is perhaps a crab salad with a cream made from fresh Valencia *tabella* beans, or some perfectly peeled and seeded tiny tomatoes filled with anchovy foam, possibly followed by a brilliantly *al dente* baby ravioli filled with *foie gras* and chestnut in a clear broth. It goes on, as does the wonderful view from the stunning terrace with its white couches—you can watch the cranes working in La Sagrada Família as you eat. The technique is brilliant, the provenance of the produce commendable. Some will love the entrance on arrival through the kitchen to meet the chef. If you'd like to catch a rising star then book a table. RC

. . . . . . . . . . . . . . . . . . . . . . . . .

## ELS PESCADORS

Plaça Prim, 1
☎ 93 225 2018
www.elspescadors.com
Daily 1300–1545, 2000–2330
**Seafood**/€€€/Cards and euros

Poblenou takes in some old neighbourhoods and one of them was a fishing area surrounding the old church of Santa Maria del Taulat. Great apartments dwarf the old town square in which old men sit and smoke under the shade of the gnarled South American Ombu trees. Els Pescadors is a fish restaurant that takes in an old tavern, circa 1898, on one side of the small square. Here they use classic elements of regional Spanish cooking and tweak them to make new dishes. For example, they take octopus, gently cook it, grill it and serve it on a bed of octopus juice jelly and a cream of smoked potatoes. It's a nod to the classic *pulpo a la gallega*. You may start with *bunyols* of eggplant served with a few paper-thin slices of eggplant. Consider the salt cod. Here they desalinate it to their *punt de sal*, meaning it's soaked just long enough to make it soft and juicy but not too long to soak all the flavour away. From this they fry up fat fillets and serve them with *suquet* and potatoes that have soaked up and concentrated the juices of the *suquet*. Although customers come here for the *suquet* and the baby lamb ribs, Els Pescadors is probably best known for its *lubina,* sea bass cooked on a bed of potatoes and onions, the juices of the fish moistening and flavouring the potatoes. This place is a good daytime choice in summer as you can pack your togs in your bag and go for a swim at the beach after lunch. RC

· · · · · · · · · · · · · · · · · · · · · · · · ·

## ELS TRES PORQUETS

Rambla de Poblenou, 165
☏ 93 300 8750
www.elstresporquets.es
Mon–Sat 1000–1600, 2030–2300
**Spanish tapas**/€€/Cards and euros
The owners of Els Tres Porquets, or The Three Little Pigs, are the adult offspring of the owners of the very well-known restaurant Can Pineda in nearby El Clot (see page 259). They have made a name for themselves in this rather nondescript part of town, known more for high-rise apartments and

listless young people than excellent tapas, but they have pulled off a classic bar with the same hospitable zing as their parents. The interior is clad with Andalucian tiles surrounding a central wooden bar with a small open kitchen at the end. Timber barrels have been renovated into tables, giving it that typical old-world tapas bar look with a few quirky little decorative items such as a small statue of rooting pigs—cute not obscene. To eat you must have a seat—you can't stand and nibble. I arrived with a mate at 9 o'clock one night and we found ourselves alone. An hour later it was packed with locals, and this place is all about the locals. They are here because the food is good and it's good value—dishes from 5€ to 11€. The menu includes cold tapas, hot tapas, seasonal dishes, braises and seafood, with eight or so really exciting selections of each, which could be Iberico pork carpaccio, tuna belly, wild mushrooms with *foie gras*, suckling pig terrine or fresh seafood from the hotplate. Also from the hotplate is their great *morcilla de Burgos*. Or just settle on the truly delicious *ccroquetas de caps*—a simple plate that alone is worth the visit. In a nutshell, truly excellent Spanish comfort food with great service and quite an exceptional wine list for this sort of bar. FC

· · · · · · · · · · · · · · · · · · · · · · · · ·

# ESCRIBÀ XIRINGUITO

Ronda Litoral, 42

☎ 93 329 4592

www.escriba.es

Tues–Sun 1100–1500;

Tues–Fri 1900–2300

**Seafood on the beach**/€€/Cards and euros

Escribà Xiringuito is right on Bogatell beach, where there's a constant stream of bathers of all body types in warmer weather, including promenading walkers, morning joggers, evening bike riders and *nudistas* before the autumn chill. It's been here since 1906 in one form or another, although the early 20th-century staff wouldn't recognise this stainless-steel and blue edifice with its airbrushed aquatic décor. This is a real crowd pleaser, with many families coming here from the elevated *barris* to eat on the shores of the Mediterranean. The staff are young and seemed to be hired more for their multilingual skills than their ability to remember an order. The food is expensive for what it is, but the quality of some dishes is good, especially the entree of steamed pippies, grilled sardines and deep-fried baby squid. Paella is the main go, but I prefer mine with a *socarrat*, a golden crust, which the paellas, cooked in the open kitchen here, just don't have. The desserts are prepared at the mothership patisserie in the old part of town and are quite reasonable. I could

# — THINGS I LOVE —
# WATER

Not far from the cathedral in the heart of Barcelona is a fountain with three round faces carved into the wall, water pouring from their mouths. Before reticulated water was piped into every apartment, daily trips to fountains like this were rituals made by the mother or children to provide the family with water to drink, cook with and wash in. Some people, perhaps through ritual or more likely economic necessity, still make the daily trip down many flights of stairs to fill up large plastic bottles with water.

Barcelona's drinking water is appalling—it makes Adelaide's water look pure and pristine by comparison—so when you're in town, drink mineral water—order either *agua con gas* or *agua sin gas*, sparkling or still. If you're thirsty it's a safer bet to ask for still water because Vichy Catalan, the default brand of sparkling mineral water they sell in Barcelona is a very mineralised water that is quite alkaline and feels slightly soapy on the lips. That said I really love the sensation. It is absolutely wonderful to sip on as it aids digestion after a rich meal but is not exactly thirst quenching. Also, look out for sparkling waters such as Solares from Cantabria and Cabreiroa from Galicia. RC

Plaça de Sant Just Gòtic

go on and quibble about the quality of food offered at every place along the kilometre stretch of beach from here to Barceloneta. But on a warm night it's easy just to sit here watching the last light of the day play on the water, drink your cold beer or glass of *cava* and remember that you're not paying for the food or service, just the cost of this beautiful piece of real estate. RC

. . . . . . . . . . . . . . . . . . . . . . . . . .

## RECASENS EL CELLER DE L'ART I EL BON MENJAR

Rambla del Poblenou, 102

☏ 93 300 8123

www.canrecasens.com

Mon–Sat 2100–2300, 2300–0100; Sat 1300–1600

**Catalan**/€€/Cards and euros

The Recasens family has been serving food from this *modernisme* corner block since 1906. You'll recognise the building as soon as it comes into view as it is the most beautifully decorated edifice in the square, with peach-coloured render and rich cream detail. The second giveaway is the huge cornucopia of seasonal vegetables at the front door. Inside is what appears to be the most overstocked deli for its size in the world, with scores of cheeses, dozens of different Catalan sausages, a hundred or so wines and 15 *cavas* in the fridge. And this is the offer: great wines by the glass and *fustes* or wooden boards covered in a variety of *fuets*, Catalan cheeses. Out the back

and upstairs is a warren of tiny rooms in which the family used to live, but which are now dining rooms. Every spare windowsill or balustrade is covered in candles, and the walls are covered in a constantly changing exhibition of cafe-quality art but also some amazingly good photography and ink drawings. The content can be adult, and that is the nature of this place. Idiosyncratic, unbending in its aim to deliver good wine and produce (many of the producers are biodynamic or organic), it is a stronghold of the purist Catalan attitude of adhering to simplicity to achieve something beautiful. RC

. . . . . . . . . . . . . . . . . . . . . . . . . .

Recasens

# MNAC

Parc Montjuïc
93 622 0376
www.mnac.cat
Tue–Sat 1000–1900; Sun 1000–1430
Free entry on the first Sunday of every month; general ticket €8.50

The great dome of the Palau Nacional sits atop a series of columns, like a Baroque version of the US Congress. The palace rises majestically at the base of Montjuïc above the Plaça Espanya. I love coming here, walking up flights of steps set in a garden rising above the city and coming face to face with the great entrance of the palace. Imagine the counts of Barcelona regaling the rooms and chambers in their finest moustachioed brilliance charming the *condesas*.

The truth is it was built for the 1929 World Fair as an exhibition building and was restored into a national gallery of art—the Museu Nacional d'Art de Catalunya or MNAC for short. It's a good place to come on rainy days or a hot day when you need a large space with lots of air conditioning that isn't a shopping mall.

To be drawn back into paintings created centuries ago is wonderful. There was a moment in the Baroque when the spiritual gave way to the secular and artists painted what was around them: landscapes, people, furniture, jewellery and food. Juan de Zurbarán's works in the MNAC are so filled with latent sexuality that they border on the erotic.

The acceptance of the food of the Americas in art comes long after they were used in kitchens. A 1700 work by Antoni Viladomat heroes a turkey surrounded by quills of cinnamon. There's a reward in seeing the familiar, recognising buildings or locations, such as a beach painting by Joan Roig i Soler of a group of boys fishing in the shallows at Sitges.

A Barcelona streetscape by Achille Battistuzzi in the late 1800s depicts La Rambla and is painted from an apartment in El Raval looking down Carrer de la Boqueria. A dark-skinned woman with a cart is cooking chestnuts over coals in exactly the same spot where South Americans now cook potatoes to sell to tourists. There is a bar next to a fountain (now blocked) with women collecting water for the house. That bar is now a clothing store. The centre pedestrian strip of La Rambla is taken over by a cart selling great sweet thick-skinned melons. So much and yet so little has changed.

Works by El Greco are worth checking out, as well as the those by modernist Ramon Casas, a particularly interesting one being of a bullfight where the bull has taken out two horses and is about to get another—perhaps an allegory for Catalan nationalism. I love seeing the progression of the city through those paintings, a city that is always changing.

The MNAC has a great coin collection, some medieval Catalan iconic works and a solid little collection of modernist works. When you have finished craning your neck, sit on the steps and watch the last light of the day play on the hills beyond and the city of Barcelona below. RC

POBLE-SEC

**P**OBLE-SEC SITS at the base of Montjuïc, a quiet residential *barri* with steep tree-lined streets and modest apartments. Poble-sec means 'dry village', and the first fountain for fresh water wasn't built until 1894. It sits just the other side of where the old city walls once stood, and this was the place for people who couldn't afford Barcelona prices. It's now divided from the old town by the broad avenue Paral·lel, which is in the city's theatre district. It is a fun area, and although it wasn't the place to go when I was living in Barcelona in the 1990s, it has undergone a really healthy urban renewal without the dreaded gentrification. Carrer Blai, which runs across the *barri*, was pedestrianised in recent years and at night it's packed with young locals.

A good way to spend half a day is to walk from the centre of Barcelona, through Poble-sec, to the *barri*'s old village, which sits just off the base of Montjuïc above Passeig de l'Exposició. Alternatively, you can take the cable car up from Barceloneta and wander down, or take the metro to Paral·lel then the venicular to the summit. Here there is a handful of artists' studios along the tiny streets. I love to wander around the garden and fortifications of Montjuïc before sauntering back down into Poble-sec for a meal. And there are some great places to eat here.

Bar Seco

## 41°/TICKETS

Paral·lel, 164
41° ( 93 292 4254
Tickets ( 93 292 4250
www.ticketsbar.es
Tue–Sun 1800–0200
**Tapas, cocktails and snacks**/€€€/Cards and euros

Such is the allure of the Adrià brothers Ferran and Albert that a few days after the opening of their new tapas and cocktail venture, 41°/Tickets, the place is filling up when the doors open at 6 pm—unusual in a city where locals don't go out until much later. In a large venue on the unfashionable Avinguda Paral·lel, the venture is split into two distinct experiences. Tickets takes care of the tapas side of things with a carnival-esque décor that is reminiscent of a village *feria*, where trestle tables are trotted out into the streets and set up with makeshift grills, *jamón serrano* stands and giant silver barrels pumping out beer into plastic cups. Next door, 41° is the antithesis of Tickets' folkloric nostalgia. In an uber-metropolitan ambiance of slate-grey textiles, steel and wall art laden with sparkling diamantes, a surprisingly old school list of cocktails is shaken and stirred by a sleekly uniformed team, while Albert elaborates the bar menu. To call these exquisite little morsels 'snacks' (as he does) is rather like describing the pyramids as 'old'. Suffice to say, most of the recipes have travelled down from elBulli and lost none of their artistry in the migration. My favourite was the *profiteroles de Grosella negra*, or featherweight blackcurrant meringues filled with a spurt of yoghurt and sporting a tuft of atsina cress. Arranged as they were on a moulded ebony plate, they reminded me of minute Easter bonnets. SW

. . . . . . . . . . . . . . . . . . . . . . . . . . .

## ⟙ BAR RAMON

Blai, 28–30
( 93 442 3080
**Late bar**/Cash

It's a bar in a pedestrian mall in Poble-sec. But wait. It might take a few years, but this part of Barcelona will be the next to go off. This is one of the vanguard bars to set up in this quite wide strip of shops below flats in the young and funky part of Poble-sec. 'The government closed the road off in 2006,' says Joan, the inked and pierced barman. Now young business people are seeing the potential and opening up here. It's not a tourist trap. The staff don't speak English, although the educated clientele do. It's fun. The late food, such as *papas arrugadas o arrugás con mojo picante*, is acceptable. But this is a chance to get away from the madding crowds just 15 minutes away from the old town. RC

. . . . . . . . . . . . . . . . . . . . . . . . . . .

## ♈ BAR SECO

Passeig de Montjuïc, 74

℡ 93 329 6374

Mon–Wed 0900–2000;
Thur 0900–0100; Fri 0900–0200;
Sat 1000–0200; Sun 1000–0100

**Bar and cafe**/€/Cash

The barista has tatts and piercings, the food is organic, the crowd young and arty, the coffee half decent and it's a light and bright room with Elvis cut-outs on the serviette dispensers. Any inner-city Australian cafe goer will recognise this sort of place from about twenty years ago. It serves some good light meals and is open until the wee hours towards the end of the week. During the day it's a good stopping point if you're walking up to Montjuïc from the metro station. At night it's a locals' bar that gets quite busy. RC

. . . . . . . . . . . . . . . . . . . . . . . .

## ♈ CELLER CAL MARINO

Margarit, 54

℡ 93 329 45 92

www.facebook.com/
cellercalmarino

Mon–Fri 1130–1500, 1900–2300;
Sat–Sun 1130–1500

**Bar bottle shop**/€/Cards and euros

There's a tradition in Catalonia of bringing your own bottle to the local *bodega* or bar-cum-bottle shop and filling it from the cask. Any bottle. I love seeing old cola bottles being filled with half-decent, good-value wine. 'I wanted

to sell wine at the correct price, not an inflated price,' says Eduard Borrull when he opened his *bodega* in 2009. He offers eight reasonable wines poured straight from the cask for around 1.3€ a glass, and eight good-quality wines from 3€ a glass. Eduard laughs that he is no cook, so follows the blokes-only Spanish bar tradition of buying great preserved product and serving it up at the old wine barrels he uses as tables. Try a red from Penedès and a little dried fig stuffed with *foie gras*, or some preserved baby scallops no bigger than soft-drink bottle tops, like the ones on the bottles that Eduard fills with *vi ranci* for the locals. It's a fun, young, less urbane and cheaper alternative to Quimet & Quimet (see page 251) around the corner. RC

. . . . . . . . . . . . . . . . . . . . . . . .

## FEDERAL CAFE

Parlament, 39

℡ 93 187 3607

www.federalcafe.es

Tue–Thur 0800–2200; Fri–Sat 0800–0100; Sun 0900–1730

**Cafe**/€/Cards and euros

One thing I really miss when I'm in Spain is good coffee and this place serves it up. Freshly roasted arabica beans, real milk (Spanish coffee is made with UHT milk) and time and care taken to make the coffee, not the *rápido* service you get in smoky bars. Anyone who has been to Bill Grainger's restaurant in

federal

Federal Cafe

VI RANCI
17°
3'15

Celler Cal Marino

Surry Hills in Sydney will recognise the décor: latte-coloured walls, cool wood and casual atmosphere. Yes—it's owned by Aussies. So if you're hanging out for Vegemite on toast or some marmalade and a pot of tea, here's the place. They do great bacon sandwiches made with British pork and a range of scrambled egg options *and* they have Berocca as well as bloody marys, perfect if you join the local crowd who come here on Friday and Saturday nights when the cafe becomes a bar. There's also a great rooftop garden where you can look out to Montjuïc or down on the older generation who just can't understand the fit-out—the casual cafe is so foreign to them. This place is for when you want to be in Barcelona but don't want to be in Barcelona. It's all about being in a comfort zone while watching the frenetic Barcelona pace through a huge window, like the 108-cm TV hanging in your apartment. FC

. . . . . . . . . . . . . . . . . . . . . . . .

## LA PERLA

Passeig de l'Exposició, 62
( 93 329 2052
Tue–Sun 0900–1700
**Traditional Catalan**/€€/Cards and euros

Miguel the mushroom hunter wanders in with a box of tiny pine mushrooms. He won't tell us where he got them, just somewhere 'up in the hills'. With his gnarled hands he takes his

beer as part payment. He's a country bloke and is the odd one out in this urban neighbourhood restaurant. It's breakfast and lunch only, and judging by the extremely well-developed paunches under their business shirts, it's an all-too-regular haunt of local businessmen. Perched on a sweeping road that follows the base of Montjuïc, this is a rather picturesque old *bodega* with barrels on the walls and a great cornucopia of produce on the bench: tomatoes, peppers, garlic, beans. The salt cod *croquetas* are the specialty. They are as creamy inside as they are crunchy outside. The mushrooms arrive sizzling on an iron plate with chunks of garlic and loads of fresh parsley. They also serve a very tame and palatable version of *cap i pota*—elsewhere it can be a visceral-looking bowl of bones and unidentifiable flesh. Here it is a sticky sweet bowl of large pieces of pig's cheek, *botifarra negra* and white beans not at all scary—just delicious. The *arroz con nécoras* comes to the table in the paella pan in which it was cooked. It remains an *arroz* and not a paella because it has been cooked slightly wet so no *socarrat* has formed on the base of the pan, but it's fabulous and all the more so because of the use of super fresh crabs that were fried in the oil before the *sofrito* was made, extracting loads of bisquey flavours. Dessert could be as simple as a plate of cheese or *garapinyades*—fresh almonds encased in brittle crust of caramelised sugar and little cinnamon. It's only a ten-minute walk to the Plaça Espanya and MNAC Catalan National Museum of Art (see pages 234–235). The other good reason to come here is to see Antonio Moreno, who claims, 'I am the best waiter in Barcelona!' RC

. . . . . . . . . . . . . . . . . . . . . .

## LA TIETA

Blai, 1

93 186 3595

Tue–Sun 1330–2400

Tiny bar/€/Cards and euros

Edgar Mestre's family had one of the last *chiringuitos* down on Barceloneta beach before the government closed them down and, well, created a beach in time for the 1992 Olympics. Old sepia photos of the family at work and play hang on the wall of his six-seater bar in the up-and-coming Carrer Blai. Edgar puts on a beautifully simple show. 'I want to keep the tradition of the *vermut* bar alive,' he says as he pours a glass of *vermut* over lemon and ice. 'This is a place for local people to just come and be.' He and his partner Elisenda Fernández offer some lovely little tapas, like a plate of *esqueixada* with pieces of onion and chunks of green pepper and salt cod. They turn out a really decent *tortilla*, perfectly golden on the outside

La Perla

# BARCELONA FOOD EXPERIENCES

Cesc Castro is a Barcelonese food and sports writer who works for the Catalan television sports news website and *Cuina* magazine and is a great mate. His brother lives in Sydney and has given him a Crumpler bag with an Aboriginal flag on the flap, and he carries it proudly around Barcelona. As a serious journalist, having covered the Iraq War for Catalan media, Cesc is not your average food writer. Even though he's a young bloke, he's not into the foams and spheres of the Catalan modernist chefs, instead preferring the traditional foods and experiences—many of which are endangered species even in Barcelona. We asked Cesc to list his favourite five food experiences in his home town. His English is still a work in progress (he swears beautifully in Catalan when he can't remember a word in English), but we love his top five recommendations.

## SALTERIO

Sant Domènec del Call, 4 (Barri Gòtic)
℡ 93 302 5028
Mon–Sun 1800–2400
**Tea house**/€/Cash

For several generations the young adults of Barcelona have come to this tea house where affairs of the mind and heart mingle. Young Catalan gentlemen pretend to read books hoping to catch the attention of local ladies, who are not impressed with the machismo of the Latin-lover stereotype, but the good music and intimate atmosphere do make a heady mix. Salterio is inside an ancient house in the very centre of the former Jewish quarter, where hostess Fàtima serves, in true Berber fashion, teas like the green tea with mint or a dark, strong and sweet Turkish coffee, as well as a few beers and wine by the glass. Ladies should, however, distrust any local gentleman who pretends to be their friend unless they want to end up like a character in the film *Vicky Cristina Barcelona*.

· · · · · · · · · · · · · · · · · · · · · · · · · · · · · ·

## XURRERIA

Plaça Eivissa, 5 (Horta, Barcelona)
℡ 93 429 6800
Wed–Fri 1000–1400, 1700–2030; Sat–Sun 1000–1500
**Xurreria**/€/Cards and euros

I am magnetically drawn here after of one of those endless Saturday nights when you need something to get through Sunday morning—you know what I mean. Situated in the main *plaça* in the residential district of Horta, get to this very popular *xurreria* too late and you won't find a table on the street terrace. This is the only place in town where you can taste the best *morro frito* or fried pork cheeks in Barcelona. These are available on Saturdays, Sundays and festival days and cost 4€ for a 200 g serve of deep-fried goodness. They are so remarkably good that they should be forbidden—calorific bombs, for sure. But as the Catalans say: *'El que no mata, engreixa'*, which could be freely translated as: 'What does not kill you makes you fatter.'

## TIO CHE
La Rambla del Poblenou, 44–46 (Poblenou)
☏ 93 309 1872
www.eltioche.com
Mon–Fri, Sun 1000–0100; Fri–Sat 1000–0200; closed Weds in winter
**Cafe**/€/Cards and euros

When the summer heat beats down on the flats of Poblenou, Tio Che is an oasis. Found in the middle of La Rambla, the main thoroughfare, this family *granja* has stood here on the corner serving iced drinks since 1940. Regulars are spoiled by the amount of choice. There's the *murcià*, a drink made with tiger lily milk—*orxata*, *horchata* in Spanish, served with iced lemonade; there's the Russian—iced coffee with vanilla ice-cream; the Cuban—meringue milk with a chocolate ice-cream ball; or the famous half and half, which is a drink made with oat milk and iced lemonade.

## MORRO FI

Consell de Cent, 171 (Eixample)
http://morrofi.wordpress.com/
Mon–Fri 1800–2300; Sat 1130–1500
**Bar**/€/Cash

Morro Fi in Eixample was established by three men passionate about the traditional food temples that the new fashionable Barcelona tried to eradicate. Their tavern is a very small, friendly venue which has become a reference spot for those food lovers who are able to appreciate the simplicity of a good *vermut*, a well-poured beer, witty conversations, *embotits*, cheese, tapas and small *platillos* such as *esqueixada*.

. . . . . . . . . . . . . . . . . . . . . . . . . . . . . . . . . . . . . . .

## SUBHASTA DE PEIX

Passeig Marítim de Montgat s/n (Montgat)
Mon–Fri 1300 until sold out
**Fish market**/€/Cash

Just 13 kilometres north of Barcelona there is the fishing village of Montgat, a quiet spot on the seaside that deserves a mandatory visit. Catch the train from Plaça Catalunya to Montgat Nord station, an easy 20 minutes along the coast. Every day (except Sunday) at 1 pm you can attend the last remaining fish auction in Catalonia, a tradition that is about to disappear. The auction is open to everyone; you can get the freshest fish of the day, caught that morning off the coast, at a terrifically cheap price. This is assuming, of course, that you are able to stop the auction at the right moment and before any of your competitors raise their voice.

La Tieta

La Tomaque

and just on the point of setting in the middle. Try a bowl of *patatas fritas* with a classic *Salsa Espinaler*—a brand of mild sweet red pepper sauce that is soused upon potato chips, anchovies and little preserved pippies. Edgar and Elisenda are very funny people and it's a bright, young bar: small, fun and friendly. RC

. . . . . . . . . . . . . . . . . . . . . . . .

## LA TOMAQUERA
Margarit, 58
Tue–Sat 1330–1545, 2030–2245
**Traditional Catalan**/€€/Cash
No phone, no cards, no web. This is as basic as it gets. I first dined at this

classic Catalan locals' joint during a trip with my partner Vanessa and friends in 2004. We were making our way down from Montjuïc on a stunning sunny day. We just kept walking down the mountain not knowing where our stomach cravings were taking us when we noticed a crowd of people waiting outside the entrance to this rustic taverna. A crowd is a good sign so we joined the queue. Fast forward to now and not much has changed except that owner Manuel has passed away. He was such an energetic force, making fun of us Australians trying to get through a bowl of snails as he manned the pans in the open kitchen. His wife still runs the same show: the same red-and-white chequered tablecloths, the great slab of bread and whole tomatoes served when you order to make your own *pa amb tomàquet*, the same smoky black wood grill roasting up delicious little quails and portions of tender rabbit and the same appalling house red that is more palatable with a fizzy *Gaseosa*—Spanish lemonade. The tiny toilet is still up a flight of impossibly narrow stairs; the place is still full of locals noisily enjoying their meals, and it still oozes old world charm. All that is missing is Manuel and his booming laugh. FC

. . . . . . . . . . . . . . . . . . . . . . . . . . . .

## MONTALBAN CASA JOSÉ
Margarit, 31
( 93 442 3143
Tue–Sun 1400–1600, 2100–2300
**Seafood**/€€/Cards and euros

Chef and owner José Rojas's simple seafood restaurant has just 24 seats, no view except the chef's head bobbing in the open kitchen and a kitsch beach mural on one wall. But it is always full. Aussie-born chef Sarah Stodhart, the harshest critic of Barcelonese seafood, stood me outside this place as the delivery man arrived and said, 'Look at those wooden boxes. They are oysters from Galicia. They were harvested last night. Beautiful. Look at those fresh prawns. They are stunning.' It took a week to get a table. There's

no menu, just a chalkboard high on one wall. Apart from prawns, mussels, razor clams and fish, you could try the cockles, which are steamed and hit the table hot. Rich, full of juice, perfect. Calamari are cleaned, sliced into rings, dusted in seasoned flour and dropped into very hot oil long enough for the flesh to set and the flour to change colour, just. Sent to the table with a wedge of lemon, they are soft, supple and delicious. José is Barcelona born and bred and learned to cook seafood in Majorca. He sends out a plate of *pimientos de Padrón*, tiny green capsicums, cooked on the grill, and a plate of French fries as a digestive. Even the chips are good here. RC

. . . . . . . . . . . . . . . . . . . . . . . . . . . .

## ⟨ QUIMET & QUIMET
Poeta Cabanyes, 25
( 93 442 3142
Mon–Fri 1200–1600, 1900–2230;
Sat 1200–1600
**Wine bar with tapas**/€/Cards and euros

This is one of the greatest tapas bars in the world. Built as a tavern at the beginning of the 20th century, it is run by a fifth-generation Quimet, a happy chap who's known as Quim. He's the chef, barman and shopkeeper. From behind his counter, he runs this little space, almost as tall as it is wide, stacked from bar height to the ceiling with an almost endless selection of wine and preserved food—it is what I thought Aladdin's cave might look like when I was 12, but with more wine than I imagined. The bar is stacked with all sorts of fishy delights: *mojama*, smoked eel, smoked salmon, *arenque* faux caviar, *bacallà*. Next to them are rectangular plates packed high with all sorts of delicious wonderments: *foie gras*, terrines, chestnuts, little mushrooms, *cecina*, plus a great range of Spanish cheeses—*Torta del Casar*, aged *manchego* and *cabrales*. There's so much food that the first time I came here early I wondered which army was going to devour this selection of gourmet treats. Soon hordes descended on the bar. Locals, old men, businessmen and tourists. Choose your bottle of wine—there are some really good Spanish wines that we just never see in Australia, and for a cost of just 2€ you can drink it at one of the small, high tables with a choice of whatever you want from the selection at the bar. Now—here's the drill. No cooking is done here. Everything is bought in and all Quim does is serve it to you on a plate. The *best* preserved meats, the *best* canned seafood, the *best* of whatever else he is serving up and all totally delicious. This place is by no means a secret but it still rocks. Don't leave Barcelona without visiting Quimet & Quimet. FC

· · · · · · · · · · · · · · · · · · · · · · · ·

## TAPIOLES 53

Tapioles, 53
☏ 93 329 2238
www.tapioles53.com
Tue—Sat 2100—2300
**Original**/€€€/Cards and euros

Sarah Stodhart has been cooking in this tiny converted old umbrella factory since 2005. The space feels very much like a quirky homely space, lots of little lamps, subdued lighting, bentwood chairs, beautiful rustic tables and a lovely view overlooking a leafy residential street. You can't pigeonhole Tapioles 53. Sarah is not a trained chef. She sits next to you at the table and explains what she is going to cook for you from her set menu, but will gladly make adaptations to suit those with allergies or religious or ethical needs. She's out on her bike at the market every day, buying ingredients for her three to five different dishes. Her menu jumps from cuisine to cuisine, and is extremely produce driven. One night I ate the most amazing fig I have ever tasted; wrapped in good *jamón* and put together with crunchy micro leaves, it was an explosion of flavour and textures. She also makes tiny round herbed gnocchi with parmesan and sage butter. Spice plays a big part in her cooking (she has travelled extensively in India and still sources the best spices for her restaurant), such as subtly spiced ginger sauce with pan-seared quail. This space has been set up in Sarah's

Quimet & Quimet

totally original way. She wanted an open kitchen and liked the look of the steel beams so didn't cover them up. Because there is a photographic studio at the back accessed through the restaurant, Sarah has to call her little place a gastronomic society in the tradition of the Basque cooking clubs to work around some of the local regulations. So at the end of the evening you will be asked to sign her registration book. This place is quirky in the most beautiful way. FC

. . . . . . . . . . . . . . . . . . . . . .

**XEMEI**
Passeig de l'Exposició, 85
( 93 553 5140
Wed–Mon 1330–0000
**Venetian**/€€€/Cards and euros

Passeig de l'Exposició sweeps around the base of Montjuïc in a tree-lined arc. Holding court on one of these corners are Venetian twins Stefano and Marc Colombo. Identical twins. From inside this snuggly gloomy room with its bare wooden tables and mismatched chairs you can watch the passing parade of dogs and their owners. Xemei turns out great quality Venetian dishes such as spaghetti with squid ink sauce, and perhaps mussels, shopping at the market for fresh produce every day. Desserts are made inhouse. If you're tired of *botifarra* (unimaginable, but anyway) and want some Italian comfort food and Italian attitude, come here. RC

. . . . . . . . . . . . . . . . . . . . . . .

Refusio 307 Poble Sec

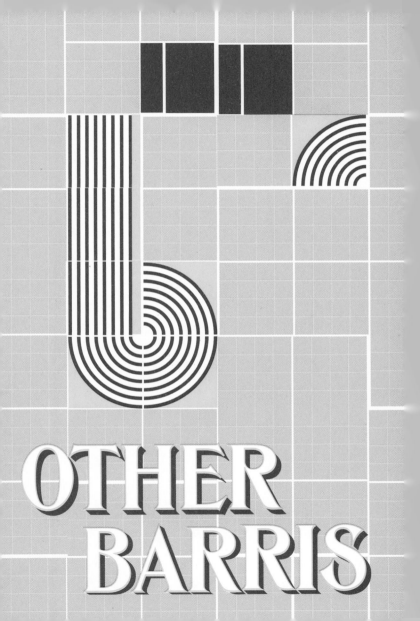

# OTHER
# BARRIS

## CAN PINEDA

Sant Joan de Malta, 55 (El Clot)
93 308 3081
www.canpineda.com
Tue–Sat 1300–1600, 2100–2300
**Produce-driven traditional
Catalan**/€€€/Cards and euros

El Clot is a bit of a cab ride from the old part of town, but if you have the time, trust me, it's worth it. It is also within walking distance of three different metro stations. Don't think that this place is totally off the tourist radar, though, because a few years ago Can Pineda featured in an American TV show about Spanish cuisine hosted by Mario Batali and Gwyneth Paltrow. However, this is no flash-in-the-pan restaurant. Opened in 1906 it is now owned by a brother and sister who run an impressively professional show, keeping their attractive waitresses on the move yet somehow giving them enough time to engage with all the customers. The plainly decorated room has an old-world feel, with a large wooden bar around which half a dozen small tables are set for diners. A more formal second room has white linen and under-plates. The printed menu has a limited number of options because the handwritten insert is what this place is about. It's sometimes hard to decipher the Spanish script in which up to 24 seasonal dishes are described. The chef uses whatever is best at the market that morning, especially the seafood. Wild sea bass, monkfish and razor clams are all on display over ice on the bar. In autumn it's fungus: morels, *trompetas de la muerte*, *ceps* and Spanish white truffle, with which they do an amazing egg dish. They could have outrageously expensive baby eels from the rivers of northern Spain. I was lucky enough to be there during snail season and enjoyed a large bowl of snails with a spiced peppery flavour, served with an amazing *allioli* and wooden picks to extract the flesh. The wine list is a lovely little selection of mostly local varieties, but there is not a lot to choose from by the glass. A long list of desserts includes a classic from Priorat—*orelletes*, a wonderful plate-sized, crisp, bubbly biscuit served with wild strawberries and *vi ranci*, a sweet wine from the same area. FC

. . . . . . . . . . . . . . . . . . . . . . . . . .

## GRANJA ELENA

Passeig de la Zona Franca, 228
(Montjuïc)
☎ 93 332 0241
Mon–Fri 1300–1600; bar open
Mon–Sat 0730–1230
**Traditional Spanish**/€€/Cards
and euros

When Cesc from *Cuina* magazine recommended this gem, I bet he thought twice about letting the cat out of the bag. Now I wish I could keep it to myself. At least it's far from the tourist crowd on a busy road that at one end intersects with Gran Via, full of eight-storey-high *pisos* or flats, and at its other is a *polígono*, Spanish for industrial estate. The nearest metro is Magòria-La Campana on the FCG. Granja Elena is the sort of place you would walk past and think 'just another generic bar' because it's never going to win any design awards, but I love this unpretentious dining room. It has a small bar to the left and about 10–12 ugly metal tables (with equally ugly chairs) set with simple white undercloths, cheap glassware and cutlery, all tightly squeezed into the room. The only clue at all that this is a great place is the occasional framed article ripped from a Spanish newspaper and hung on the white wall. The menu is a daily list of twenty-odd dishes that—wow—are what you'd find in a Michelin-starred restaurant, with the same immaculate ingredients and amazing technique. Imagine a tartare of langoustines with tomato sorbet and cucumber gazpacho, or a *foie gras* terrine with truffle, a soup of cream of artichokes with a slow-cooked egg or an incredibly generous selection of pan-fried wild mushrooms, *rossinyol*, *trompetas de la muerte*. There's suckling pig, its entire back leg boned, skin crisp, the meat aromatic, moist and tender. 24€—amazing! This is Michelin-quality cooking but with large portions, great prices and no pretentions at all. No wonder it's packed all the time and the locals love it. FC

## H. TOMÁS RESTAURANT

Padre Pérez del Pulgar,
1 (La Trinitat)
☏ 93 345 7148
www.htomas.com
Mon–Sat 1300–1600; Tue–Sat 2100–2300; closed August
**Traditional Spanish**/€€/Cards and euros

Trinitat is not a pretty place but it has a certain charm. It's an old milling village on the banks of the Besòs River that was engulfed by suburbia in the 1960s. Hermanos Tomás was recommended to us by the late Santi Santamaria (see Racó de Can Fabes, page 280), who apparently was coming the next morning for a breakfast of fried chorizo. From the outside at night it looks like the set of one those Tarantino films where the waiters turn into vampires. Relax. It's more bizarre than that. This is a meat and cigar restaurant and there is not a right angle in the joint. The wallpaper is made entirely of lottery tickets donated by the local residents since the restaurant opened in 1970. Not a lot has changed since then. This is a Spanish place—not Catalan. Don't ask for a menu, just let co-owner and host Julián Tomás look after you. Julián is a great laugh and a great communicator—he'll speak to you in such beautiful Spanish that the words will permeate your skin and you'll feel what he is saying. That said, go with the *cecina*, the beautifully deep-red cured meat

streaked with yellow fat. Make sure you get some of the *morcilla* from Burgos and the obscenely plump preserved asparagus from Rioja. There could be two halves of whole pot-roasted partridge previously cooked in *escabeche*. But it is the 25-day-old lamb and real Galician beef the regulars come for. The Hermanos part relates to Julián's dad, also called Julián, who partnered with his brother to start the business in the 1970s. They split, but the name remains, and old Julián comes in and talks to the clients just as he has done for the past four decades. It's a 15–20€ cab ride from town, but the Casa de l'Aigua metro station is only ten minutes' walk away. RC

## LLUERNA

Rafael Casanovas, 31 (Santa Coloma de Gramenet)

( 93 391 0820

www.lluernarestaurant.com

Mon–Sat 1300–1600, 2100–2300; closed 3 weeks in August

**Modern Catalan**/€€/Cards and euros

If this little restaurant was in the centre of the city rather than the outlying suburb of Santa Coloma de Gramenet, we would be talking about one of the most popular restaurants in Barcelona. But the 30-minute metro ride makes Lluerna go pretty much unnoticed. Far from regretting it though, chef Víctor Quintillà and his wife Mar

Gómez have remained faithful to their original location and have overcome this handicap by stepping outside the trendy gastronomic fashion of throwing out tradition for the sake of the new. The result is a constant conversation between the kitchen and the seasonal produce that delivers unbeatable quality and satisfaction for the price. There are dishes suitable for the gourmand, such as *botifarra del perol,* the pork sausage sourced from Els Casals (see page 279), cooked with potato, mushrooms and organic eggs. And then there is the conversely austere plate of mackerel marinated with citrons, and the simple *coca* with vegetables, cured bacon and *manchego* cheese. There could even be a succulent duck magret with pistachios. Each course seems better than the last and you find yourself in constant praise of such sensory delights. While holding fast to the past, some modern creative spells have been cast, like the solid *mojito aperitivo* or the fake *tarte tatin*. If you feel the temptation of these more imaginative options, just choose the Surprise Menu. It will certainly not disappoint you. CC

Sure it's in the burbs, but that's what makes this taverna so appealing. You would never guess that in this little tree-lined street hides one of the most appreciated cuisines of Barcelona. This average-looking tavern, housed in a two-storey building with a pale grey stone façade, could be easily overlooked were it not for the fact that it keeps alive the spirit of the antique *fondes de sisos*, the old-fashioned food houses that have been the foundations of the gastronomic tradition of the city. Can Roca's food is simple, humble and popular. In order to fully embrace it, there is nothing better than to let it seduce you with its *esmorzars de forquilla*, or the worker's breakfast—it is truly remarkable. Any true foodie will make the effort to start one day of their Barcelona visit here, sitting around a table with a succulent menu that Josep Maria recites out loud. The options are really tempting: stuffed calamari, braised pork cheek, or honey-baked cod. A few dishes are a must, such as the *peus de porc*, succulent pig's trotters with *romesco*, the *cap i pota* with *samfaina* and parmesan cheese and the meatballs with beans and squid. To be consistent, any of these options should be sluiced with a strong Priorat wine served in a *porró*. And in order to rightfully finish the feast, we cannot help but order the traditional *café*, *i copa* or a coffee and a liqueur. After that breakfast, you will have a great day—I promise. CC

. . . . . . . . . . . . . . . . . . . . . . . . .

## TAVERNA CAN ROCA
Gran de Sant Andreu, 209
( 93 346 5701
Mon–Fri 0800–1800; Sat 1300–1500
**Classic Catalan**/€€/Cards and euros

# DAY TRIPS *from* BARCELONA

Sometimes a restaurant serves such wonderful food or has some-thing so wonderfully beautiful or even quirky about it that you'll travel a long way just to try it out. A beautiful old dining room overlooking a courtyard and the sea with a three-Michelin-star meal at your table could be just a 45-minute train ride away. Heading out of the centre of town through the suburbs and outlying districts, it's quite astonish-ing to see just how concentrated and dense the population is. For kilo-metre after kilometre, massive apartment buildings pass by, and then you find yourself in the heart of an ancient village, once far from the city's boundaries. Sometimes going off the beaten track takes a little planning, but I assure you, it's worth the effort.

Girona

# GIRONA

. . . . . . . . . . . . . . . . . . . . . . . .

Girona is about an hour and a bit's drive from Barcelona. Trains leave from Barcelona Sants train station roughly every hour and take about an hour or an hour and a half, depending on the service. It makes a great day trip, but I'd recommend staying overnight. The coloured houses of Girona line the slowly flowing Onyar River, built right to the edge of the bank, their muted reds, pinks and yellows reflecting in the clear water. Behind them the white tower of the cathedral cuts into the blue of the sky. Girona is one of Catalonia's most beautiful cities, with almost 100 000 people living in and around its medieval heart. The ancient beauty of its old Jewish quarter is captured in the film *Perfume*. The mostly pedestrianised central old town provides a relatively quiet respite from the human pressure that can make Barcelona seem giddyingly busy. From the steep steps of the cathedral one can see across the countryside to the snow-covered Pyrenees and towards the French border. Local affluence is reflected in the number of Michelin-starred restaurants in the area, like the magnificent El Celler Can Roca. Evenings are when the city is at its most beautiful. Shoulder-wide alleys cut through stone archways bathed in soft yellow light, with small bars and restaurants around just about every corner. We've listed just a few restaurants to encourage visitors to use Barcelona as a base for exploring more of this incredible region.

## DIVINUM

General Fournàs, 2
( 87 208 0218
www.divinum.cat
Wed—Mon 1300–1600, 2000–2400
**Modern Catalan**/€€/Cards and euros

This place is out there, but in a good way. Any chef who creates a sauce out of *sobrassada*, cream, onion and potato and serves it with the very robustly-textured monkfish obviously loves experimenting. Initially this is a confronting dish, but given time to settle in with a reisling or a light Tempranillo, it is dare I say it, a masterpiece. This corner restaurant right in the heart of Girona's old town has quirky décor: theatre lights, a Buddha's head, arty videos played on one wall and rows of wine stored in the restaurant and the cellar off the side. Owner is Joan Murillo, an unashamed vinophile who has decent wines from 2€ a glass to more finessed wines for around 4€. Joan worked under the late Santi Santamaria for many years and shares the same market-to-table philosophy, so expect seasonal indulgences such as asparagus in spring, fungus in autumn, and nuts later on. The seconds of seasonal best, such as black trumpet mushrooms, might be blended with a béchamel and rolled into slightly sweet and rich *croquetas*. There could be some langoustines cooked on the grill with a sharp and strong *allioli*.

Girona

The Catalans are fond of their pasta, and you'll find handmade pastas such as *canelons*, stuffed with baked pumpkin with a cream and bacon sauce. What Joan specialises in, however, is Catalan cheese. He accesses some of the smallest and funkiest cheesemakers in the region, some of whom offer him experimental batches—raw milk and cave ripened—like El Cremós d'Alba from Mas Huguet in Terradelles, a sharp and funky cow's milk cheese with a fine washed rind and a smooth, broken-down interior. Like the cheese, Divinum is worth the risk. RC

. . . . . . . . . . . . . . . . . . . . . . .

## EL CELLER DE CAN ROCA

Can Sunyer, 48
☎ 97 222 2157
www.cellercanroca.com
Tue–Sat 1300–1500, 2100–2300
**Modern Catalan**/Three Michelin stars/€€€€/Cards and euros

People come from all around the globe to make the pilgrimage to El Celler de Can Roca. With elBulli gone, this is the last bastion of high-end progressive cuisine left in this northeast corner of Catalonia. Thirty chefs work side by side crafting delicious little morsels to delight the jaded palates of middle-aged global gastronomes. It's the Roca family business, with Juan and Jordi in the kitchen and brother Josep the sommelier. The restaurant sits on the outskirts of town in a beautiful 19th-century home to which a triangular dining wing has recently been added. At the heart of this is a small forest, encased in glass, seemingly growing out of a layer of *llicorella*, the famous stone that gives the wine-growing area of Priorat its flinty textures. Ask to see the cellar, the above-ground temple to Champagne, German reisling, burgundy, Priorat and sherry housed in rooms clad in old wine boxes. The wine

# — TOP FIVE —
# PLACES TO TAKE THE KIDS

**1** **BARCELONETA BEACH,** keep away from the nudists at the southern end.

**2** **MAGIC FOUNTAIN,** the spectacular light and water show where you have to hold your kids up like the locals.

**3** **GAUDÍ'S PARC GÜELL,** a great place to let kids loose.

**4** **PARC JOAN MIRÓ,** another lovely park with swings and wonderfully bizarre sculptures.

**5** **EL TIBIDABO AMUSEMENT PARK** still has some of the original rides it had when it opened in 1901, but there are no frightening ones, just a nice atmosphere; the venicular ride to get there is an adventure in itself.

Parc Güell

list is two weighty phonebook-sized editions—they have to be wheeled to the table. You have to love a place that offers magnums of Chateau d'Yquem. In the kitchen the Rocas carefully and artfully blend the food of the market with hi-tech cooking. You can order à la carte, but look, you've come all this way, so just commit to the tasting menu at around 110€. Expect a bonsai olive tree with toffee-encrusted olives hanging from its limbs to be presented at the table. More small treats from the kitchen follow, such as a jellified *tortilla* and a pigeon liver bonbon. This is serious cooking with a playful approach that mixes the well known with the novel. It could be fungus soup on a bed of Pedro Ximénez jelly with a little piece of *foie gras* and ripe fig. Joan took me through the kitchen and I was amazed at the sheer number of cooks, divided into clear sections, with a good ten working on preparation alone. Joan pointed out the pride and joy—a wood oven and grill at the back of the kitchen slowly burning oak logs. Although the Rocas have pushed the boundaries of food and are standouts in the world of modern cuisine, the thought that they still burn oak to produce their amazing food, just as countless generations of Catalans have before them, flags to me that they are traditionalists at heart. RC

# OCCI RESTAURANT

Mercaders, 3
☎ 97 222 71 54
www.restaurantocci.com
Mon–Sat 1300–1530, 2030–2300
**Modern Catalan**/€€/Cards and
euros

Occi is a young and contemporary dining space with an urban feel in the heart of the old town. Walking into the dining room you are surrounded by rustic marble columns, stacked crates of wine, and festoons of suspended corks. In the corner of the room, which is below street level, lies an open kitchen. Here you can see the young crew working with quality seasonal ingredients, carefully preparing Catalan food using high technique. I like their hot baby-prawn soufflé, served with Avruga faux caviar, balancing full flavour and lightness. Slow-cooked baby octopus with Gironese red wine, saffron and freshly shelled baby peas is a harmony of soft flesh and the crunch of green peas. It's a good-humoured affair, with one of the young owners proudly showing off his regionally inspired wine collection and punctuating this with a punchline: a bottle of Penfolds. Occi is good value and worth checking out. SM

. . . . . . . . . . . . . . . . . . . . . . . .

Tower of Sant Bartomeu i Santa Tecla

# SITGES

Sitges is a pleasant day trip south of Barcelona, well set up for tourists. It's a 45-minute train trip or about an hour's drive along the coast, depending on the traffic. I prefer the train as it takes you through the suburbs, the industrial estates and then the villages of the Mediterranean coast before the train pulls in at Sitges.

When it's hot and you need some real sand under your feet and a few waves around your thighs, Sitges beckons. It's an old fortified seaside town with a gothic church, Sant Bartomeu i Santa Tecla, built by the cliffs overlooking the Mediterranean. It's close enough to be considered a suburb of Barcelona, but relaxed enough to be a getaway from the crush of the city. Sitges is all about the beach, the seaside lifestyle, whitewashed buildings and dazzling bright-blue sea. This is also party central for lots of people and has become a gay mecca following in the footsteps of the 19th-century bohemian set who once called Sitges a second home. Scores of restaurants huddle around a tiny half-moon beach, Platja de Sant Sebastià. It's worth dropping into the old town market, now a Bacardi bar, for a Rum Capriana (Sitges was the birthplace of the founder of the Bacardi Rum label). The Cau Ferrat Museum, former home of one of the leaders of Catalan modernism, artist and writer Santiago Rusiñol, is also in the town.

## AL FRESCO

Pau Barrabeig, 4

( 93 894 0600

www.alfrescorestaurante.es

Daily 2000–2330 (May–Oct); Thur–Sat 1300–1600, 2000–2300 (Nov–April)

**International**/€€/Cards and euros

Although you may eat better elsewhere, Al Fresco embodies the vibe of Sitges, capturing all the features of a Mediterranean seaside village. Recommended to me by the boss of a nearby *cava bodega*, the restaurant was once a large house and still has the heavy timber doors, terracotta floor tiles, walls covered in centuries of whitewash and large open courtyard garden. It marries theatre and kitsch. The clientele are mostly northern Europeans, and English is the lingua franca. Tables are covered with white linen and the room is lit with candles. The menu has been put together by a local guy, owner Xavi, and a French chef who has spent time cooking in England. They offer an eclectic global mix of mezze plates, perhaps parpadelle with veal ragout, Indian chicken curry or swordfish with caponata. Fresh, delicious and priced at 22€ for one plate and 35€ for two. Don't confuse this place with its sister establishment, Cafe Al Fresco, at the top of the lane. FC

## LA SALSETA

Sant Pau, 35

( 93 811 0419

www.lasalseta.com

Tue–Sun 1330–1530;
Wed–Sat 2000–2330

**Catalan and Mediterranean/**
€€/Cards and euros

La Salseta is a restaurant located in a narrow lane in the centre of Sitges, close to the seaside strip el Passeig de la Ribera, but far from the usual tourist-oriented offerings in town. The street is filled with low, quaint *pisos*, some of them elegant *modernisme* buildings. Don't be fooled by this establishment's appearance, which is not luxurious at all. What was once a barber's shop is now one of the strongholds of *Garraf* cuisine, a type of cooking typical of the nearby coast. Owner Valentí Mongay is one of the Catalan supporters of the Slow Food movement and has helped to position La Salseta as a bastion of food ethics and sustainable cuisine. Here you can taste typical but revamped Catalan and Mediterranean dishes. The distinguishing feature, though, is their Km 0 label: an initiative that promotes local, ecological and free-range products where possible. The menu is a compendium of the most precious vegetable garden, poultry and sea products, all 100 per cent seasonal and with plenty of options for vegetarians. There's the traditional *xató*, Penedès boneless rooster with prunes, and cod with confit cloves of garlic and tomato, sheer pleasure to the palate. These are pure flavours that arrive crisp, clear and fresh. For the gourmet visitor a couple of options are a must: the Catalan artisan cheese platter (diverse and delicious!) and the Sitges Malvasia, a unique indigenous wine that is perfect to accompany the desserts. CC

. . . . . . . . . . . . . . . . . . . . . . . . . . .

## TAMBUCHO 2

Port Alegre, 49

( 93 894 79 12

Daily 1300–1630, 2000–2330

**Seafood/€€/Cash and euros**

The dazzling blue of the Mediterranean is mesmerising. To sit by the beach as the waves crash is a pleasure in itself. Then there's a bottle of oak-aged white Macabeu on ice. We're here in this small restaurant, one among scores along the shore, for the flesh fest on the beach and the fish fest from the kitchen. It's about prawns from the grill, baby calamari and langoustines, but the main event is paella. Not the paella you cook up in the hills with friends but the best type of paella you can get in a tourist mecca. The *sofregit* is sauted well, the starchy rice perfectly cooked, and the prawns and mussels are juicy. But this place is about the view, not the food. If you can't book *una mesa para dos en la terraza* (a table for two on the terrace), try another place with a view. Also in Sitges is Tambucho 1, Passeig de la Ribera, 56. RC

. . . . . . . . . . . . . . . . . . . . . . . . . . .

# PRIORAT

You'll probably need to hire a car to get to Priorat, or El Priorato as they call it in the rest of Spain. It's about one and a half hours' drive to the west of Barcelona, in a series of valleys surrounded by the Montsant (Holy Mountain) ranges about thirty kilometres from the Mediterranean at Tarragona as the crow flies. From here the clouds roll in over the hills from the sea, occasionally drenching the stony ground, which is covered in little fingernail-like stones and flat broken tiles that make up the local soil known as *llicorella*.

Vines here—old-growth Garnacha, Cariñena and Cabernet Sauvignon—cling to the steep hills and seem to suck the very essence of stone from the soil, reflecting it back in wines so texturally rich they have become some of the most sought-after Spanish drops in the world. It's one of the reasons to make the pilgrimage—that and the sheer beauty of isolated villages like Falset and El Masroig rising from hilltops, colourful, sun-drenched versions of places like San Giminiano in Tuscany. This region would be overrun with tourists by now if it weren't for the narrow winding roads: tourist buses are limited to travelling on the coastal *autopista*, making this a relatively remote destination.

Priorat's history dates to the 12th century, when Carthusian monks constructed a monastery at Escaladei and, building on

the wine heritage of the Romans, started making communion wine for the church. By the late 19th century, Priorat was exporting commercial wine across Europe. Then phylloxera struck. The first vines were affected in 1893, and within about five years the industry was wiped out. The steep vineyards were replanted with nut trees and the area descended into poverty and depopulation.

During this period, while the rest of the Western world was moving away from traditional farming, preserving and cooking, the people of Priorat made do and created a hearty cuisine based on beans, greens, salt cod, eggs, chicken and pastry, where nothing is wasted and any natural bounty is embraced as it ripens. It is food that is ingeniously frugal while being warmly generous.

Since the recovery of the wine industry, Priorat's renaissance has been led by top-end wines such as L'Ermita and Clos Mogador, but the local cooperatives have been the real backbone of the industry, making wines for the masses throughout the 20th century.

In the town of Falset rises what appears to be a modernist cathedral. The Falset-Marçà Agrícola, made of brick and concrete, was designed by Cèsar Martinell, a friend and student of Antoni Gaudí. So it is a blend of the wine, the food, the architecture, the sheer beauty of the countryside and the relative remoteness of the region that draws me here time and time again.

## EL CELLER DE L'ASPIC

Miquel Barceló, 31, (Falset)

( 97 783 1246

www.cellerdelaspic.com

Thur–Tue 1300-1500;
Mon–Sat 2000–2300

**Catalan**/€€/Cards and euros

Chef Toni Bru is a champion of Catalan food and, like his neighbour Matías Fernández, proudly labels local food on his menu with a Km 0 or zero-kilometre mark, a reflection of the produce's food miles. Toni showed me how to cook a spinach and white bean *tortilla* a few years ago. 'This is real poverty food,' he told me as he fried off some garlic in oil, then added some flour to start a basic sauce. 'In Catalonia, anything with a sauce instantly becomes a main meal, as you need bread to soak up the sauce. *Truita amb suc* is a traditional way of extending some eggs, beans and greens from a snack to a main meal.' His food is basically old-fashioned Catalan food served in a modern fashion, which is very friendly to the great local wines on his wine list. FC

. . . . . . . . . . . . . . . . . . . . . . . . . . .

## QUINOA

Miquel Barceló, 29 (Falset)

( 97 783 0431

www.restaurantquinoa.com

Wed–Mon 1300–1500;
Wed–Sat 2000–2300

**Modern Catalan**/€/Cards and euros

This great little restaurant right in the heart of Falset is called Quinoa because the chef, Matías Fernández, took over a health-food store run by his mother, quinoa being the South American grain favoured by health-food types. The food here is light and modern and run to some pretty strict Slow Food philosophies about sustainability. The prices are aimed at locals as well as out-of-towners, so lunch can cost as little as 12€. Fernández does fun dishes like chicken and *jamón* with caramelised almonds and hazelnuts, and desserts that reflect the produce of the region, so expect lots of apples and nuts. RC

. . . . . . . . . . . . . . . . . . . . . . . . . . .

## EL RACÓ DEL PRIORAT

Priorat, 9 (La Vilella Baixa)

( 97 783 9065

Wed–Mon 1300–1500, 2000–2300

**Classic Catalan**/€€/Cash

Maria Victòria Masip cooks over a wood fire and turns out good old-fashioned Catalan food. She starts with a plate of *canelones*, thick cannelloni stuffed with chicken, veal, pork loin, pork liver, onion and garlic, flavoured with olive oil and bay leaves and served with a light béchamel, a reflection of both the Italian and French influences on Catalan cuisine. Next, she sends out a local dish of sardines slow-cooked with red beans and onions; some ham and melon; a plate of assorted charcuterie; juicy salt cod with *romesco*, made with roasted red peppers and toasted hazelnuts; a gratin of preserved asparagus; pig's trotters and beans; grilled lamb loin. The 'simple' comes at the end: a dessert in the form of a handful of mixed nuts soused with a splash of *vins dolços*. 'This is *postres de músic*,' Maria Victòria explains, 'or the musician's dessert. You see, musicians are always so poor this is all they can afford.' Then she sits down next to me and sips a cup of black coffee, talking of all the other rich dishes of the Priorat and ensuring we eat every last almond. RC

. . . . . . . . . . . . . . . . . . . . . . .

## CATACURIAN

El Masroig
℡ Spanish 97 782 5341
℡ English 93 802 2660
www.catacurian.net
**Cooking school/tours/boutique hotel**/Tours from around 130€ per person per day

Catacurian is a fourth-generation family home, built from stone by Alicia Juanpere's great-grandfather in the little town of El Masroig. From here she and her husband run tours, take cooking classes and look after their live-in guests. You can buy a one-day tour and see food being grown and wine being made in the valleys of the Priorat, then come back to the house and learn how to cook an authentic Catalan meal for your lunch … or you can live in for six days and really get to know the area. RC

. . . . . . . . . . . . . . . . . . . . . . .

## RACHEL RITCHIE

℡ 97 783 0784
www.rachelritchie.com
**Guide**/Around 200€ per day

Rachel Ritchie is the person I use for information about the Priorat region and I wholeheartedly recommend her as a guide. She's Lancashire born but is married to a local man and raising a family here. She understands the nuances of small communities and has a great network of food and wine professionals as friends, so a tour with her is a day spent dropping in on lovely people who share their oil, olives, wine, smallgoods and little morsels of gossip with you. Rachel has an encyclopaedic knowledge of local history and a great sense of humour. RC

# OTHER AREAS

## CAL XIM

Plaça de Subirats, 5 (Sant Pau d'Ordal, Penedès)

℡ 93 899 3092

www.calxim.com

Daily 1330–1600; Fri 2030–2330

**Classic Catalan**/€€/Cards and euros

The reason to go to Sant Pau d'Ordal is Cal Xim. Situated in the main square of this village halfway between Barcelona and the seaside town of Sitges, this classic restaurant has been in the same family since 1934. The food here is simple and rustic Catalan fare, based around the stunning charcoal grill that is open to the back dining room. It is really, really good, which is why I will rave on about it. There is a strong seasonal focus, and at certain times of the year this is the place to come to try snails, mushrooms, game and, in February, *calçots*. These are long, thin baby onions, cooked on charcoal, wrapped in paper and served with a special *calçot* sauce. Santi, the charming owner, gives instructions to the uninitiated. Everything I tried here was good. No, wonderful! The best dish I tried was an amazing *escalivada* that made the many *escalivades* I have eaten in my time pale into insignificance. Here they do the dish the traditional way, cooked over wood coals to create wonderful smoky eggplant, sweet collapsed tomatoes, soft and silky deep-red peppers and sweet baby onions, combined into a fantastic vegetable salad of charcoaly, smoky goodness finished with fine arbequina oil and a hit of salt. And the hamburgers! Forget buns and cheese—that's for the Americans—here they are petite patties of gelatinous boneless pig's trotter meat, and white *botifarra* braised in a rich gravy. And while the food is great, the wine list is seriously impressive. The owners have an award-winning collection of wines, mostly Catalan, but plenty from France and the New World. Being in the DO of Penedès, expect a great range of *cava* and Penedès whites, as well as less common local grape varieties. As of mid-2010 another Cal Xim opened in Barcelona at Girona, 145, just off Avinguda Diagonal, phone 93 459 2030. FC

## ELS CASALS

Sagàs

℡ 93 825 1200

www.hotelelscasals.com

Daily 1300–1600, 2100–2300

Winter hours Wed–Sun 1300–1600; Fri–Sat 2100–2300

**Seasonal Catalan**/One Michelin star/€€€/Cards and euros

They don't give the address to Els Casals, they simply give directions. It's a centuries-old stone farmhouse in the hills of the Berguedà region in the foothills of the Pyrenees about an hour north of Barcelona by car. It is beautiful country, all narrow winding roads cutting through stunted pine and oak forests and crossing over little streams. But come for dinner and stay the night in the hotel in another old farmhouse on the 300-hectare Rovira family property. The family have been living here for 700 years. Oldest brother Jordi is the farmer and his younger brother Oriol is the chef. Other family members work on the farm, and neighbours deliver honey and fungus, including some lovely local truffles. Everything served on the plate comes from the farm. The meal might start with a little pork rind and *jamón* from Jordi's Iberico pigs, which graze in pens in the forest. He runs a separate charcuterie and makes some stunning *chorizo* and *sobrassada*. Oriol will use the best seafood, but in this one Michelin starred restaurant, one is struck by the predominance of veges in Catalan food, especially fresh beans and greens. At Els Casals there's also eggs, pork, a little beef from the herd of local *Bruna dels Pirineus* cattle—they look like a horny version of French Limousin. You can see the herd from the dining-room window, the snowcaps of the Pyrenees beyond them. It is a wonderful experience dining here. The staff are good, and Oriol is as charming a master of the food of his family farm as he is

of the modern Catalan dining scene. RC

## RACÓ DE CAN FABES

Sant Joan, 6 (Sant Celoni)

[ 93 867 2851

www.canfabes.com

Wed–Sun 1330–1515;
Wed–Sat 2030–2230

**Modern Catalan**/Three Michelin stars/€€€€/Cards and euros

When we were in Spain several years ago researching our *MoVida Rustica* book, all hell broke loose when chef Santi Santamaria publicly criticised Ferran Adrià, then the world's most famous chef and father of molecular gastronomy, for using too many chemicals in his food. The 'polemic', as it was known, was on everyone's lips and was a topic of discussion in bars and taxis throughout Spain. He died suddenly of a heart attack early 2011. His chef Xavier Pellicer took over and the team are determined to keep the 'fires alight'. Expect good things. The à la carte menu offers the best of the season—mushrooms, spider crab, game, piglet—for around 70–80€ for two courses plus dessert, aperitifs, water, bread, coffee and *petits fours*. The set menu is about 230€ but this offers about twenty different courses served at a reasonable, but not pressured, pace. You might start with the merest shavings of French pork fat on parmesan grissini. There could be ellipse of raw tuna belly wrapped in y leek with green and black olives. tamaria's understanding of texture umami is exemplified in a tiny amic bowl lined with a custard of urchin, whole fresh raw cockles, a tle chive foam and the juice of the kles. He may follow this with a all piece of toast with a disk of just-warm beef marrow—sheer poetry. wls of translucent pork fat may iceal fat prawns and boletus caps iched with scant coconut sorbet freshened with bitter greens and rop of lime juice. It all works. Yes, dishes get heavier and there are ie reduced stocks that darken the al, but this is only a reminder that y were conceived to have different ies as their companions, which t extra. This level of dining is a nmitment to taste and sensuality highly recommended to any visitor Barcelona. Diners who show an rest in technique may be invited the stunningly beautiful kitchen, a ce that flows on from the old stone-led dining room on one side and the a-modern room on the other.

Racó is Catalan for 'corner' and s is a modern box-like room that been added to an old stone corner ding in a pretty little town called it Celoni about an hour north Barcelona. Take the train from celona Sants to Sant Celoni on the ona line. It's 60 kilometres but takes

about an hour. The lunchtime train gets in 20 minutes before the kitchen opens, giving time to explore Sant Celoni's city square with its *modernisme* town hall, Baroque church and array of little food stores. There is accommodation at Racó de Can Fabes from 257€ per double. Because of the sad passing of Santi, things may change here. RC

. . . . . . . . . . . . . . . . . . . . . . . . . .

## SANT PAU
Nou, 10 (Sant Pol de Mar)
( 93 760 0662
www.ruscalleda.com
Tues–Wed and Fri–Sat 1330–1530;
Tues–Sat 2100–2300; closed first
3 weeks in May and November.
**Catalan**/Three Michelin stars/€€€€
Cards and euros

Take the train from Barcelona to this restaurant, about 50 kilometres north to the seaside town of Sant Pol de Mar, and you will see the Catalan countryside that dictates chef Carme Ruscalleda's life and cuisine. She was brought up in this county between the shores of the Mediterranean and the stunning hills of the Serralada Litora. The restaurant is in an old seafront townhouse with a garden courtyard which looks out through a stand of plane trees and out to the sea. Chef Ruscadella's cuisine is precise and subtle, with strokes of artistic reference such as the 'Gastronomic Mondrian', a simple codfish brandade with capsicum and olive tapenade plated up to be an exact reproduction of one of the paintings of the Dutch abstract artist. The *lloritos amb pa amb tomàquet*, a traditional seaman's meal, has been converted in a spectacular dish—a delicate piece of small fish with bread and tomato. Simple but beautiful. She might make ravioli with fine strips of zucchini, carrot and *jamón* instead of pasta, perhaps a dish of prawns with artichoke, or even some game such as loin of deer with pear and apple. This is how she mixes the vegetable garden with produce from the hills or fish from the sea. Her patisserie, dessert and cheese selection is stunning. In all she builds a set of flavours that are at once clean and as natural as possible while still treating the food on the plate as pieces of sculpture or paintings.

Sant Pol is connected to the Renfe Rodalies train network, with trains arriving directly from Barcelona Sants station and Maçanet in Girona. Sant Pau is a block's walk from the station. CC

Juan and Jordi Roca of El Celler de can Roca

# HOTELS

During the 18th century, European travellers reported back on the sheer awfulness of Spanish inns. It took a century or so for things to change, and while you may still find a few nicotine-stained lobbies with moth-eaten rooms elsewhere, Barcelona has created the most exciting hotel scene in the country, from family-run hostels to eclectic boutique hostelries and five-star palaces. We hope the selection you find in this chapter reflects this diversity.

Although you'll be spoilt for choice, the problem may be getting what you want. There is often more demand than supply in the fourth-most visited city in Europe, particularly during big business events or even a Barcelona–Madrid football match. To a certain degree, the self-catering accommodation boom in Barcelona has eased the pain. To book a short-term apartment, the internet is your first port of call, but do ask a lot of questions on location and hidden costs. Reputable agencies with a great selection of flats in Barcelona include www.holiday-velvet.com and www. suitelife.es.

Hotels in Barcelona have widely adopted a sort of 'budget airline' approach to their rates, meaning that prices will vary wildly depending on when you want to go and whether it includes a weekend, public holiday or the like, so check out their websites before booking. Unless breakfast is included in the rate, I would generally advise you to forgo a hotel breakfast and instead enjoy a cheaper, more local experience in one of the multitude of bars that are never more than a few steps from your front door.

**Suzanne Wales**

Price key (for double rooms)

| | |
|---|---|
| € | Under 100 euros |
| €€ | 100–150 euros |
| €€€ | 150–200 euros |
| €€€€ | Over 200 euros |

## ABOVE DIAGONAL

. . . . . . . . . . . . . . . . . . . . .

### ABaC

Avinguda Tibidabo,1
℡ 93 319 6600
www.abacbarcelona.com
€€€€

The existence of fifteen luxe hotel rooms adjacent to the ABaC restaurant (see page 31) is almost as mysterious as the lower-case 'a' in the establishment's name. Are they there to accommodate dinner guests who have overindulged on the wine pairing? A loud 'no', asserts the management. The ABaC hotel has been conceived for those wanting a very private, almost clubish experience. Located in a lovely garden setting in a 19th-century mansion, the spacious rooms at ABaC possess all the trimmings you'd expect for the price. Perhaps most interesting though is the chance to witness first hand the workings of a Michelin-starred restaurant (you actually enter the rooms via the kitchen) and really pig out on exceptionally good breakfasts.

. . . . . . . . . . . . . . . . . . . . .

### ELS JARDINETS GUEST HOUSE

Gran de Gràcia, 27
℡ 69 039 3593
www.guesthousejardinets.com
€

Carla Mora and her partner Maarten preferred staying in B&Bs during their

286

years of travel, so when they returned to Barcelona they decided to open one themselves. Els Jardinets Guest House is one of the very few places to stay in Gràcia, and the neighbourhood's boho chic vibe is reflected here, with hardwood floors, bright cushions and throws, cheerful prints on white walls and the strong smell of incense in the air. Guests can choose to take breakfast at whatever hour they like (convenient if you have been hitting the great little bars in Gràcia the night before) and it goes beyond the usual 'continental' fare, with herbal teas and real espresso coffee. With only five rooms (all with shared bathrooms) El Jardinets is often full. If so, ask about Carla and Maarten's other B&B in nearby Eixample.

## BARCELONETA

### W BARCELONA HOTEL
Plaça de la Rosa del Vents, 1
☏ 93 295 2800
www.w-barcelona.com
€€€

The global group of W hotels promises a no-holds-barred party atmosphere, and while this landmark sail-shaped building perched on the Mediterranean's edge has raised a few eyebrows among the city's traditionalists, international party animals are lapping it up. More a resort than a hotel (meaning that for many there is little reason to leave), a sleek, white-shaded wet deck overlooks the sea, the penthouse Eclipse bar hosts some of the most

Villa Emilia

talked-about nights in town and Carles Abellán's great steak house Bravo 24 (see page 72) is situated on the first floor. Rooms are spacious and modern in a retro sci-fi sort of way, with decoration kept to a minimum so as not to distract (we are told) from the wonderful sea views they afford.

## WILLOWMOON

Marina Port Vell, Escar, 26
www.willowmoon.uk.com
( 69 979 4983
€€

Barcelona has a sizeable community of boat dwellers in its central marina, and you can be part of this niche on an art deco sailing boat. You'll be greeted at the gate by British couple Lisa and Vick, who then lead you onboard for your welcoming drink on the *Willowmoon*'s wonderful deck, adorned with plants, old ship lanterns, bunting and a jumble of other nautical contraptions from the golden age of sailing (that is before it all went digital). There are two wood-lined cabins underneath the wheelhouse; one has a double bed and the other is suitable for a (small) child. Although Lisa and Vick also live onboard, they hand the deck over to guests (breakfast is also served here), and certainly there is nothing finer than pulling up a couple of chairs on the bow for an evening G&T.

# BARRI GÒTIC

## BONIC GUESTHOUSE

Josep Anselm Clavé, 9, 1°, 4ª
( 62 605 3424
www.bonic-barcelona.com
€

Bonic means 'pretty' in Catalan and this little B&B just off La Rambla is as bright as a button. Once buzzed into the courtyard entrance, Portuguese owner Fernando comes bounding down the stairs and then shows you to one of four rooms in this huge 19th-century apartment. Fernando has done a super job of tarting it up with sunny yellow walls, potted palms, Moroccan objects and an overall ambiance more fitting to the south of Spain than the north. The rooms are not overly big, but are comfortable enough, while the shared bathrooms are spacious and immaculately kept. Fruit, croissants, ham, cheese and other goodies are served for breakfast in a sunny gallery.

## DENIT

Estruc, 24–26
( 93 545 4000
www.denit.com
€€

Situated a minute's walk from Barcelona's principal shopping and transport hubs, the Denit couldn't be more convenient. And despite being

W Hotel

located on a quiet and narrow street, the all-white, very metropolitan interior creates an ambience of light and space. The lobby is terrific, with a large table for free wi-fi use and meetings. Rooms are compact and contained, with walk-in showers, wardrobes tucked behind translucent screens, natural wood and textiles and not a thing out of place. (If available, book room 501, which has its own private terrace.) The only real drawback is the windowless, basement breakfast room.

## EIXAMPLE

. . . . . . . . . . . . . . . . . . . .

### ANA'S GUEST HOUSE

Avinguda Diagonal, 345 Principal, 1ª

℡ 93 476 1141

www.anasguesthouse.com

€

Stepping into Ana's Guest House on a chilly day my heart was immediately warmed, not only by the homespun atmosphere of the place but also by the greeting bestowed by hosts Ana

Casa Camper

d her daughter Natalia. This B&B
ns with comfort, from the polished
oden floors and waffle throws on
 beds to the cosy breakfast room
t glows with light filtered in from
 original leadlight windows. Located
 the first floor of a 19th-century
idential building, guests can either
e breakfast or just chill out back
 the narrow terrace that overlooks
untypically verdant (for Barcelona)
an garden. The only drawback here
he noise from the busy Avinguda
gonal, so best to forgo a balcony and
uest an interior room instead.

## OSTAL GIRONA

ona, 24, 1º, 1ª
3 265 0259
w.hostalgirona.com

ny horror movies have been shot
this building,' says Isabel, one of
 second-generation owners of
stal Girona. It's easy to see why;
s art nouveau building is gothic
nspiration, with an ornate carved
ircase, columns and plenty of
ly wrought-iron features casting
oky shadows. (Even the building's
ncierge looks otherworldly.)
wever, the interior of the hostel is
t like stepping into an antiques fair,
h etched mirrors, brass lamps and

carved mahogany furniture spit-and-
polished to perfection. The rooms are
more ad hoc, and most have wooden
bedheads, damask throws and marble
surfaces here and there. Hostal Girona
has a faithful following that it has built
up over 25 years of service, so book
well ahead.

. . . . . . . . . . . . . . . . . . . . . . . .

## HOTEL OMM

Rosselló, 265
( 93 445 4000
www.hotelomm.es
€€€€

If Spanish *Vogue* were a hotel, it would
be the Omm. Home of the gastro-chic
Moo restaurant (see page 184), the
best spa in town, the most fashionable
lobby-bar scene, the slickest rooms,
the best-looking staff and stratospheric
cotton counts, the Omm comes
up trumps on all the cool meters.
The décor mixes Zen minimalism
with handmade carpets, textiles and
masterful lighting that somehow makes
you look good from every angle. The
rooftop terrace has views of a handful
of the Eixample's signature buildings
(including La Sagrada Família) and a
fab little plunge pool. Despite its hip
assets, the Hotel Omm has an air of
informality, which is one of the reasons
it has remained so perennially popular.

. . . . . . . . . . . . . . . . . . . . . . . .

## HOTEL PULITZER

Bergara, 8

( 93 481 6767

www.hotelpulitzer.es

€€

This buzzy and friendly boutique hotel is situated withing spitting distance of La Rambla, and pretty much in the centre of everything. The rooms are not overly large (enquire if rooms 306 or 506 are available, both have balconies), but make up for it by being super-swish, with sunken bathtubs, slate floors, striking pieces of modern art and furniture that generally makes you feel as if you are living inside a spread from a design magazine. The Pulitzer was one of the first hotels in Barcelona to make its roof terrace available to the public, so during the warm weather the outdoor sofas and armchairs fill up with the per behinds of the city's cool set, sippin; cocktails and admiring the jumbled skyline of downtown Barcelona.

. . . . . . . . . . . . . . . . . . . .

## MANDARIN ORIENTAL

Passeig de Gràcia, 38–40

( 93 151 8888

www.mandarinoriental.com/ barcelona/

€€€€

There is a sense of occasion whe you arrive at Barcelona's Mandarir Oriental. You ascend from the posl Passeig de Gràcia via a catwalk-lik ramp and enter into a sumptuous *mis en scène* created by top Spanish designe Patricia Urquiola. Converted from former bank, the Mandarin Oriental'

east-meets-west culture has been interpreted beautifully by Urquiola, using Asian antiques, rich, hand-woven carpets, contemporary art and an abundance of eye-catching little design details at every turn. Even if your budget doesn't stretch to the Zen-inspired sophistication of the rooms, treat yourself to a coffee in the breathtaking Blanc, the lobby-lounge featuring a hanging garden.

. . . . . . . . . . . . . . . . . . . . . . . . .

## PRAKTIK RAMBLA

Rambla de Catalunya, 27
( 93 343 6690
www.hotelpraktikrambla.com
€€

The Praktik Rambla is one of the new wave of cheap-and-chic design hotels in Barcelona, located in a grandiose mansion on the upmarket Rambla de Catalunya. Designer Lázaro Rosa-Violán does miracles with abstract prints and large lamps (he also fitted out the Market Hotel, see page 297). Many original details have been preserved, such as baroque carvings, moulded ceilings, arabesque mosaic flooring and, best of all, a fountain on the hotel's wonderful rear terrace that wouldn't look out of place on the set of a Wagnerian opera. The rooms emanate a sort of New York elegance, with shiny black surfaces, big tiled bathrooms and super-high ceilings. It's definitely worth paying extra for a suite here, as the standard rooms can be somewhat pokey and dark.

. . . . . . . . . . . . . . . . . . . . . . . . .

## THE5ROOMS

Pau Claris, 72, 1°

( 93 342 7880

www.the5rooms.com

€€

When Yessica Fritz bought a neo-classical, 400-square-metre apartment in the Eixample, her intention was to renovate it for her own dwelling and pottery workshop. Plans changed and four years later her boutique B&B has become so successful she has expanded it into the apartment upstairs. This vibrant woman has impeccable taste, and has put her heart and soul into the5rooms (now actually 12), decking it out with beautiful furniture (some design pieces, others reclaimed and made over), striking modern art, hardwood floors and an overriding feeling of seamless comfort. She has even gone as far as soundproofing all the rooms, and if the dozens of Polaroids of beaming guests at reception is anything to go by, a good night's rest here is assured.

. . . . . . . . . . . . . . . . . . . . . . . .

## VILLA EMILIA

Calàbria, 115

( 93 252 5285

www.hotelvillaemilia.com

€€

Villa Emilia could well be lost in the wash of 'design hotels' in Barcelona were it not for the obvious dedication of its lovely staff. This hotel is privately owned and situated in a very un-touristy part of the Eixample, and going by my first visit, there is no request too bothersome for the charming director Pere. The public areas drip with a mix of Venetian-style antiques and contemporary art and curios, including a pair of intriguing straw dressmaking dummies. Rooms are more restrained—very comfortable but not as eclectic—but do have floor-to-ceiling glass windows should you wish to be entertained by the street life below from the comfort of your bed (rooms with numbers ending in 4 or 5 have the best corner vistas). The icing on the cake here is a compact little roof terrace filled with big plants and plush sun beds.

# EL RAVAL

. . . . . . . . . . . . . . . . . . . . . . . .

## CASA CAMPER

Elisabets, 11

( 93 342 6280

www.casacamper.com

€€€€

Hailing from Mallorca, the Camper shoe brand has been extended to the hotel business. There are two to date: one in Berlin and the other in Barcelona's inner-city Raval. The company's eco-friendly culture is evident throughout the quirky, urban décor of the hotel, with an indoor garden, signs reminding you to conserve water and take the stairs, and rental bikes dangling from the ceiling. You'll find this tree-hugger attitude either irritating or inspiring, though many Euro-hopping new-media types love the private lounge adjacent to every room (great for brainstorming with colleagues) and the 24-hour, free buffet of soups, salads and healthy snacks in the lobby.

## HOTEL BARCELÓ RAVAL

Rambla del Raval, 17–21
( 93 320 1494
www.barcelo-raval.com
€€

La Rambla del Raval is a microcosm of Barcelona's inner-city street culture. You'll find it all here: hipsters piling out of cool bars, kids kicking footballs, pickpockets and entire Moroccan families taking in the evening breeze. The (very large) blip in this urban landscape is the Hotel Barceló Raval, a striking elliptical-shaped building that towers over its neighbours. The lime and fuchsia lobby of the hotel is whimsical and slightly mad (a giant black horse—not real—greets you at the entrance), but the rooms are spacious and comfortable (in a *Lost in Space* sort of way) and will appease gadgetry freaks. At the very top, a telescope-equipped terrace offers 360-degree views and hosts a lively bar scene come sundown.

## HOTEL ESPANYA

Sant Pau, 9–11
( 93 550 0000
www.hotelespanya.com
€€€

The grand old Hotel Espanya languished in a Cinderella state for decades, its magnificent *modernisme* (or art nouveau) dining room and bar dusty shadows of their former selves. In late 2010 it reopened with a makeover that sensitively combines the building's breathtaking period details with tasteful and smoothly comfortable rooms. It's the more interesting common areas, however, that will transport you to the *fin de siècle*. Breakfast is served in 'the fishtank', so-called because the room is wrapped in a whimsical mural of watery nymphs (the work of Ramon Casas, one of the *modernisme* movement's foremost artists) and the ornate dining room has opened its doors as Fonda Espanya, a gourmet restaurant with topnotch Basque chef Martín Berasategui overseeing the rebirth.

## WHOTELLS

Joaquín Costa, 28
( 61 658 1780
www.whotells.com
€

Fans of the Japanese homewares chain Muji will be tickled to know that you can live surrounded by their products

Villa Emilia

at these short-term apartments in Barcelona (the founder also owns the Spanish franchise for Muji, so presumably got the stuff at a good price). As expected the apartments are all blond-wood furniture, bone-white china and slate-grey floors and textiles, with the odd black-and-white photograph or lime-green wall brightening up the minimalist scenario. Practical they are, and spacious too—and with some apartments featuring two bathrooms they are perfect for families or large groups. There are three locations: the Eixample, the old maritime hood of Barceloneta and the inner-city Raval, the latter providing front desk should you need any information about the city.

## POBLE-SEC

. . . . . . . . . . . . . . . . . . . .

## MARKET HOTEL

Passatge de Sant Antoni Abad, 10
93 325 1205
www.markethotel.com.es
€

The lovely little Market Hotel was one of the first boutique hotels in Barcelona to position itself in the budget category, and it has remained one of the best and most popular, so book well ahead). It takes its name from the Sant Antoni market next door, which at the time of writing was going through a long and

very noisy renovation process. (To be on the safe side, ask for an interior room or, better still, room 904, the Junior Suite with the largest terrace.) The décor is a mix of hardwood floors and Asian-inspired furniture, with bright abstract art and oversized lampshades lending a smooth, contemporary feel. A buffet breakfast is served in the ground-floor Market Restaurant, and Rosso, the hotel's pint-sized bar, provides a cosy setting for a nightcap.

## OTHER AREAS IN BARCELONA

. . . . . . . . . . . . . . . . . . . .

## INOUT HOSTEL

Major del Rectoret, 2
℡ 93 280 0985
www.inouthostel.com
€

If the idea of staying in a beautiful rural setting and giving something back to the community appeals, then consider this great hostel, located only a 15-minute train ride from central Barcelona. InOut, which operates as an NGO, is staffed almost entirely by people with physical or intellectual challenges, providing jobs for those who are largely shut out of the workforce. Dorms and rooms (all with bunks for ten, six and four people) are bright and clean, and an eclectic collection of flea-market curios

brightens up the common areas and sunny restaurant. Although it mainly caters to groups, families would have a fine time here, hanging out in the large pool or walking through the beautiful Collserola nature park, whose entrance is adjacent to the hostel.

## HOTELS OUTSIDE BARCELONA

. . . . . . . . . . . . . . . . . . . . . . . . . .

### HOTEL HISTÒRIC
Bellmirall, 4a (Girona)
( 97 222 3583
www.hotelhistoric.com
€€

Tucked away in the bowels of Girona's dark and moody old city, the family-run Hotel Històric lives up to its name by featuring fragments of original 9th-century stone walls in some of the rooms. Luckily the amenities have been upgraded since then and you'll find modern and functional furniture, gleaming marble bathrooms and heartwarming details such as wooden-beamed ceilings and really effective central heating. In addition to the eight rooms there are seven attractive self-catering apartments.

. . . . . . . . . . . . . . . . . . . . . . . . . .

## HOTEL LA NIÑA

Passeig de La Ribera, 65–68
(Sitges)

( 93 811 3540

www.laninahotel.com

€€

Boutique it isn't, but for my money La Niña offers the best location in Sitges, right on the Passeig Marítim. It's definitely worth paying a bit extra for a sea-facing room, with its own small private terrace and table and chairs (you can even have your breakfast brought up here at no extra charge). La Niña's décor hasn't changed much since the 1970s, and if chenille bedspreads and teak furniture bring back cringe-worthy memories of family holidays in motor inns, then stay away. If full, enquire about La Niña's sister hotels, called (you guessed it) La Pinta and La Santa María.

## HOTEL RURAL ELS CASALS

Sagàs (Berguedà)

( 93 825 1200

www.hotelelscasals.com

€

For an earthy taste of life on the farm, bed down for the night in the guesthouse attached to the restaurant Els Casals (see page 279). This ancient *masia* (farmhouse) has been divided into ten rooms (two with their own private lounge rooms) and fitted out with a mishmash of rural-chic antiques and modern comforts. Kids will love the *bestiari*, with pigs, chickens and calves (just don't let them get too attached, as much of the livestock ends up on the dinner table). Various options are available here, from bed and breakfast to full board.

## MAS ARDÈVOL

Carretera de Falset a Porrera Km 5, 3 (Falset)

( 630 32 4578

www.masardevol.net

€€

Gemma Peyri is one of the hospitality pioneers of the still underdeveloped (in touristic terms) Priorat region, and her *casa rural* is as personal and welcoming as her restaurant. Beautifully situated between the villages of Falset and Porrera, and cradled by the craggy Serra de Montsant, five rooms have been tastefully decked out with brightly coloured textiles and decorative details while still retaining original stone walls and wooden beams. A bucolic menu of activities is at your doorstep, from snoozing on a hammock in the lovely garden to hiking through the Priorat's distinctive *llicorella* terraces.

# GLOSSARY

Here is a glossary of some words with which you might be unfamiliar—some Catalan and Spanish words, as well as some cooking terminology. We have given the Catalan word first and then the Spanish word. Sometimes the word is same in both languages. Sometimes we give the Spanish only, as this is the most commonly used or the way the word or phrase is generally presented.

*agua*—water.

*agua con gas*—water with gas, or as we would call it, sparkling mineral water. Great to have with food, as it aids digestion.

*agua sin gas*—water without gas, or still mineral water. Good for your thirst.

*ajo blanco*—translates as 'white garlic' but refers to a smooth cold white soup made with almonds, bread, garlic, extra virgin olive oil and a little salt. It's from the south but it's so good chefs in Barcelona can't help but make it.

*allioli/alioli*—an emulsion of oil, garlic, salt and sometimes egg. Imagine very garlicky mayonnaise.

*amb/con*—with.

*angel's hair/cabello de ángel*—a filling for pastries made from the thread-like fibres from a large gourd (*cucurbita maxima*), which are crystallised in sugar.

*aperitivo*—aperitif, a little something to sharpen the appetite before the main meal.

*arbequina*—a type of olive grown in Catalonia. They are crushed to make olive oil that is lightly sharp and delicious.

*arròs/arroz*—*see* page 48.

*asador*—both a roasting house (a place where you find delicious roasted pigs, lambs and goats and other meats) and the man who does the roasting. This is more an Aragonese tradition than Catalan.

*bacallà/bacalao*—*see* page 48.

*barri/barrio*—an urban neighbourhood; actually 'hood' describes it nicely. People associate very strongly with their *barri* and each one, although cheek by jowl with the other, has a distinct character and feel; some even have their own specific dishes.

*bellota*—in this sense refers to acorns on which pigs are fed to create tasty meat. The flesh from an Iberico pig fed on acorns will carry the name *Ibérico de bellota*, and produces delicacies such as *jamón*, *paletilla* (cured foreleg), *secreto* (fresh meat from the secret cut of the forequarter near the neck) and *costillas* (pork ribs). So, from little things big things grow.

*bistronomy*—the term used to describe the trend of restaurants serving really great, top-level food, but not going to the cost of investing in a good dining room with expensive linen and tableware. They charge half the price. It's one good thing to come out of the global financial crisis.

*bocadillo*—a small crusty baguette filled with *manchego* cheese or fresh *tortilla* or a few slices of *jamón*.

*bocata*—another word for *bocadillo*.

*bolets*—*see* page 48.

*bombes*—*see* page 49.

*borracho*—drunkard. When a dessert is soused with liquor it is called *borracho*.

*botifarra*—*see* page 51.

*botifarra negra*—*see* page 51.

*brochetas*—skewers. The French call them *brochettes*. Long, thin steel shafts onto which chunks of meat are threaded and grilled.

*bull*—a cousin of Catalonia's *botifarra*, made with pork, blood and tripe.

*bunyols/buñuelos*—*see* page 51.

*cabrales*—blue cheese from the north, made from cow's or perhaps goat's milk.

*calçots*—*see* page 51.

*canelons*—*see* page 52.

*capipota*—*see* page 52.

*cargols*—*see* page 52.

*Cariñena*—The red grape variety the French call Carignan. In Priorat it is used with Garnacha to make wonderful textural reds.

*casa*—house. If we had a *La Casa de Juan* we'd probably call it 'John's place'. Bars in small towns tend to be named after their owners. Not to be confused with the Catalan *mas*, which also means house, but there it is a large country homestead. This is sometimes used today to describe an old house that has been converted into a winery, restaurant or B&B.

*Catalunya/Cataluña*—Catalonia. I know you worked it out but there might be some people out there who can't.

*cazuela*—cooking pot, generally made from terracotta.

*cebiche/ceviche*—a way of cooking protein, generally fish, using citric acid, generally from limes, but sometimes from lemons or other citrus. The acid denatures the protein and changes its colour and texture. Yum.

*cecina*—air-dried beef. As the beef dries it develops aromas and flavours from microflora, just like *jamón*. We can't make dried beef as good as this in Australia because of government regulations.

*cep*—a delicious mushroom called *boletus edulis*, which is harvested wild. The Italians call them *porcini*.

*charcutería/chacinería*—a business that

sells *charcuterie*, the French word used to describe smallgoods; by definition they specialise in pork products. You might also *see* this spelt *xarcuteria*.

*chiringuitos*—on the beaches around Spain, especially in the south, there are little bars, some bordering on beach shacks, that sell basic seafood dishes and beer and perhaps cocktails. The Barcelonese version is more urbane.

*chistorra*—like a little *chorizo* but always served fresh, not cured.

*chorizo*—sausage made from ground pork and pork fat, with added salt, garlic and *pimentón*. Cured *chorizo* is served as a *tapa*; fresh *chorizo* is used in cooking, like a meaty, spicy stock cube. The best *chorizo* is made with *pimentón* from La Vera in Extremadura.

*chumbera*—fruit of the prickly pear, also known as *higo indio* or Indian fig.

*cigala*—scampi.

*cim i tomba*—traditionally a fisherman's dish of *sofregit* or *sofrito* cooked up with any unsold fish at the end of the day.

*coca*—*see* page 54.

*comedor*—dining room (not a car).

*confit*—a French term for slowly cooking something in fat. Typically it refers to a poultry such as duck, cooked in its own fat, but in these ever-changing times it can also mean anything cooked slowly in fat or oil. Usually delicious.

*conched*—a term used in making chocolate in which liquid chocolate is constantly rolled or pounded to break up the cocoa particles to make them smoother and smoother on the tongue.

*conservas*—conserved food. Spanish people don't put anything but the best into cans or jars. If someone is serving *conservas* in a bar, they are probably serving the best they can get for the price.

*cortador*—a man who cuts *jamón* for a living. Yes, it's a real job.

*costillas*—ribs.

*crema catalana*—*see* page 54.

*croqueta*—croquette. Béchamel flavoured with whatever is good or around at the time, rolled in breadcrumbs and deep fried.

DO—Denominación de Origen. A bit like the French AOC or the Italian DOC. It's a way of defining where a food or wine is grown or made. Some *see* it as a way of defining excellence, others *see* it simply as a marketing tool. For me it's a label and one should educate one's sense of taste and then trust that.

*embotits/embutidos*—smallgoods, often served in a selection on a *fusta* and often experienced in very generous serves.

*entrepà*—*see* page 54.

*ensaïmada*—an *escargot*-like pastry made with lard and a cloak of glacé sugar.

*ensaladilla rusa*—Russian salad made with diced potato, mayonnaise, perhaps some peas, canned tuna and *piquillo* pepper, usually kept cold in a fridge by the bar and served as a little *tapa*. From my experience some are fresher than others.

*escabeche*—food preserved in vinegar. Long before electricity and fridges were invented, people preserved food using vinegar. These days the vinegar has been toned down and balanced by sugar. A few spices are thrown in to make the dish tastier. Fish and small wild birds are most likely to be served *en escabeche*.

*escalivada*—*see* page 57.

*escudella i carn d'olla*—While the Madrileños have their *cocido* and the Asturians have their *fabada*, the Catalans have their *escudella i carn d'olla*. It's a hotpot of meat and pasta that will fill the emptiest stomach for days. Chickpeas, cabbage, vegetables, sausage and pork are cooked low and slow. It should come with a wild wind warning.

*esmorzars de forquilla*—a strong breakfast, the kind of breakfast that requires time, a table or a bar to sit around, forks, bread and wine. An important meal in Catalan food tradition, it became popular with workers in the 19th century. For a low price they could eat their way through meals such as pig's trotters, codfish, *capipota*, *fricandó* (veal stew). Enough to keep them going all day.

*espardenyes*—*see* page 57.

*espigalls*—a member of the cabbage family that looks like a cross between a Chinese broccoli and endive. It's a native of the Garraf region, a coastal area south of Barcelona. It is only available in winter and often served with hearty fare like *botifarra* and potatoes.

*esqueixada*—a salad of torn salt cod (*esqueixada* comes from the Catalan verb 'to shred'). This is often served with onion, tomato, olives and some *romesco*.

*estofat*—*see* page 57.

*fideuà*—*see* page 58.

*flautes*—Catalan for flute. Long bread, like a thin *bocadillo*.

*foie gras*—a fat liver from duck or goose, a French term to described the livers of ducks or geese that have been force fed until their livers expand to six times their normal size.

*fondes de sisos*—inns or taverns that offer meals.

*fuet*—*see* page 58.

*fusta*—wooden board on which sausages are served.

*garrapinyades*—nuts rolled in a light crunchy toffee.

Garnacha—the French call it Grenache.

*granja*—means farm, but in this case a *granja* is a like an old-fashioned milk bar. A family place.

*guiso*—a slow-cooked dish. *See* this on a menu and expect something hearty and sticky.

*higo/figo*—fig. Spanish figs are delicious.

*kataifi*—Greek pastry—think shredded *filo*.

*leche merengada*—sweet milk infused with cinnamon and citrus rind, a classic flavour of this part of the world. Sometimes frozen and served like a milky granita.

*llicorella*—the slaty, stony soil of the Priorat.

*loncha*—a slice or rasher, a beautiful little piece of hand-cut *jamón*.

*lloritos*—pearly razorfish.

*lubina*—sea bass.

*magdalena/madalena*—a little cake, a madeleine. Wander down to the bakery from your *piso* or apartment, order a few of these and take them back and enjoy leisurely with lots of coffee.

*Malvasia*—a white grape variety.

*manchego*—the cheese from La Mancha, made from the milk of sheep native to the area. It's the default cheese of Spain and often served as a *tapa*.

*mar i muntanya*—see page 58.

*marcona*—a variety of almond grown extensively in Catalonia. Fat, with a broad round bottom, it is a truly delicious nut.

*menú del dia*—menu of the day. A very cheap fixed-priced lunch menu, usually two courses and a glass of wine for around 12€. Some are great value for money, others less so.

*migas*—hand-torn breadcrumbs of various sizes. A great way to use up stale bread.

*modernisme*—Catalan for modernism, but here a uniquely Catalan cultural movement.

*modernista*—a modernist. An artist, architect or any other member of the influential movement that rose in Barcelona and across Catalonia in the early part of the 20th century.

*mojama*—air-dried tuna, the *jamón* of the sea.

*mojito*—a rather addictive drink of rum, lime, mint and sugar. Perfect on a hot day and popular in Barcelonese bars.

*molecular cuisine*—a cooking phenomenon of the early 21st century that saw chefs such as England's Heston Blumenthal, USA's Thomas Keller and Spain's Ferran Adrià combine modern food technology with traditional restaurant cooking. All movements have their day.

*montadito*—a little mounted open sandwich.

*morcilla*—Spanish blood sausage. Depending on where it comes from, it may have a lot of rice, onion or other texture. It generally has a nice hit of salt and a little cinnamon. A good *morcilla* should puff up a little when grilled. It's just delicious.

*morro*—a word for both for a knob of land or something that juts out, or in this case, a vealer's face, the face of a calf. Slow cooked, it is sweet and gelatinous. If you can handle the guilt, order it, because it is so succulent and great with wine.

*morro frito*—fried *morro*.

*músic*—see page 58.

*nécora*—crab.

*nudista*—a nudist. A lot of nude old people line the beach in summer. You'd think they'd retire in the winter, but oh no, they stick it out year after year.

*orelletes*—literally, small ears. In this case, large crisp pastries made with olive oil and sweetened with sugar.

*orxata/horchata*—a delicious nutty earthy sweet drink made from tigernuts, the tuber of a sedge. Restorative on a hot summer's day.

*pa amb tomàquet*—*see* page 60.

*paella*—*see* page 60.

*patatas bravas*—fried potatoes with a spicy sauce and *allioli*.

*perol*—a deep metal pan for making wet rice dishes.

*peus de porc*—*see* page 61.

*phylloxera*—a disease that affects grape vines.

*pimentón*—dried and ground red peppers, the spice of Spain. In La Vera in Extremadura they smoke the peppers over oak to dry them out. It is the foundation spice-note to many dishes and smallgoods.

*pimientos de Padrón*—imagine a very small green pepper or capsicum. Fried or grilled and heavily salted, they are a delicious snack. One in ten are ridiculously hot. Good luck.

*pintxo*—Basque tapas. Generally seafood and mayo on a slice of baguette left on a plate, unrefrigerated, for people to help themselves to. Some, however, can be very good.

*piperrada*—Spanish version of the French *piperade*, from the Basque country. Sauce of cooked down onions, tomatoes and peppers.

*pisos*—flats, apartments.

*pista*—dance floor.

*pisto*—sauce of cooked down onions, tomatoes, eggplants, zucchini and peppers.

*plaça/plaza*—town square.

*polígon/polígono*—industrial estate.

Sometimes a place, however, where artisanal food factories can be found. Don't write them off.

*pop/pulpo*—octopus. Pulpo is the name of our great bar and restaurant in the International Terminal of Melbourne Airport.

*porró*—drinking vessel.

*postres de músic*—a musician's dessert. Apart from AC/DC, The Beatles, Elton John and Michael Jackson … oh, and Justin Bieber, it is a well-known fact that all musicians are poor. The Catalans serve their musicians a mix of dried fruit and nuts soused with sweet wine.

*pulpo a la gallega*—a dish from Galicia of octopus over discs of potato, seasoned with salt, dusted with *pimentón* and drizzled with extra virgin olive oil.

*PX/Pedro Ximénez*—sweet sherry.

*rabo de toro*—tail of the bull; we'd call it oxtail.

*ración*—a plate to be shared. 'Raciones' is plural of *ración*. A *media ración* is a smaller portion from a shared plate.

*recuit*—*see* page 61.

Ribera del Duero—a lovely red wine.

*romesco*—a sauce made from roasted hazelnuts, almonds, dried peppers, garlic, olive oil and as many recipes as there are chefs.

*rossinyol/rebozuelo*—Catalan/Spanish for Girolle mushrooms.

*salpicón*—a salad of summer vegetables.

*samfaina*—the local version of *ratatouille*.

*sarsuela*—see page 62.

*secador*—a drying room. *Secadores* for curing *jamón* in some regions are in the middle of town and look like blocks of flats.

*serrano*—from the *sierra*. In a culinary context refers to *jamón* cured in the hills, but not the top-end stuff. That said, the best *jamón serrano* is better than the crappiest *jamón ibérico*.

*sierra*—means saw, but when someone is pointing to a hill in the distance, they'll be referring to the mountain range, which looks saw-like.

*sobrassada*—see page 62.

*socarrat*—the golden crust of rice that forms on the base of a paella pan. Some people freak out at a little burnt bit—if you *see* it, relax; it's not only normal, it's desired.

*sofregit/sofrito*—a rich, slow-cooked mix that is usually made up of onions, tomatoes and peppers. This is then used as a foundation for paella and other rice dishes.

*spherification*—a process in molecular cuisine where a clear gel made from algae extract forms around solid or liquid. It's basically a chemical reaction that creates a novel food. Some delicate palates can feel a bit battered by the chemicals used.

*suc*—Catalan for sauce or juice.

*suquet*—see page 62.

*torta del Casar*—a wonderful raw sheep's milk cheese from near Cáceres in Extremadura. What makes this a standout cheese is that the curds are set with a tea made from cardoon flowers, a bit like a thistle instead of rennet. Sticky and weirdly delicious.

*tortilla*—see *truita*.

*tripa/callos*—tripe, slow cooked in a rich tomato-based sauce. It is really a dish from further south, but still a rich, sticky way to punctuate a cold day.

*trompetas de la muerte*—death trumpets. Tasty little fungus as black as the inside of a cow and, thankfully, not at all poisonous.

*truita/tortilla*—a moist egg dish, a bit like a fritatta only better.

*turrón*—nougat. A mix of egg whites folded through hot honey or sugar syrup and punctuated with roasted almonds. The best is said to come from Jijona near Alicante.

*umami*—Japanese term for savoury. Scientists have proved that apart from salt, sugar, bitter and sour, the tongue can detect amino acids found in foods like asparagus, mushrooms, *jamón*, seafood, matured cheese and a host of other ingredients central to Catalan and Spanish cuisine.

*vermut*—vermouth. In old bars you *see* a glass of vermouth being passed to a customer with a glass soda siphon for them to top up their drink. Not my normal tipple, but strangely goes well with the food and atmosphere wherever you are.

*vi dolç*—see page 194.

*vi ranci*—see page 194.

*xurreria/churrería*—a place that fries and sells churros.

*xuixo*—a pastry cone filled with sweet custard.

# ACKNOWLEDGEMENTS

The authors would like to thank the following people for their generous suggestions and kind help: Paul Guiney, Cesc Castro, Suzanne Wales, Sarah Stodhart, Louisa Biviano, Susan Healy, Melbourne Private Tours, Casey Death Bisnaga Tours, Scott Wasley from The Spanish Acquisition, Stephanie Masterman, Dallas Cuddy, Stephen Pannell, Tony Tan, Nici Wickes, Simone Gordon, Pete Dillon, Suzy and David McDonald, Matt Wilkinson, John Lethlean, Max Allen, Rodrigo Garcia, Adam Melonas, Richard Seymour, Keppell Smith, Jane Willson, Emma Poole, Oscar Lerena, Phillippa Grogan, Natalie O'Brien, Natalie Lleonart, Cherry Ripe, Richard Mohan, Paul Wilson, Tim White, Amanda Schulze, Pat Nourse, Anthony Puharich, David Mackintosh, Neil Perry, Barbara Santich, Cathy Boirac, Mónica Brun, Elisa Berg, Gillian Hutchison, Miriam Rosenbloom, Victoria Alexander, Veronica Ridge, Antonio Boza, Andrew and Mandy Gray, Cathy Baker, Shaun Levin, German Aroyo, Shannon Bennett, Mary Ellis, Alimentaria, Andy McMahon, Peter Bartholemew, Emma Ragheb, Liz Carey, Alfons Serra, Denise Tan, Susan Wright, Fernando Córdoba, Will Studd, Jill Dupleix, Rhonie Wray, John Newton, Andrew McConnell, Melanie Young, Rachel Ritchie, Alan Benson, Sonia Martínez Muñoz, Kate McGhie, Con McMahon, Juanjo Sagnier, Willy Moreno.

The authors acknowledge the generous support of the Moritz Brewery, Barcelona.

The authors would like to thank their partners and their children for allowing them to spend so much time away from them to be able to research this book.

# INDEX

# ABOVE DIAGONAL

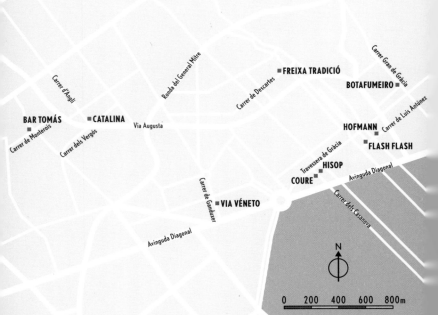

Parc Güell

EL ASADOR DE ARANDA

Avinguda del Tibidabo

Ronda de Dalt

ABAC

Parc del Turó del Putget

Carrer Gran de Gràcia

Ronda del General Mitre

FREIXA TRADICIÓ

Carrer de Descartes

BOTAFUMEIRO

Carrer d'Anglí

BAR TOMÁS

CATALINA

Via Augusta

Carrer de Luis Antúnez

HOFMANN

Carrer de Monteroïs

Carrer dels Vergós

FLASH FLASH

Travessera de Gràcia

HISOP

COURE

Avinguda Diagonal

Carrer de Ganduxer

VIA VÉNETO

Carrer dels Casanova

Avinguda Diagonal

N

0   200   400   600   800m

Hospital del Mar

AGUA

SET PORTES

Pla del Palau

CAN PAIXANO

Ronda del Litoral

Carrer de Ginebra

BAR JAI-CA ■ ■ CHERIFF

Passeig Marítim de la Barceloneta

1881 PER SAGARDI

Carrer del Baluard

Carrer de la Maquinista

MUSEU D'HISTÒRIA DE
CATALUNYA

Passeig de Joan de Borbó

VINOTECA VORAMAR

MERCAT DE LA BARCELONETA

FORN BALUARD ■ ■ LLUÇANÈS

Carrer de Sant Carles

Espanya

ROSA CANINA ■ ■ ABSENTA

CAN SOLÉ ■ ■ LA COVA FUMADA
SOMORROSTRO

SIT

Carrer del Mar

CAN MAJÓ

Carrer de l'Almirall Aixada

VIOKO GELAT
XOCOLATA
EXPERIÈNCIA

SUQUET DE L'ALMIRALL

BARCELONETA

Mediterranean Sea

N

Passeig de Joan de Borbó

0   50   100  150  200m

BRAVO 24

# BARRI GÒTIC

SAUC

Via Laietana

NEYRAS RESTAURANT

ELS QUATRE GATS

KOY SHUNKA

Carrer de Montsió

SHUNKA

Carrer de la Princesa

Via Laietana

LA COLMENA

Carrer del Pi

PLAÇA DEL PI FARMERS' MARKET

COOK AND TASTE

FORMATGERIA LA SEU

CAELUM

BAR GINGER

Carrer dels Banys Nous

VILA VINITECA

Carrer dels Lledó

Via Laietana

XURRERIA MANUEL SAN ROMÁN

LA GRANJA

Carrer de Ferran

Via Calle de Raurich

AGUT

Carrer d'En Gignàs

Carrer d'Avinyo

LES QUINZE NITS

EL PIPAS

Carrer dels Escudellers

PITARRA

La Rambla

LOS CARACOLES

N

0    50    100    150    200

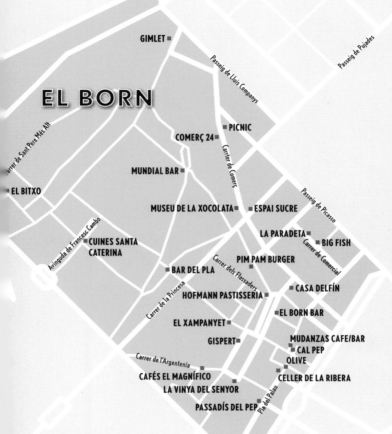

SANTA ■

GIMLET ■

**EL BORN**

Passeig de Lluís Companys

Passeig de Pujades

Carrer de Sant Pere Més Alt

PICNIC ■

COMERÇ 24 ■

Carrer de Comerç

MUNDIAL BAR ■

■ EL BITXO

Passeig de Picasso

MUSEU DE LA XOCOLATA ■ ■ ESPAI SUCRE

LA PARADETA ■ ■ BIG FISH

Carrer de Comercial

Avinguda de Francesc Cambó

■ CUINES SANTA CATERINA

Carrer dels Flassaders

PIM PAM BURGER ■

■ BAR DEL PLA

Carrer de la Princesa

■ CASA DELFÍN

HOFMANN PASTISSERIA ■

■ EL BORN BAR

EL XAMPANYET ■

■ MUDANZAS CAFE/BAR

GISPERT ■ ■ CAL PEP

OLIVE

Carrer de l'Argenteria

CELLER DE LA RIBERA

CAFÉS EL MAGNÍFICO ■

LA VINYA DEL SENYOR ■

Pla del Palau

PASSADÍS DEL PEP ■

N

0   50   100   150   200m

Carrer dels Tallers

KASPARO BAR AND
RESTAURANT

La Rambla

BETTY FORD'S

DOS PALILLOS

GRANJA M.VIADER

EL QUIM DE LA BOQUERIA

NEGRONI

BARCELONA
REYKJAVIK

AVINOVA

L'ESTEVET

KIOSKO UNIVERSAL

Carrer de Joaquín Costa

Carrer dels Àngels

EL RINCÓN
DE ARAGÓN

PINOTXO

ÀNIMA

MERCAT DE SANT JOSEP/LA BOQUERIA

Carrer del Carme

ANTIGUA HOJALATERÍA
SUCESOR DE PEDRO
APOLLARO

PASTISSERIA ESCRIBÀ

BAR MUY BUENAS

La Rambla

MAM I TECA

Carrer de la Riera Alta

MENDIZABAL

Carrer de l'Hospital

ISSERIA LIS

BIBLIOTECA
RESTAURANT

Carrer de la Unió

BAR CAÑETE

CASA LEOPOLDO

EL RAVAL

CAFE DE LES DELÍCIES

Carrer Nou de la Rambla

Carrer del Comte Borrell

CA L'ISIDRE
Carrer de les Flors

N

0   50   100  150  200m

Av del Paralelo

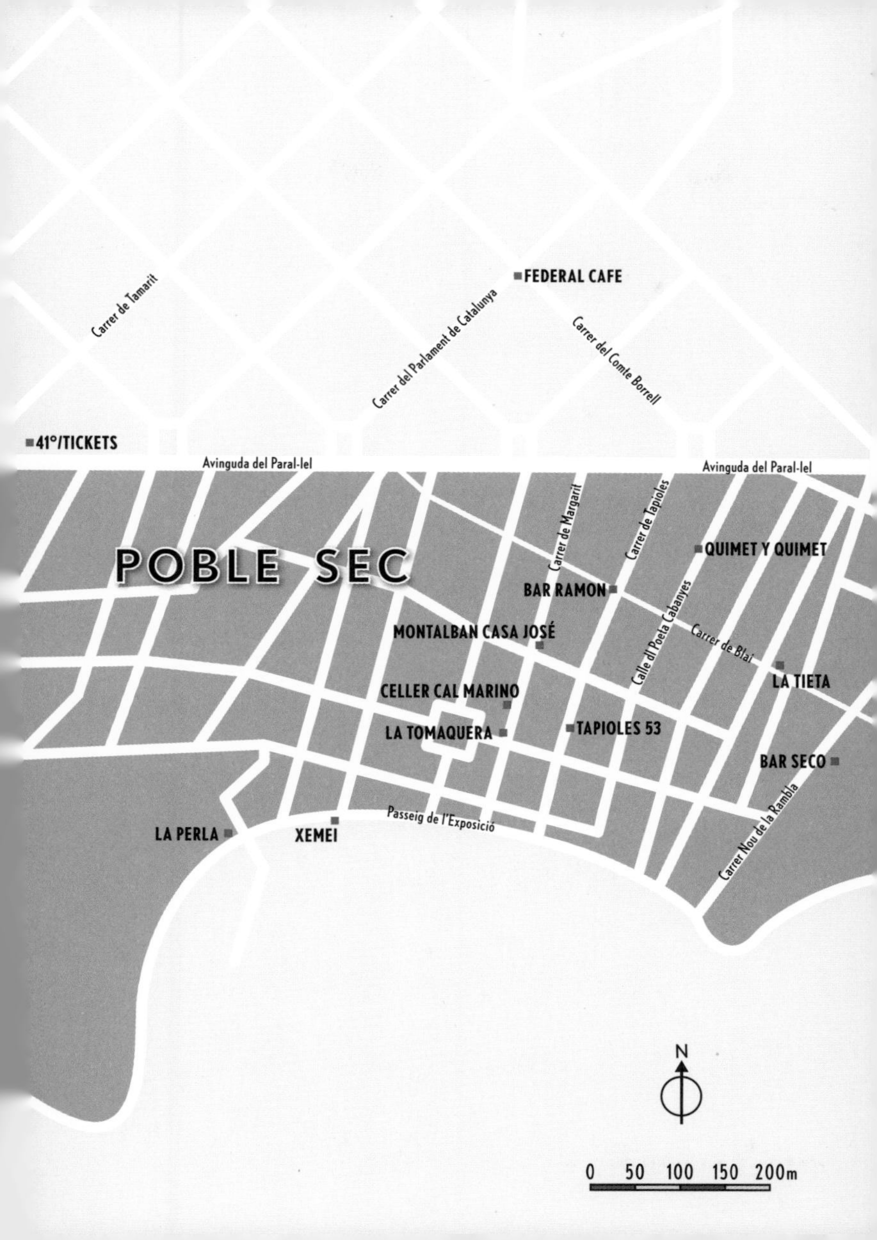

■ FEDERAL CAFE

Carrer de Tamarit

Carrer del Parlament de Catalunya

Carrer del Comte Borrell

■ 41°/TICKETS

Avinguda del Paral·lel

Avinguda del Paral·lel

POBLE SEC

Carrer de Margarit

Carrer de Tapioles

■ QUIMET Y QUIMET

BAR RAMON ■

Calle d'l Poeta Cabanyes

Carrer de Blai

MONTALBAN CASA JOSÉ ■

CELLER CAL MARINO ■

LA TIETA ■

LA TOMAQUERA ■

■ TAPIOLES 53

BAR SECO ■

LA PERLA ■

XEMEI ■

Passeig de l'Exposició

Carrer Nou de la Rambla

N

0   50   100   150   200m

THE MIEGUNYAH PRESS

This book was designed by Miriam Rosenbloom.
The text was typeset by Miriam Rosenbloom and Pauline Haas.
The text was set in 10 point Dante MT with 13 points of leading.
The text is printed on 120gsm woodfree.

This book was edited by Cathy Smith.